D1008175

Federated States of
Micronesia
and Palau

Other Places
Federated States of Micronesia
and
Palau

Ben Cook
Michael Gall, Chad Lathe, Christy Lejkowski,
Richard Lejkowski, Lorry Marvin, Megan McCrea

Published by
OTHER PLACES PUBLISHING

First edition
Published August 2010

*Federated States of Micronesia
and Palau*
Other Places Travel Guide
*Written by: Ben Cook, Michael Gall, Chad Lathe, Christy Lejkowski,
Richard Lejkowski, Lorry Marvin, Megan McCrea*
Cover designed by: Carla Zetina-Yglesias
Published by:
Other Places Publishing
www.otherplacespublishing.com

ISBN 978-0-9822619-3-4

The Authors

Ben Cook *Lead Writer (Pohnpei)*

After graduating from Emory University, Ben Cook served as a Peace Corps volunteer in Micronesia on Pingelap atoll, where he enjoyed teaching English, talking to local friends, and catching flying fish. Since returning to the United States, Ben has written this book as a way to share his passion for Micronesia. Among his other pursuits are writing software for students of ancient languages and studying political theory at the University of Texas.

Michael Gall *Contributing Writer (Chuuk)*

Michael Gall was proudly raised in Toledo, OH. He began his travels in high school and has not settled down since. From 2007-2009 Michael served in the Peace Corps on the tiny island of Ta in the Mortlocks of Chuuk. While there he taught ESL and formed lasting relationships with his host family, whom he misses dearly. Michael will be attending graduate school in the fall to receive his Master's in Social Work.

Chad Lathe *Contributing Writer (Yap)*

Chad Lathe became a Peace Corps volunteer after graduating from the University of Louisville in Kentucky and, like many other philosophy students before him, realizing that the real world waited. While serving on the island of Falalop with his wife Lorry, he definitely experienced real life and the joys and tribulations of island living. He also took the opportunity to travel throughout the state, seeing many of the rarely visited neighboring islands of Yap state. During his time in Ulithi, Chad became infatuated with the people and wildlife of Yap and its neighboring islands, and he is counting the days until his next visit. Chad now works and plays in Sacramento, California.

Christy Lejkowski Contributing Writer (Palau)

Christy served as a Teaching English as a Second Language and Community Development Volunteer in Palau. When she was not busy at school, she worked with the Palau Red Cross Society to design an HIV anti-discrimination puppet show and form a Youth Volunteer Corps. She also enjoyed running, hiking, kayaking, snorkeling, and biking around the islands of Palau and fell in love with the people, atmosphere, culture, and environment. She is happy to share her secrets with readers in hopes that they will come to appreciate her tiny island as much as she does.

Rick Lejkowski *Contributing Writer (Palau)*

Hailing from the suburbs of the Jersey shore, Rick received his Bachelor's Degree from Rowan University. Following a stint working in construction, Rick escaped to the opposite side of the world with his wife Christy as a Peace Corps Volunteer. Rick spent 2007-2009 teaching high school English on the Pacific Island of Palau. In addition to teaching and working with a variety of community organizations, Rick spent his two years in paradise seeking adventures on both the land and sea of Palau. Rick has since returned to New Jersey and is currently preparing to begin a Master's Degree in Literature.

Lorry Marvin *Contributing Writer (Yap)*

Lorry shipped off to the Federated States of Micronesia in 2007 and taught English on the tiny island of Falalop of the Ulithi Atoll in Yap State. She became proficient in many local skills, learned the local language, and participated in many different traditional ceremonies. While on visits to Wa'ab, she took advantage of island resorts, scuba diving, kayaking, and hiking trails. She remains close to her Yapese friends and host family members, and misses warm nights with full moons, walking on Falalop's runway, and philosophical discussions with her host mother. Lorry is currently living and working in Sacramento, California.

Megan McCrea *Contributing Writer (Kosrae)*

A native of colorful Colorado, Megan McCrea contracted the traveling fever even before she had gained the ability to form memories. After graduating from Duke University, Megan spent a year with the Peace Corps on Kosrae, then another on Palau. She treasures memories of trading stories and jokes with her host dad, hiking around Kosrae with her fellow volunteers, and knocking around a volleyball with her neighbors. During her time in the islands, she gained an admirable tan, a voracious appetite for fresh seafood, and an ability to throw rocks with astonishing accuracy at close range. This fall, the wanderer will head to Berkeley, CA, to pursue an internship in publishing.

Acknowledgments

Many people contributed to researching, writing, and publishing this book. Without their help, the authors could never have completed it.

We owe a debt of gratitude to our families and friends for supporting us in this endeavor. They have always been patient with us as we have moved from one hare-brained, low-paying job to the next.

It would not have been possible to write this book without first serving as Peace Corps Volunteers in the Federated States of Micronesia and Palau. Therefore, we thank the Peace Corps staff and our fellow volunteers who made this possible.

Also, we are grateful to our friends in Micronesia and Palau, especially the families and communities that hosted us during our terms of service. These people opened their homes to us and taught us about Micronesian life and culture not because they thought we would write a travel guide but because it is in their character to share with others. We thank them for their generosity and warmth.

Specifically, the authors would like to thank Chris Beale of Other Places Publishing and Nick Noble. In addition, Ben Cook thanks Largo Edwin, Lois Englberger, and Matthew Britten for their help in collecting information for the guide.

Megan McCrea wishes to send a big "kulo, suo luhk" to Baba Isaac, Nina Delona, Mia, Frinlang, Double, Kutkut, and Karie for the incredible experience on Kosrae. For research help, she thanks Sally and Katrina. For amazing research material as well as for camaraderie and kindness, she also thanks Mark and Maria. She appreciates the Jane Lifties for supporting her as she worked through her chapter as well as 40 hours a week together. She also wishes to thank Alex, Valerie, Esteban, Scott, Sue, and the rest of her second family at Mountain Grind. Finally, she thanks Madi for the writing tips; Talbott for the inspiration; Mom and Dad for playing their role of a two-person editing, cookie, research, and morale department; and Slava for the love and encouragement.

Michael Gall would like to thank and send his love to: Mom, Dad, Grandparents, B.J., Lindsey, the Nobles, Jake the Virginia Creeper, Jessie, Elizabeth, David, and all the PCVs and Peace Corps staff he served with. He also says, "Kalisou Chapur" to Windsor, Cintia, Obit, Santa, Imaou, Suzi, Kester, Innoce, Thesco, Igko, Senelyn, Meleny, Ketreen, Tian, Julies, Sony, George, Taichi, Toprez, Windcy, Tavid, Mary Ann, Steven, and Sammy. Finally, he sends his love and thanks to everyone on Ta.

The authors of the Yap section offer their sincerest gratitude to Garrett Johnson, Tori Stannard, Seema Shah, Stephanie Lott, and Rachel Rogers for providing Yapese language assistance and local business contact information. They also thank Regina Raigetal and Michaela Logwar for their endless support, kindheartedness, and hospitality, and Elizabeth Neason for providing guidance and focus.

The authors of the Palau section thank Christa Daly, Amber Fricke, and Laura London for their contributions to the chapter. They would also like to thank Pauleen Kumangai, Isabella and Truman Ngirmang and the staff of both Palau High School and Meyuns Elementary School for showing them the sights and teaching them the "local way" to live in Palau. Finally, they would like to thank their families for letting them explore the world and experience all the adventures it has to offer.

We ask forgiveness of those whom we have forgotten to name here but who nevertheless contributed to work on this book. Lastly, thanks to you, the reader, for your support and interest in Micronesia and Palau.

Quick Reference

Official name: Federated States of Micronesia (FSM); Republic of Palau, in Palauan *Beluu er a Belau* (ROP)

States: *Micronesia:* Kosrae, Pohnpei, Chuuk, Yap; *Palau:* Aimeliik, Airai, Angaur, Hatohobei, Kayangel, Koror, Melekeok, Ngaraard, Ngarchelong, Ngardmau, Ngatpang, Ngchesar, Ngeremlengui, Ngiwal, Peleliu, Sonsorol

Nearby countries: territory of Guam, Northern Mariana Islands, Marshall Islands, Philippines, Papua New Guinea

Population (2009 estimate): *Micronesia:* 107,434; *Palau:* 20,796

Capital: *Micronesia:* Palikir, Pohnpei; *Palau:* Melekeok

Government: *Micronesia and Palau:* constitutional governments in free association with the United States

Ethnic groups (2000 census): *Micronesia:* Chuukese 48.8%, Pohnpeian 24.2%, Kosraean 6.2%, Yapese 5.2%, Yap outer islands 4.5%, Asian 1.8%, Polynesian 1.5%, other 6.4%, unknown 1.4%; *Palau:* Palauan 69.9%, Filipino 15.3%, Chinese 4.9%, other Asian 2.4%, white 1.9%, Carolinian 1.4%, other Micronesian 1.1%, other or unspecified 3.2%

Languages: *Micronesia:* English (official), Chuukese, Kosraean, Pohnpeian, Yapese, Ulithian, Woleaian, Nukuoro, Kapingamarangi, others; *Palau:* Palauan (official on most islands), Filipino, English, Chinese, Carolinian, Japanese

Religions (2000 census): *Micronesia:* Catholic 50%, Protestant 47%, other 3%; *Palau:* Catholic 41.6%, Protestant 23.3%, Modekngei (indigenous Palauan religion) 8.8%, Seventh-Day Adventist 5.3%, Jehovah's Witness 0.9%, Mormon 0.6%, other 3.1%, unspecified or none 16.4%

GDP (2008 estimate): *Micronesia:* $238.1 million; *Palau:* $164 million

GDP per capita (2008 estimate): *Micronesia:* $2,200; *Palau:* $8,100

Life expectancy at birth: *Micronesia:* 70.94 years; *Palau:* 71.22 years

Adult literacy rate: *Micronesia:* 89%; *Palau:* 92%

Currency: U.S. dollar *All prices in this book are in U.S. dollars (USD).*

Calling codes: *Micronesia:* +691; *Palau:* +680

Postal codes: *Kosrae:* 96944; *Pohnpei:* 96941; *Chuuk:* 96942; *Yap:* 96943; *Palau:* 96940

Electricity: 120V, 60 HZ with plugs and sockets of the Type A (ungrounded, "two-prong") and Type B (grounded, "three-prong")

Time: *Kosrae/Pohnpei:* GMT +11; *Chuuk/Yap:* GMT + 10; *Palau:* GMT +9

If you travel to Micronesia or Palau from the Western hemisphere, you will cross the International Date Line. This means that you will jump forward one day as you travel west and jump back one day as you travel east. There is no Daylight Savings Time in Micronesia or Palau.

Measurements: U.S. standard measurements are the official measurement system in Micronesia and Palau, but due to Japanese and Korean influence, the metric system is also used in the countries.

Holidays: In addition to the national and state holidays listed here, some municipalities and individual islands have their own holidays. The following days are holidays in 2010. The dates are approximate for other years.

National holidays

Micronesia
New Year's Day, January 1
Good Friday, April 2
Easter, April 4
Constitution Day, May 10
United Nations Day, October 24
Independence Day, November 3
Veterans Day, November 11
Thanksgiving, November 25
Christmas Day, December 25

Palau
New Year's Day, January 1
Youth Day, March 15
Senior Citizens Day, May 5
President's Day, June 1
Constitution Day, July 9
Labor Day, September 1
Independence Day, October 1
United Nations Day, October 24
Thanksgiving Day, November 25
Christmas Day, December 25

FSM state holidays

Kosrae
Constitution Day, January 11
Liberation Day, September 8

Pohnpei
Pohnpei Culture Day, March 31
Liberation Day, September 11
Constitution Day, November 8

Chuuk
Liberation Day, September 23
Constitution Day, October 1

Yap
Yap Day, March 1
Tree Planting Day, June 1
Constitution Day, December 24

Contents

Introduction 15

Environment 17, History 18, Government and economy 21, Culture and people 23

Basics 27

Getting there and away 27, Customs and entry requirements 29,

Communication and media 30, Money 31, Weather 32,

Travelers with special considerations 33, Accommodations 33, Food and drink 34,

Shopping 36, Activities 36, Health and safety 37, Responsible travel 42

Kosrae 49

Highlights 53, Geography 53, History 54, Culture and people 57,

Travel information 62, Getting around 63, Where to stay 64, Where to eat 66,

What to do 67, Nightlife 75

Pohnpei 77

Highlights 80, Geography 77, History 81, Culture and people 86,

 Travel information 90, Getting around 92, Where to stay 94, Where to eat 95,

What to do 97, Nightlife 104, Outer islands 105

Chuuk 113

Yap 141

Palau 173

Book Icons

Author recommended accommodation or eatery	Clinic
Accommodations	Ferry Dock
Airport	Hospital
Bank or ATM	Information Office
Bar or Nightclub	Landmark or Sight
Beach	Mountain
Bus Station or Stop	Pharmacy
Capital	Point of Interest
Church	Police
City or Village	Post Office
	Restaurant or Eatery

Federated States of Micronesia

200 km

N

Guam (U.S.)

MARSHALL ISLANDS

Wa'ab

Ulithi

Fais

YAP

Woleai

Olimarao

Elato

Satawal

Namonuito

Pulap

Puluwat

Houk

CHUUK

Hall Islands

Nomwin

Murilo

Weno

Nama

Losap

Namaluk

Etal

Moch

Kuttu

Lukunor

Oneop

Ta

Satawan

Nukuoro

Kapingamarangi

Oroluk

Sapwuahfik

Pakin

Ant

Pohnpei

Mwoakilloa

POHNPEI

Pingelap

KOSRAE

Kosrae

CHINA

TAIWAN

PHILIPPINES

PALAU

GUAM (U.S.)

INDONESIA

FEDERATED STATES
OF MICRONESIA

MARSHALL
ISLANDS

PAPUA NEW GUINEA

SOLOMON
ISLANDS

PAPUA NEW GUINEA

About this Book

The authors of this book have cumulatively spent over 13 years living and working in the islands of the Federated States of Micronesia (FSM) and the Republic of Palau. Before officially beginning to research this travel guide, the authors visited the places reviewed in this book, ate in the restaurants, stayed in the hotels, and learned the cultures and languages of various islands from locals generous enough to teach them. As such, the information in this travel guide represents intimate, first-hand knowledge of these countries, knowledge which will help you discover a side of Micronesia and Palau that most visitors do not see. Throughout the book, we have included tips for cultural sensitivity and integration, recommendations for authentic interaction with local cultures, and a handful of our own stories from the islands.

> Micronesia and Palau are fairly expensive destinations. Tickets alone are too high for many travelers. As much as possible, however, we have tried to highlight options for budget travelers in this guide.

You do not need to read this book from beginning to end. Instead, we recommend that you use the table of contents and the index to find the sections that are most interesting to you. The Introduction includes general information about the FSM and Palau, including a brief history, political and economic profiles, and an introduction to the cultures and peoples of these islands.

The following chapter offers practical travel information that applies to all areas of the two countries. You will also find information on issues facing Micronesia, organizations that are making a difference and volunteer service opportunities during your visit for those so inclined.

The next five chapters give information specific to the four states of the FSM (Kosrae, Pohnpei, Chuuk, and Yap) and to Palau, including island-

Micronesia vs. The Federated States of Micronesia

In common usage, the term *Micronesia* can refer either to the Federated States of Micronesia or to the much broader region of Micronesia, which includes the FSM, Palau, Guam, the Marshall Islands, the Northern Marianas, Kiribati, Nauru, and a few outlying U.S. territories. In this book, which is about the FSM and Palau, the term *Micronesia* refers to the FSM, unless otherwise noted. When used as an adjective referring to an ethnic group, however, *Micronesian* refers to the people of the broader region as distinct from other Pacific ethnic groups, such as Melanesians or Polynesians.

specific cultural and historical sketches and practical information for visitors. Finally, you will find some suggestions for further reading, a few local phrases, and the index.

The recommendations in this guide represent the opinions of the authors. We hope that you use these recommendations when planning your travel. Your experiences, however, will likely be different than ours, and you should take into consideration your own circumstances and desires when planning your itinerary.

Introduction

The archipelago of several hundred islands in the Western Pacific is literally not on maps. While the names of South Pacific islands like *Samoa* and *Tahiti* have become familiar, names such as *Kosrae*, *Chuuk*, and *Babeldaob* remain foreign to the ears of all but a handful of diving fanatics. Micronesia and Palau are hidden gems, well-kept secrets unknown to the vast majority in the developed world. This makes these countries ideal destinations for travelers interested in adventure, in the romance of isolated Pacific islands, in getting off the beaten track, or in escaping the fast-paced developed world.

The islands of Micronesia and Palau have much to offer. From the moment one steps off the plane, one is transported, not only physically, but also emotionally and spiritually, to a place of wonder and imagination. One cannot help but be awed by the physical landscape, whether it is the soaring mountain peaks of Kosrae, the mysterious jungle of Pohnpei, the enchanting Rock Islands of Palau, or the untrammeled beach of an empty coral atoll. The underwater landscape is just as impressive; Micronesia and Palau feature some of the world's most pristine coral reefs, varied and colorful marine life, and incredible wrecks.

Shortly after arriving in Micronesia and Palau, one begins to look beyond the physical landscape to the peoples and cultures of the islands. Micronesia and Palau have been touched very gently by globalizing trends, and thus the unique cultures of these islands are preserved to an unusual extent. While the capital towns of Micronesia and Palau offer visitors many conveniences of modern life, one can also find remote corners where people live much as they have for centuries. What is more, Micronesians are not merely willing but truly eager to share their traditional cultures and languages with anyone who shows an interest. In fact, it would be nearly impossible to visit these islands without having some authentic interaction with the indigenous cultures, something which cannot be said for other islands in the Pacific.

Upon returning from Micronesia or Palau, acquaintances may not understand the magic of these islands. If, however, you ever meet someone else who has visited these hidden gems of the Western Pacific, a smile and a nod will suffice to indicate that you, too, are in on the secret of Micronesia and Palau. If you are planning a trip to Micronesia or Palau, prepare yourself to step into a place like no other on Earth.

Highlights

ISLAND CULTURES

One reason to visit Micronesia and Palau is to experience the diverse island cultures found across these two countries. Elsewhere in the Pacific, traditional ways have been brushed aside in favor of Westernization. In Micronesia and Palau, however, you cannot avoid coming in contact with local traditions, which islanders are constantly striving to preserve in a changing world.

Although Micronesians and Palauans can be shy, it takes only a little prodding to discover that they are eager to share the unique traditions and cultures of their home islands with foreigners. Start a conversation with a local, and soon you will find yourself learning age-old strategies for fishing in Palau, chewing betel nut with a group of Yapese men, helping a Kosraean woman make coconut cream, or drinking *sakau* with a Pohnpeian chief.

DIVING

It is no exaggeration to say that some of the best dive sites in the world are found in the Federated States of Micronesia and Palau. These countries include every kind of island environment: continental islands, coral atolls, high volcanic islands. Their tropical waters are home to many pelagic species, and in the reefs surrounding the islands, one can find countless species of plants, coral, fish, sharks, rays, crustaceans, and other sea life. In addition, the legacy of World War II has left many wrecks for divers to explore.

Each area of these two countries has something unique to offer divers. In Kosrae, which sees few tourists, divers of all levels can explore the fringing reef in seclusion. Pohnpei's pristine, undamaged reef is one of Micronesia's best-kept secrets. Chuuk Lagoon is world-famous as home to the "ghost fleet" of Japanese World War II wrecks. In Yap, one can dive with manta rays 15 to 20 feet (5 to 6 meters) across, and Palau offers an unparalleled variety of sea life and topography along with a developed tourist industry. Divers really cannot go wrong anywhere in the Federated States of Micronesia or Palau.

PACE OF LIFE

Though the culture of each island in Micronesia and Palau is distinct, one thing they share in common is that things operate on "island time." These islands do not disappoint visitors who come looking for an escape from the hectic pace of life in developed countries. Whatever your purpose for visiting Micronesia, you can expect to have enough time at the end of the day to relax and enjoy your surroundings.

Environment

The islands of Micronesia are geologically diverse. Some islands, like Pohnpei and Kosrae, were formed by volcanic activity. Others, like Yap, are a part of a continental shelf that is pushed above sea level. Still other islands in Micronesia and Palau are coral atolls.

Many people are aware that coral are actually colonies of small, stationary animals that produce calcium carbonate deposits over time. These deposits eventually become coral reefs. Coral atolls are formed when a ring of coral grows up around the summit of an aging volcano. As the summit of the volcano erodes and recedes into the ocean, the coral reef grows up until it pokes above the surface of the water, often forming an enclosed lagoon protected from the open ocean. If enough sand and soil accumulates on the exposed reef, the coral atoll can sustain plant and animal life.

Charles Darwin first hypothesized this origin of coral atolls.

As might be expected, the tropical climes of Micronesia and Palau are home to a huge number of flora and fauna, many of which are endemic to the region or the islands on which they are found. The high islands are covered by tropical rainforest. Taro, yams, breadfruit, and coconuts are among the most common produce of these islands. Plant life on coral atolls is usually more limited due to the shallow, brackish water table, but low-lying shrubs, and coconut, breadfruit, and pandanus plants are common here as well as on the high islands.

Micronesia and Palau are not known for their terrestrial animal life. While these islands are home to a wide variety of insects, reptiles, amphibians, and other small critters, including both native and introduced species, these are likely to be of great interest only to hobbyists or biologists. Moreover, almost all mammals in Micronesia and Palau are introduced; the only native terrestrial mammals are bats.

Some visitors may be interested in the sea and forest birds of Micronesia and Palau. Approximately 225 species of birds are found in the region of Micronesia, including 18 endemic species. Birds that have been recorded in the region include short-tailed and black-footed albatrosses, a variety of petrels, storm-petrels, shearwaters, sandpipers, and terns, several species of boobies, ducks, geese, cormorants, and many others. Some species, such as the Pohnpei Lorikeet, are endemic to particular islands. If you are interested in learning more about the birds of Micronesia, check out Harold Pratt's *Field Guide to the Birds of Hawaii and the Tropical Pacific* or Harvey Gordon Segal's *Birds of Micronesia.*

What Micronesia and Palau may lack in terrestrial fauna, they more than make up for with marine life. The tropical waters of Micronesia are frequented by many pelagic species including fish, sharks, dolphins, and manta rays, which can reach up to 20 feet (6.1 meters) or more across. Eagle rays, yellowfin and skipjack tuna, mahi mahi, barracuda, and whitetip sharks are very common.

The green turtle and hawksbill turtle are both found in the waters of Micronesia and Palau. A few islands, including Ulithi Atoll in Yap, serve as turtle nesting grounds.

Additionally, most islands are fringed by coral reefs, which serve as homes to various invertebrates, fish, eels, skates, and turtles. The colors and variety of hard and soft corals alone is simply astounding, to say nothing of the animal life that lives in and among the coral. On any given dive, you might encounter lionfish, Napolean wrasses, brightly colored triggerfish, moray eels, humphead parrotfish, stingrays, nudibranchs, as well as green, hawksbill, or loggerhead turtles. You could also run into a grey or blacktip reef shark. In Palau, it is also possible to see the dugong, a rare animal similar to a manatee.

History

To learn more about the history of particular islands, see the chapters on the various states of the FSM and Palau.

While the history of Palau and each state of the FSM is distinct, these islands were subject to many of the same historical forces. The history of this area can be broken into a few periods, including pre-contact history, history of European contact and colonialism, and, most recently, the history of the FSM and Palau as independent nations.

PRE-EUROPEAN CONTACT

Because the peoples of Micronesia and Palau did not have a writing system before the arrival of Europeans, much of what scientists suspect about pre-historical Micronesia and Palau is based on archaeology, racial and cultural studies, and traditional legends and stories. Scientists hypothesize that Austronesians from the Philippines and what is now Indonesia began moving into Palau and Yap, possibly forced out by Malay tribes. As these small islands became full, people from these islands settled Chuuk, Pohnpei, and Kosrae over a period of hundreds of years.

These intrepid voyagers sailed across broad stretches of open ocean without the benefit of compasses or sextants. Indeed, how early Pacific islanders found new land without maps or prior knowledge of other islands in the area is a mystery and a testament to human ingenuity.

Over the next few millennia, the people who settled Micronesia and Palau formed societies based on subsistence fishing and agriculture. Although the cultures of the various islands differ significantly, there are similarities. All of the cultures of Micronesia and Palau emphasize the importance of the family. During this time, islanders did occasionally sail to other islands in the region to trade.

EUROPEANS AND COLONIALISM

The first Europeans to visit the islands of the region of Micronesia were Spanish and Portuguese explorers. Magellan landed in Guam in 1521 on his attempt to circumnavigate the globe. He did not, however, visit any of the islands of modern-day Palau or the FSM. A few years later, Dioga da Rocha, a Portuguese explorer, became the first European to visit what is now the FSM. He happened upon what was probably Ulithi Atoll east of Yap after being blown off course by a storm and spent four months there.

Over the next 300 years, exploration of Polynesia and the South Pacific continued, but Micronesia and Palau were visited only occasionally by European beachcombers and traders. Christian missionaries, however, became a regular presence on the islands during these years.

Beachcombers were often escaped prisoners, mutineers, or deserters who tried to live on Pacific islands with the natives.

In the 1800s, European traffic in the area began to pick up considerably. Spain, which had claimed ownership of the islands of Micronesia and Palau as early as 1565, was officially granted control of the islands in 1885 by the Pope after Spain's rule was contested by the Germans. Although, Spain was forced to defend its Pacific claims in Guam and the Philippines, its presence in Micronesia and Palau was hardly felt, except through its missionaries. After the Spanish-American War, Spain sold the islands of Micronesia and Palau to Germany. The Germans cared primarily for using the islands for profit through the copra, cotton, and shell trades. Islanders tended to bristle more under German rule than they had under the Spanish, and the years from 1899 to 1914 were characterized by hostility and, in some cases, violent conflict between islanders and the Germans.

When Germany was defeated in World War I, Japan occupied the islands of Micronesia and Palau. The years leading up to World War II were fraught with tension. The islands of Micronesia and Palau were fortified by the Japanese in preparation for World War II. The strategic importance of Micronesia and Palau in the Pacific theater varied from island to island and from month to month, but a number of the islands were bombed. The island of Peleliu in Palau was the site of an important and deadly battle. To learn more about the Battle of Peleliu, see pg 180.

The Yap Crisis

In one flare-up known as the Yap Crisis, it was reported that the Japanese were treating islanders cruelly on the island of Yap. U.S. President Woodrow Wilson argued that Yap's port should be opened to all nations. Japan agreed to this demand but promptly stopped development of the island.

World War II had a lasting impact on the FSM and Palau. Most of the large islands and some small islands saw conflict, including bombing, naval battles, and, in the case of Peleliu, full scale invasion. The physical remains of Japanese and U.S. military installations are scattered throughout the islands. Even more lasting, perhaps, is the toll that World War II took on the people of the FSM and Palau. While the early years of Japanese administration were relatively peaceful and prosperous, the years just prior to and during World War II were extremely difficult times. The Japanese exploited the resources and people of Micronesia and Palau. Moreover, there were extreme shortages of important goods during World War II and in the year following Japan's surrender. While Micronesians are generally not bitter toward either the Japanese or the Americans, those old enough to remember World War II speak about it as a difficult and harsh time.

With World War II over, the United States took control of Micronesia and Palau, along with many other Pacific islands. These islands were organized by the United Nations into the Trust Territory of the Pacific, which was governed first by the U.S. Navy and later by the U.S. Department of the Interior. Over the next three decades, the United States oversaw the development of many important political and commercial institutions in Micronesia, which set the stage for independence.

INDEPENDENCE

The years from the mid-1970s to the present are characterized by a continuing transition from U.S. governance to self-government for the islands of Micronesia and Palau. The states of the FSM voted to form an independent nation in 1978, and the Constitution of the FSM went into effect in the following year. Over the next few years, the United States government transferred power to the national and state governments of the FSM, and the FSM was officially recognized as an independent state in 1986, when the United States and the FSM formed a Compact of Free Association. This Compact was renewed in 2004. Since 1986, the FSM has met with mixed success economically, and unemployment is a major concern throughout the islands. Smaller states, such as Kosrae and Yap have tended to fare better economically while Chuuk, the most populous state, has faced many problems related to unemployment and poverty. The FSM joined the United Nations in 1991.

Palau voted in 1978 to form an independent government rather than join the FSM. Like in the FSM, a Compact of Free Association was approved in 1986, but pointed political battles prevented ratification of the Compact until 1993. Since the Compact went into effect, the Republic of Palau has fared much better economically than the FSM. Palau joined the United Nations in 1995.

While Micronesia and Palau are both recognized as independent nations by the United Nations and the global community, there is a long way to go to true self-governance for these islands. The governments of both countries rely heavily on U.S. funds distributed under the compacts of free association. It is unlikely that either country will ever become economically independent in this interdependent world; the islands are simply too small to produce any exports on a large scale. There is hope for the development of these islands, however. Palau has already become a major tourist destination in the Pacific, and if the FSM invests in the development of facilities to serve tourists, it could become a destination as well. Moreover, the natural resources of both nations are still reasonably intact, and in difficult economic times, the citizens of the FSM and Palau rely, as they have for centuries, on the fruit of the land and seas.

Government and Economy

Both the FSM and Palau were formerly parts of the Trust Territory of the Pacific. Now, they are independent countries with constitutional governments in compacts of free association with the United States. Under these compacts, the United States provides aid to government agencies in Micronesia and Palau in exchange for the right to use land for military purposes, though the United States currently maintains no significant military presence in the countries. In addition, the compacts allow citizens of the FSM and Palau to immigrate to the United States and serve in the U.S. military.

The governments of Micronesia and Palau are similar in many respects. Both are representative democracies with a president, legislature, and independent judiciary. There are currently no active political parties in either country, and elections are often won on the basis of personal reputation. Both countries have rather large bureaucracies and spend a significant portion of their annual budgets on education.

Micronesia differs from Palau in that it lacks national cohesiveness. The FSM is divided into four distinct states, which are geographically and culturally distant. Indeed, the people of these states are accustomed to thinking of themselves as citizens of the state but not of the nation. Palau is also divided into states, but these are small, administrative districts which are culturally similar and, for the most part, located on the same island. This lack of a national identity has made it difficult for the government of the FSM to develop effective policy. Still, the government of the FSM, like that of Palau, is generally a positive force in the lives of citizens. It provides services, such as waste management, transportation between islands, and education, that would otherwise be nonexistent. Moreover, both governments are inclusive democracies that observe constitutional protections of individual rights.

Government Corruption

The state and national governments in the FSM, especially the Chuukese government, are considered by some observers and citizens to be corrupt. The lack of relevant laws that promote access to information make this practice widespread and largely unprosecuted. Some examples of government corruption include the case of a former ambassador who was charged in connection with a passport fraud scheme in 2007 and a senator who after being indicted for corruption in 2004 retained his seat in the next election. He was later removed from his seat after being charged with embezzlement of funds in 2008.

OCCUPATIONS AND LIVELIHOODS

For better or worse, geographical isolation has prevented much economic development in the FSM. Subsistence agriculture and fishing are still the most common sources of livelihood. For most citizens of these countries, daily life still resembles the lives of islanders several hundred years ago. Men are usually responsible for fishing, hunting, caring for livestock, building houses and canoes, and harvesting the abundant tropical fruits as they ripen. Women spend their time cooking, cleaning, and caring for children, and they sometimes participate in fishing and raising livestock as well. Where daily life has changed for islanders is in diet and food preparation (imported foods are much less time-consuming to prepare) and in leisure time activities (watching TV and movies is very popular).

A large number of citizens are also employed by the national, state, and municipal governments. Even on small outer islands, there is usually a mayor's office, a legislative council, at least one judge, a postmaster, and several other government jobs. The government, in turn, is funded by the United States under the Compact of Free Association. Sale of commercial fishing rights to Japanese and Chinese fishing vessels also accounts for a large portion of the FSM government's revenue, although most agree that the government sells these licenses for a fraction of what they are worth.

If the FSM and Palau implement sustainable policies for their reefs and fisheries, selling commercial fishing licenses could become a significant source of income for the future.

In addition to subsistence farming and fishing, businesses supporting the tourist industry provide a major source of income for the people of Palau. Tourism is one reason that Palau's per capita GDP is almost four times that of the FSM.

Like the FSM, Palau also receives financial support from the United States under a Compact of Free Association, and its national and state governments employ many Palauan citizens. Palau is also home to many Philippine and Bangladeshi immigrants, who fill mostly low-paying jobs.

Culture

The family is central to life in Micronesia and Palau. Most people live on compounds with a number of their extended family members, and many young people live with their parents long after they get married and begin to have children. Almost every part of daily life, including working, socializing, eating, and sleeping, is undertaken with family. Beyond the family, Micronesians consider themselves a part of a village or community located in a geographical area. Many times, this community is headed by a traditional chief or hierarchy. In turn, this village might be a part of a larger municipality or island.

Although traditional ways have taken a toll with the increasingly influence of Western culture, there are strong movements on all the islands to preserve local ways and cultural knowledge. The people of Micronesia and Palau, who are generally warm and open toward visitors, particularly admire foreigners who display knowledge of and respect for local customs.

ARTS

Carving is one of the most important art forms in Micronesia and Palau. On Pohnpei, for example, one finds many small carvings of sea animals, while in Chuuk, traditional love sticks and masks are still carved by hand. In Palau, elaborately carved storyboards depicting traditional stories, which once adorned houses, are now made in smaller, portable forms.

The people of Micronesia and Palau are expert canoe-builders. In contrast to Polynesian canoes, which are elaborately decorated, Micronesian canoes are simple and functional. Micronesian canoes are invariably carved from breadfruit trees, and have at least one outrigger, which works to keep the canoe upright when conditions at sea are rough. Although fiberglass motorboats are now the most common form of water transportation, traditional canoes are still used across the FSM and Palau for fishing or sailing.

In Yap, islanders still practice the art of navigating across the open ocean in sailing canoes, as the first people to populate the islands of Micronesia did thousands of years ago.

Borrowing and Privacy

If you spend much time in a local's home in the FSM and Palau, you will notice that notions of privacy and borrowing are very different than in the United States and Europe. If, for example, you leave a bag in a local's house, you may discover that children or adults will explore its contents to satisfy their curiosity. What is more, if you loan something to a Micronesian, you cannot assume that it will be returned. These customs, considered rude or even criminal by some Westerners, are simply what is expected of friends and family members in Micronesian cultures. If you find yourself the "victim" of these customs, consider yourself privileged to be counted among the friends or family of a local.

Micronesians have largely adopted Western clothing, except on some of Yap's outer islands, but traditional clothing, including grass skirts and loin cloths, is worn during traditional dances and ceremonies. Tattoos, once symbols of power and authority, have all but disappeared from the islands of Micronesia and Palau due to the influence of Christian missionaries. Micronesian tattoos, which could cover a person's entire body, are now relatively rare, but some Yapese still bear traditional tattoos.

Music in Micronesia and Palau is a living art form as religious choral singing is important to modern worship on many islands, especially Kosrae. Traditional dance is also a very important and constantly evolving art form. In Micronesia and Palau, traditional dances are usually performed by a group in unison and may involve chanting or rhythmic instruments, such as sticks or paddles.

LANGUAGES

Twenty-one distinct languages, including English, are spoken in Micronesia and Palau. Some languages have several dialects. In some areas of these countries, each separate island has a unique language that may or may not be intelligible to the people of nearby islands. For example, in Pohnpei state, the majority of citizens speak Pohnpeian, of which there are two dialects. Outer islanders in the state speak various languages that share a great deal of vocabulary with Pohnpeian but which are nevertheless distinct.

In general, the languages are classified as Malayo-Polynesian. Since Micronesia was settled both by Polynesians from the east and southeast Asians from the west, it is unsurprising that Micronesian languages share features of Polynesian languages as well as languages spoken in East Asia. Nevertheless, as a group Micronesian languages are distinct from both.

There is some fear that the languages of the FSM and Palau may be dying. Certainly, many specialized and honorific words have already been forgotten. Also, many English words have infiltrated Micronesian languages, in some cases replacing native words in common usage. Pacific Resources for Education and Learning (www.prel.org), a nonprofit organization that produces educational materials for Pacific islands associated with the United States, has several publications aimed at preserving these languages.

One interesting feature of many Micronesian languages is the importance put on location. Many languages in the region have elaborate sets of words and suffixes to express the locations and orientations of people and objects. By contrast, many of these languages do not have precise ways to express time. Pohnpeian, for example, has no past or future tense in the way that English does. Instead, the time of a verb is usually inferred from context.

Most English-speakers have difficulty picking up these languages. Luckily, English is spoken on every island in Micronesia, especially by businesspeople or government officials. Also, hotel and restaurant employees usually know enough English to help a visitor with simple questions. Indeed, almost everyone born after World War II knows a few words in English. However, many Micronesians are shy or fear that they may appear unintelligent if their English is not flawless. They are more at ease with English-speakers who know even a few simple phrases in the local language. See pg 223 for a language reference.

RELIGION

The vast majority of citizens of the FSM and Palau belong to various Protestant or Catholic denominations. On most islands, the inhabitants are split roughly in half along Protestant-Catholic lines, though Catholics predominate in Palau and Chuuk. On some islands there are very small communities of Mormons, Baha'i, Muslims, Jehovah's Witnesses, Seventh Day Adventists, and other missionary religions. Missionaries of all of these religions are active to this day in Micronesia and Palau. The number of missionaries varies depending on the island.

Almost all Micronesians have given up the most evident practices associated with traditional religion or spiritual beliefs. Indeed, since missionaries began arriving in Micronesia and Palau, Micronesians adopted Christian beliefs and practices relatively wholeheartedly, and a church service in Micronesia or Palau will seem familiar to any visitor who has attended a Protestant or Catholic service back home. Nevertheless, Micronesians deeply respect the spiritual beliefs of their ancestors. Even Micronesians whose families have practiced Christianity for generations may profess a belief in "magic," retain knowledge of traditional healing beliefs, or avoid profaning a place held to be spiritually significant.

In most Western societies, a typical question to ask a new acquaintance is "What do you do?" In Micronesia, however, you will inevitably face the question, "What is your religion?" Or, more directly, "Do you believe in Jesus?"

Protestant and Catholic churches abound throughout Micronesia and Palau, and travelers will not have trouble finding a place to attend church on Sunday mornings. In fact, attending church can be a worthwhile and memorable cultural experience. Visitors are often impressed by the choral singing of Micronesian congregations, especially on Kosrae.

On Palau, a small number maintains the religion known as Modekngei. This religion, a hybrid between Christianity and traditional beliefs, is the only form of native religion openly practiced in Micronesia or Palau.

See Native Religion on Palau *on pg 207 to learn more about Modekngei.*

The Basics

Getting There and Away

It is not easy to reach Micronesia or Palau. The costs of travel, distances, and traveling time involved all conspire to make these beautiful countries out of reach for many travelers. However, these countries are also protected from the crowds and extensive economic development associated with mass tourism, and if you can afford to travel here, it is well worth the difficulty of arranging an itinerary.

AIRLINES

Continental Airlines ((800) 231-0856, www.continental.com) is the only major carrier servicing the four states of Micronesia. China Airlines, Japan Airlines, and Asiana Airlines, in addition to Continental Airlines, sometimes offer charter flights to Palau. Continental flights leaving from Guam, Hawaii, and Manila in the Philippines hop from island to island, stopping in Palau and all the FSM states.

On Continental flights through Micronesia, it is necessary for half of the plane to disembark at each stop so that the cabin can be searched, except at Kwajalein in the Marshall Islands.

If you are going to Kosrae from the United States, flying through Hawaii is probably easier than going through Guam. Otherwise, travelling through Guam is recommended as doing so avoids two extra stops in the Marshall Islands. If you are flying to Palau through Asia, you will probably want to take the flight from the Philippines.

When departing from Kosrae, Pohnpei, or Chuuk, you will face an airport tax of $10-15. In Palau the fee is $35. Airline baggage fees will also apply. Continental Airlines currently allows each passenger to check one bag up to 70 pounds for no additional charge. Airline baggage policies change frequently though, so be sure to check with Continental Airlines before packing your bags.

Avoiding Jet Lag

Needless to say, if you are travelling from the U.S. or Europe, you will face significant jet lag. A good strategy is to set your watch for the time at your destination as you board your plane to depart. Throughout the flight, periodically check your watch, and, as much as you can, sleep, stay awake, and eat meals according to the times at your final destination.

CRUISES

Cruises have sometimes stopped at some islands in Micronesia, specifically Pohnpei, Chuuk Lagoon, and some of the outer islands of Yap. Though such cruises offer a great chance to see the Federated States of Micronesia and Palau, they are not necessarily the best way to experience these countries. One of the biggest attractions of Micronesia and Palau is that they do not have extensive tourist industries, and seeking out the authentic experiences that makes visiting Micronesia so memorable takes time and freedom that cruises may not allow. As of this writing, the authors are not aware of any cruises making regular stops in Micronesia or Palau.

Suggestions on What to Pack

- Antibiotic ointment and bandages: for small cuts and scrapes
- Antifungal cream: for fungal infections
- Medications: a large supply of any over-the-counter or prescription medications you take regularly
- Multivitamin: particularly if you are traveling to remote areas for an extended period
- Oral rehydration salts: to treat dehydration from diarrhea or the sun
- Over-the-counter medications for pain, motion sickness, diarrhea, and nausea or upset stomach
- Contact supplies or an extra pair of prescription glasses: these are usually not available locally
- Insect repellant and sunscreen
- Sunglasses
- Diving and snorkeling equipment: including mask, snorkel, fins, wet suit (not necessary for warmth but recommended as a protective layer)
- Dry bag: if you plan on traveling over water, this will keep your belongings dry
- Flashlight: power outages occur on all the islands from time to time
- Flip-flops: the only practical footwear on the islands
- Sealable plastic bags: these will protect your electronics and valuables from humidity or water

FIELD TRIP SHIPS

Within the FSM, it is possible to join one of the government-owned ships on a field trip. These field trip ships carry passengers and goods, including emergency supplies, to outer islands. Field trips, which can last from a week to over a month, usually depart from Pohnpei on round-trip journeys to Kosrae, Chuuk, Yap, or the small islands south of Pohnpei. The ships always stop at outer islands along the way. Usually, these ships travel during the night and stop during the day at various islands to load and unload passengers and cargo. As a passenger, you can accompany one of these ships and hop from island to island, a truly amazing experience and one of the best ways to see the outer islands.

However, planning to join a field trip is next to impossible if you are not on an extended visit to Micronesia. Field trips are routinely cancelled or delayed for weeks, even at the very hour of the scheduled departure. Wildly varying rumors about when ships are leaving abound, and even port officials are often mistaken about crucial information.

Tickets can be obtained from the port authority several weeks before a trip leaves for $10 and up, depending on the length of the journey. Accommodations on the ships are not comfortable. A few cramped cabins are available, but the cheapest way to travel is to sleep on the crowded deck. The latter option is not for those who are concerned about Western notions like personal space or physical comfort, but traveling in this way affords ample opportunity to meet locals. These ships do have kitchens, where you can buy a meal for $5-7, but most passengers bring their own food and water. Contact the **Pohnpei Port Authority** (320-2682) for schedules and tickets.

If you want to take a field trip ship, start planning several months in advance. Two weeks before the ship is scheduled to leave, begin calling the port authority every day for schedule changes. Most importantly, be very flexible with your plans.

Customs and Entry Requirements

The FSM and Palau require all visitors to have a passport that is valid for a period after the date of arrival (6 months in Palau, 120 days in the FSM). Also, both countries require proof that one can leave the country; a ticket showing the intended date of departure suffices. Tourist visas for 30 days are issued upon arrival in either country, and visas can be extended for a fee with approval from the immigration office. Citizens of the United States, FSM, Guam, Northern Mariana Islands, or Marshall Islands can obtain visas for up to one year upon arrival. If you are traveling by yacht or other private craft, you must visit the capital town in Palau or the FSM state and pass through customs before visiting any island. Importation of controlled substances and weapons is prohibited.

In the FSM, you will have to pass through customs in each state that you enter.

Though marijuana is widely used in Micronesia and Palau, it is illegal in both countries.

IMMUNIZATIONS

If you are traveling from an area with cholera or yellow fever, you must have proof of immunization. It is also strongly recommended that you enter the country with up-to-date immunizations for tetanus and diphtheria, polio, typhoid, hepatitis A, and hepatitis B.

Communications and Media

CELL PHONES

Cell phones can be used on the main islands and some of the outer islands of Palau. Cell phone service is provided by the FSM Telecommunications Corporation in Micronesia and by a few providers in Palau. Service is fairly reliable in the towns, but it can be spotty elsewhere.

INTERNET

There are a few establishments on each of the main islands offering wireless or wired internet access, often for a fee. As might be expected, internet access is very limited on outer islands, if it is available at all.

MAIL

The FSM and Palau use their own stamps rather than U.S. stamps.

Both the Republic of Palau and the Federated States of Micronesia are serviced by the U.S. Postal Service. Mail service is fairly fast and reliable. Mail to or from the United States follows standard U.S. domestic rates while international rates are sometimes higher than those in the United States.

PRINT MEDIA

A few English-language local newspapers are available in Micronesia and Palau, such as the *Kasalehlie Press* (Pohnpei), the *Micronesian Alliance* (Kosrae and Chuuk), the *Yap Networker* (Yap), and the *Island Times*, *Palau Horizon*, and *Tia Belau* (Palau), all of which are published on a weekly, biweekly, or monthly basis. The *Pacific Daily News*, published in Guam, is also readily available. Other newspapers are difficult to find on the islands.

RADIO

Outer islands use radio to communicate with the major islands. Most, though not all, outer islands have a municipal office on the main island in their state, and if you need to get a message to an outer island, you should try going through this municipal office.

TELEPHONE

Prepaid phone cards are available on all the main islands from FSM Telecom or Palau National Communications. Telephones are in most hotel rooms. Additionally, most stores, restaurants, and hotels are happy to let you borrow their phone for a local or prepaid long-distance call.

International Calling

To call an international number from the FSM or Palau, dial 011 + country code + area code and number. To call the FSM, dial your country's exit code + 691 + seven-digit number. To call Palau, dial your country's exit code + 680 + seven-digit number.

TELEVISION AND RADIO

On the main islands, English-language cable television is widespread. Most islands also have a few local radio stations in English or the local language. There is also a healthy market of bootleg and legitimate English, Japanese, Filipino, and Korean DVDs.

Money

BANKS AND ATMS

In Palau, there are banks in Koror but not on Babeldaob or the outer islands. In the FSM, there are banks only on Kosrae, Pohnpei, Weno, and Yap proper. ATMs are common in Palau, but they are few and far between in the FSM; moreover, ATMs often run out of money or break down. As such, it is a good idea to always carry cash on your person or stashed in a safe, secure place. If you are uncomfortable carrying a large amount of cash while traveling to Micronesia, bring some cash and a supply of traveler's checks. If you are in a pinch, Western Union wire transfer services are available on Pohnpei, Weno, and Yap proper.

Credit cards

Some establishments in the FSM accept credit cards, but most do not. In Palau, credit cards are more widely accepted. Even if you plan to use a credit card, it is advisable to carry some cash with you, as credit card machines can be unreliable even at establishments where they are accepted.

BUDGETING

Your budget will vary widely depending which islands you visit during your stay, what kind of hotel you choose, and what activities you want to participate in. In general, Palau is more expensive than the islands in the FSM. Obviously, airfare to and from Micronesia and Palau as well as among the islands will be the most expensive aspect of your travel.

Lodgings are also not cheap. A double occupancy room will cost you at least $60 per night, and rooms at the higher end hotels in Yap and Palau can be as much as $300 per night. If you choose to eat out frequently, you should expect to spend at least $30 per person per day on food. If you prepare some of your own meals, you could save quite a bit.

If you plan to dive, you will want to budget $150 or more per day per person (sometimes the cost of a dive trip includes food). The costs of other activities vary widely. Seeing a cultural site or a museum on your own might be free or might cost only a few dollars per person. Going there with a tour guide could be $40 or more for a group. Hiring a boat (with gas and a driver) for a day might cost $150 or significantly more.

If it is your first time to Micronesia, you might consider staying at one of the higher end "eco-resorts," such as the Kosrae Village Resort, the Village Hotel on Pohnpei, or the Blue Lagoon Resort in Chuuk. While these hotels are fairly expensive, they sometimes offer convenient transportation around the island, they have the most knowledgeable tour guides, and some services may be included with your room. If nothing else, staying at one of these resorts is the easiest way to see the most of a given island in a short time. To save money, you could stay at one of these resorts for a few nights, take advantage of their tours and dive shop, and then move to a cheaper hotel, from which you could explore on your own.

CURRENCY

Both the Republic of Palau and the Federated States of Micronesia use U.S. dollars. There are money changers at the airports, but you may wish to change some currency before arriving in case the money changers are not working when you arrive.

Weather

Any time is a good time to visit Micronesia and Palau! Though the islands tend to be wetter from June to October, the weather of these countries varies little throughout the year.

The islands of Micronesia and Palau are tropical. Average daily high temperatures are about 80° Fahrenheit (27° Celsius) all year. The summer and early fall months tend to be the wettest, but it is fairly wet throughout the year, especially on the high islands. Nevertheless, Micronesia and Palau do have droughts from time to time.

Typhoons, tropical storms in the western Pacific Ocean that are called hurricanes when they occur in the Atlantic or eastern Pacific, are not frequent. Pohnpei and Kosrae are very rarely hit by a typhoon, although they do experience major storms when typhoons pass the area. Chuuk, Yap, and

Palau are at a greater risk of a direct hit. Typhoons pose the greatest danger to thatch and tin-roof houses and to low-lying coral atolls.

Travelers with Special Considerations

CHILDREN

Micronesia and Palau are great places to travel with children. Children can accompany adults while swimming, snorkeling, hiking, and appreciating the culture of these countries. In addition, though Micronesian children may be initially shy, they are generally eager to make friends with foreign visitors of all ages.

DISABLED

There are almost no facilities in Micronesia or Palau designed with disabled travelers in mind. Kosrae Village Resort and Dolphins Pacific in Palau are the only exceptions of which we are aware.

LGBT

There are really no businesses or services intended specifically for gay travelers in Micronesia and Palau. Homosexuality and transgender issues are not openly discussed in either of these countries, and Micronesians and Palauans tend to view both homosexual and heterosexual displays of affection as inappropriate in public.

SENIORS

The cultures of Micronesia and Palau hold elders in high esteem, and senior travelers in good health will enjoy a trip to either country. If access to medical care or special services is important, then Palau is to be preferred to the FSM, and the outer islands should be avoided entirely.

Accommodations

HOTELS

Micronesia and, to some extent, Palau are relatively new tourist destinations. All of the main islands, however, have at least a handful of hotels and resorts. Unfortunately for the budget traveler, there are no hostels, and rates tend to run a little high. When making your plans, be sure to ask hotels about any specials that they might offer. See pg 32 for information on budgeting for your lodgings.

HOMESTAYS

Camping is not common in Micronesia or Palau. If you do wish to camp, be sure to ask the landowner for permission beforehand.

Staying with a local family is certainly the best way to experience local culture in Micronesia and Palau. If you are not acquainted with any locals, it can be difficult to arrange a homestay on the main islands, where visitors usually stay in hotels. Still, Micronesians like visitors, and if you strike up a friendship with a local, he or she will likely invite you over. If you feel comfortable visiting the person, do not hesitate to accept!

It is slightly easier to secure a homestay on the outer islands. If you plan on journeying to the outer islands, talk to the municipal office for the island you plan to visit or radio ahead and ask about arranging a homestay.

Any time you visit a local at home, it is appropriate to bring a small gift of food. On outer islands especially, it is appropriate to offer a gift of food or cash for any help you receive.

Toilets

Fully functional toilets are available in all hotels and in the capital towns of every state in the FSM. On outer islands or in remote areas of main islands, there may or may not be a flush toilet available to you. Outhouses, or pit latrines, are common in these areas. If you are traveling in remote areas, carrying your own toilet paper is a good idea, but a banana leaf or a scrap of paper can serve in a pinch.

Food and Drink

TRADITIONAL FOOD

Micronesian diets have changed drastically with the importation of rice, livestock, and canned food, but many families in Micronesia and Palau still eat traditional, local foods much of the time. Taro, a starchy root that grows in the tropics, is a staple. Boiled or baked, it appears in many Micronesian dishes. It is, in addition, vitamin and mineral-rich. Yam is also an important root on some islands, especially on Pohnpei, where yams are a symbol of prestige.

Micronesia and Palau are home to a wide variety of fruits. There is a seemingly endless diversity of bananas, most of which make the yellow variety found in the grocery stores of developed countries seem bland. Breadfruit, a starchy but delicious and healthful fruit that is always eaten cooked, is culturally important on many islands. Soursop, an exceedingly sweet fruit sometimes eaten as a dessert, is found on some islands here. Also common are papaya, plantain, starfruit, crab apples, mangos, watermelon, pineapple, and, of course, the ever-present coconut.

Not surprisingly, Micronesians also take their sustenance from the fruit of the sea. Pelagic fish, such as yellowfin tuna, skipjack tuna, rainbow runner, and mahi mahi, as well as reef fish are staples in Micronesian diets. Mangrove crab, coconut crab, and small shellfish are also very common. Some Micronesians enjoy sea cucumbers, but foreigners generally find these unpalatable.

RESTAURANTS AND STORES

Restaurants in Micronesia and Palau rarely serve local food. Instead they exist largely to serve American and Asian patrons, and thus borrow heavily from American, Japanese, Korean, and Chinese cuisine. Burgers, fried chicken, rice, and tuna sashimi are very common. Regrettably, canned meats such as Spam and corned beef hash are also very popular. The one local food that is consistently found in restaurants is fish, and the fish in Micronesia and Palau is among the freshest and most delicious that can be found anywhere.

Like restaurants, stores usually offer mostly imported foods. Canned foods, ramen noodles, pasta, and snack foods are all staples. Many fresh fruits and vegetables are also imported, but if you do not happen to go into a grocery store immediately after a shipment has arrived, you are likely to find only a few rotten leftovers. Local fruits, on the other hand, are plentiful and delicious, but they are more often sold in small stalls or by individuals than in grocery stores. Fresh fish can be purchased in some grocery stores, but for the freshest fish, go to the local market in the late morning after the fishermen have returned from their morning fishing trips.

Spam is sometimes substituted for chicken or beef, even when the menu says otherwise. If you are opposed to eating Spam, be sure to ask before ordering anything with "chicken" or "beef."

DRINKS

Imported soft drinks, beer, wine, and liquors are popular in Micronesia and Palau, and it is easy to find a variety of brands marketed and sold in the United States. The local drink of choice is coconut milk. Coconut milk, which varies from fizzy to sweet depending on the coconut, is nature's alternative to soft drinks. If you are feeling dehydrated or thirsty, ask for a coconut and drink the milk straight from the shell. When you are done, toss the biodegradable container on the ground. You may need to ask for help when opening a coconut.

Coconut milk is excellent for replenishing fluids lost through sweat and exposure to the sun.

A variety of intoxicating beverages are enjoyed on certain islands. *Sakau*, a muddy, narcotic drink similar to kava, is central to Pohnpeian culture, and drinking it is more of a religious experience than a culinary one. Tuba, fermented coconut milk, is popular on some islands. Beverages based on fermented yeast are also found on certain outer islands. Palau and Yap have micro-breweries that are worth trying.

Tipping

Tipping is becoming more commonplace in Micronesia and Palau, and while it is not expected at every establishment (in fact, there is no tipping anywhere on Kosrae), it is always appreciated. Tipping 10% after a meal is usually sufficient; in Palau it is common to tip up to 20%, though again this is not expected. It is also polite to leave a couple dollars per day in your hotel room for the housekeeping staff. At some hotels this gratuity may be included in your bill, so be sure to check before leaving a tip. Tour guides, including dive guides, appreciate tips as well. You do not need to tip taxi drivers.

Shopping

It is possible to buy a variety of local goods and handicrafts from individuals or from stores in Micronesia and Palau. Popular souvenirs include small carvings of sea animals, grass skirts, especially the brightly colored skirts from Yap, Chuukese masks and love sticks (see pg 121), woven baskets, Palauan storyboards (see pg 214), and a variety of decorative and functional items. One popular souvenir is a carved stool with a knob on one end. Functional, Spartan versions of these stools are used daily on many islands to grate coconuts, but artistic, polished versions are also available in some shops.

Activities

Visitors who love water sports and outdoor activities will find plenty to enjoy in Micronesia and Palau. The countries are world-renowned among divers, and there are great spots for diving and snorkeling on every island. Surfing is also popular, especially on Pohnpei. It should not be surprising that Micronesia and Palau offer opportunities for fishing using either foreign or traditional techniques. There are also abundant opportunities for kayaking, especially on Palau. For those who prefer to stay on land, hiking and biking are great ways to see the islands.

For travelers wanting to experience Micronesia and Palau at a little slower pace, there are plenty of opportunities to interact with local culture. Cultural tours on Yap are famous, but other islands have much culture to share as well. Photography is a great way to capture your experiences of the natural and cultural landscapes of Micronesia and Palau, though sometimes you will need to ask permission before taking pictures. Bird watchers and those interested in biology will find plenty to keep them busy. Last but certainly not least, Micronesia and Palau offer many opportunities simply to relax and watch the world pass by.

Health and Safety

In general, the Federated States of Micronesia and the Republic of Palau are very safe countries. Still, when traveling in unfamiliar territory, it helps to follow a few precautions. Some general information is given below. In each of the following chapters, there is information specific to health and safety concerns in Palau and the states of the FSM.

There is no rabies, yellow fever, or malaria in Micronesia and Palau.

CIGUATERA POISONING

Ciguatera poisoning results from eating fish that have consumed too much of certain types of toxic algae. Locals, including those working in restaurants, usually know which fish are safe to be eaten. Very large fish, turtles, and sharks tend to accumulate ciguatera more than other species, but small fish can be dangerous as well. Symptoms of ciguatera poisoning include numbness, paralysis, nausea, cramps, diarrhea, and sometimes death. If you suspect that you have been poisoned from eating fish, vomit as much as you can and seek medical attention immediately.

CUTS AND SCRAPES

Wash cuts thoroughly with soap and use an antibiotic ointment to prevent infection. Cuts take longer to heal and become infected more easily in the tropics.

Embassies and Immigration Offices

	FSM	Palau
Embassy in United States	1725 N Street, NW Washington, DC USA 20036 (202) 223-4383	1701 Pennsylvania Ave., NW Suite 300 Washington, DC USA 20006 (202) 452-6814
U.S. embassy in country	Box 1286 Kolonia, Pohnpei FM 96941 320-2187	PO Box 6028 Koror, Palau 96940 587-2920
Australian embassy in country	PO Box S Kolonia, Pohnpei FM 96941 320-5448	None
Immigration office	Main office: 320-5844 Kosrae office: 370-3051 Chuuk office: 330-2335 Yap office: 350-2126	488-2498

DENGUE FEVER

If you plan on spending the night in a remote area or on an outer island, it is a good idea to sleep under a mosquito net. Insect repellant is also helpful while exploring the islands during the day.

Dengue fever is a serious and sometimes fatal disease transmitted by mosquitoes primarily during the day in urban areas. It is rare, but it is found on some islands in Micronesia and Palau. Its symptoms include a sudden high fever, nausea, vomiting, muscle and joint pain, headache, and, in severe forms of the disease, excessive bleeding. If you suspect you may have dengue fever, seek medical attention immediately for diagnosis and treatment.

DIET

If you follow a typical Micronesian diet during your visit, you may find you are not getting enough fruits or vegetables. There are plenty of fresh fruits around, but they are often sold in stalls beside the road rather than in grocery stores or restaurants. Taking a multivitamin can also help to balance your diet.

DIGESTIVE PROBLEMS

Be sure to bring a large supply of all prescription and over-the-counter drugs that you use regularly.

It is very common for visitors to Micronesia and Palau to suffer from bouts of diarrhea. Often these bouts are minor, and the only treatment needed is hydration. It is important, though, to recognize the signs of a serious illness.

Any time you experience diarrhea, you should increase your fluid intake. You should treat severe cases of diarrhea with oral rehydration salts, which are available over-the-counter. Consuming bananas, toast, tea, or apples can also help. Drugs designed to stop diarrhea, such as loperamide or diphenoxylate, are only recommended if you are traveling somewhere where you cannot use the restroom.

You should seek medical attention immediately if you experience any of the following symptoms:

- blood or mucus in the stool
- severe diarrhea
- diarrhea lasting over 48 hours
- diarrhea with a fever

In these cases, you need to see a medical professional and have your stool tested to determine the cause of the diarrhea.

If you do not suffer from a bout of diarrhea, you may experience constipation during your trip due to the low levels of fiber in Micronesian diets. Constipation rarely poses a serious health threat, but it can be uncomfortable. Drinking water, eating foods high in fiber, such as breadfruit, and consuming fiber supplements can help alleviate this discomfort.

DOGS

On many islands, dogs are allowed to roam freely. These dogs can be quite frightening, and dog bites do occur. There is no rabies in Micronesia or Palau, however, and dog bites are rarely serious. If a dog barks or charges at you, it is important to keep your cool. Often, a dog will run off if you simply pretend to bend down and pick up a rock. If this does not work, try waving a stick or throwing rocks, and do not hesitate to kick a dog if it comes within range.

FUNGAL INFECTIONS

Fungal infections, marked by an itching, burning, or easily irritated rash, are common in the tropics, usually on the scalp, hands, feet, or groin. If you experience a fungal infection, treat the affected area with an over-the-counter antifungal ointment, expose the area to the open air as much as possible, and wash your hands frequently to prevent spreading the infection to other parts of your body. Cotton clothing is better for preventing fungal infections than synthetic materials.

HEAT

The heat and sun near the equator can be oppressive for visitors, especially when one first arrives in the tropics. In order to avoid heat exhaustion, it is important to drink liquids frequently and to replenish electrolytes (found in fruits like bananas) that are lost in sweat. If you experience fatigue, headache, or muscle cramps, try slowing your pace, drinking water, and eating something salty. If exposure to heat is prolonged it can lead to heatstroke, a serious condition that requires professional medical attention. The symptoms of heatstroke are decreased sweating, a high temperature, severe headaches, and sometimes mood disruptions.

PARASITES

As long as you drink only bottled water and eat only foods that are prepared in restaurants or that you cook yourself, you are relatively safe from parasites. If you do not, there is a small but real chance that you will acquire a parasite, such

Emergency Numbers

	Kosrae	Pohnpei	Chuuk	Yap	Palau
Police	911	320-2221	911	911	911
Ambulance	370-3012	320-2213	320-2444	350-3446	488-1411
Hospital	370-3012	111	330-2444	350-3446	488-2558

as giardiasis. Symptoms of a parasite can appear intermittently over a period of weeks or months, but if you experience severe cramps, bloating, or excessive diarrhea or gas during or after your trip to the region, you should see a doctor to be tested and possibly treated for a parasitic infection.

SEA SICKNESS

If traveling over water gives you motion sickness, then it is a good idea to take some over-the-counter sea sickness medicine with you.

STDS

Sexually transmitted diseases, such as HIV/AIDS, gonorrhea, syphilis, and hepatitis B, are a growing concern in Micronesia and Palau. Safe sex practices are not widespread in these countries. Protect yourself against STDs during your visit by abstaining from sex or using a condom.

Despite growning concerns, HIV infection rates are very low, with less than 25 cases reported in FSM and less than 10 in Palau (2004 stats).

HIV can also be spread during blood transfusions or by using a needle after a person with HIV has used it. The hospitals in the FSM and Palau are reasonably safe, but check to see that needles are unwrapped in front of you to protect yourself from HIV infection. If you are seriously injured, do not refuse a blood transfusion out of fear of HIV infection.

SUNBURN

Wearing a T-shirt, even while swimming, offers some protection against the sun in addition to being culturally sensitive.

Sunburn is a common health issue for visitors to Micronesia and Palau. Wearing sunscreen is essential to avoid sunburns if you are going to be under the sun for any length of time. If you are not picky about the brand or the quality of sunscreen that you use, you can purchase it at some stores in Micronesia and Palau. Otherwise, you may want to bring some from home. In Palau, you can find sunblock for prices similar to what you can find in the United States, but usually the bottles are much closer to their expiration dates and brands are much more limited. Wearing sunglasses and a hat will help to protect your eyes and face from damage caused by the sun.

WATER

Water-borne diseases and poor waste management are common in some areas, making tap water unsafe to drink. Cholera outbreaks are not common, but they do occur from time to time. Check the health and safety section in each of the following chapters for information specific to each state of the FSM and to Palau. Bottled water is readily available in stores and restaurants on all the major islands. If you are visiting a remote area, you should bring enough bottled water for your trip or boil your drinking water for several minutes to kill any pathogens. Filters by themselves do not make water safe to drink; if you choose to use a filter, you should do so in combination with a chemical agent such as iodine. Water filters and iodine are not available in Micronesia or Palau.

WATER SAFETY

Enjoying the water is one of the best parts of visiting Micronesia and Palau. In order to keep yourself safe in the water, it is helpful to follow a few precautions.

If you are going to be traveling outside a protected reef on the open ocean in a motorboat, ensure that the boat has spare gas, more than one outboard motor, and life jackets. It is quite easy for a single motor to break down or run out of gas, leaving you lost at sea. Even the most experienced local fishermen respect the sea and fear the possibility of becoming adrift in the open ocean.

When diving or swimming, be careful to avoid cutting yourself on coral. It goes without saying that coral can be very sharp. In addition, some coral is poisonous.

Sharks

Sharks are not the aggressive, man-eating predators that they are reputed to be. Still, they can be dangerous animals. If you see a shark while swimming or diving, do not panic. Keep your distance and try tapping the top of the water to get it to go away.

Most species of sea life are not dangerous. On the other hand, some species, including certain fish, jellyfish, shellfish (especially conefish), urchins, rays, and coral, are poisonous, and it is better not to find out that a certain species is poisonous the hard way. In general, do not touch any underwater creature unless you know that the particular species is safe. Also, to minimize the risk of bites or stings, do not put your hand into crevasses or under rocks where you cannot see it.

Some ocean currents, particularly those in breaks in a reef, can be quite strong. Do not tire yourself by swimming directly against a current. Instead, swim across a current diagonally until you reach a relatively calmer stretch of water.

Diving Safety

Before diving in Micronesia or Palau, you should, of course, be certified for the depth you wish to dive. Some dive shops in Micronesia and Palau offer quick dive certification courses, but you might consider taking a longer, more comprehensive certification course before you come to the islands, especially if you plan to dive below 40 feet. A longer dive certification course will ensure that you fully understand how to protect yourselves from the risks inherent in diving.

When possible, bring your own equipment. Though the equipment at most dive shops is reasonably reliable, using your own equipment can give you some extra peace of mind. Finally, bear in mind that some dive shops cater to a Japanese-speaking clientele while others serve mostly English speakers. Ensure that you can communicate with your divemaster.

Responsible Travel

ISSUES FACING MICRONESIA AND PALAU

Environmental issues

Endangered species such as mangrove crabs, a variety of fish, and giant clam as well as protected species such as sea turtles are often poached and eaten. Local restaurants may even offer endangered or threatened species such as mangrove crabs on their menus.

In Chuuk, the large population has led to unsustainable fishing practices. One egregious practice involves using dynamite to destroy parts of coral reefs in order to catch fish. By destroying coral reefs, an important habitat for fish, some Chuukese fishermen are jeopardizing their long-term livelihoods for the sake of a few fish in the short term.

> Most Micronesians use sustainable fishing practices. Unfortunately, the Japanese and Chinese fishing boats in the same waters do not.

Another major concern for islanders in the Pacific is the threat of rising sea levels. Scientists have long worried that rising average global temperatures will cause polar ice caps to melt. In turn, sea levels will rise, swallowing up coastal lands. This is a concern for low-lying coral atolls in particular, which could be submerged if sea levels rise even a small amount. High islands could also be affected if the arable land near the coast becomes submerged, forcing islanders to move into the uncultivated jungle.

There is disagreement in the scientific community as to how much or how quickly sea levels might rise. Anecdotal evidence from the islands, however, suggests that sea levels, at least in some places, are rising. From time to time, one can even see buildings that were presumably built above water some years ago but are now partially underwater at high tide.

One way that islanders cope with this problem is to use trash to make new land. This practice not only provides room for population expansion but also recycles waste.

Social Issues

The quality of **education** available to children in Micronesia varies widely from place to place. On some islands, decent, though not great, schools are available. On others, schools are highly dysfunctional. Nearly all schools in the FSM and Palau struggle to find enough qualified teachers and up-to-date textbooks. Education in speaking, understanding, and writing English is particularly important, as English is the language of business and government.

Among the many **public health** issues facing Micronesia and Palau are drug and alcohol abuse, the spread of STDs, and diseases associated with poor diet and obesity.

The importation of white rice, which is relatively cheap and much easier to prepare than local foods, has contributed to a diabetes epidemic in Micronesia and Palau. It is hypothesized that Micronesians are genetically programmed to conserve blood sugar; this combined with increasingly sedentary lifestyles and consumption of imported foods high in sugar and fat has made diabetes a leading cause of death.

Opportunities for Women

Although traditional hierarchies on many islands in Micronesia and Palau were based on matrilineal descent, women paradoxically have few opportunities for political or economic advancement on these same islands. One particularly abhorrent manifestation of women's lack of power is the prevalence of domestic abuse. It is difficult to say how big of a problem this is, as shame and silence surround the issue. Sadly, however, it is an issue on many islands in this region.

TIPS FOR RESPONSIBLE TRAVEL

Dining

Tourists are urged to educate themselves on the endangered and threatened species in Micronesia and to abstain from eating these animals. In restaurants, stay away from mangrove crabs and all types of sea turtles.http:///   On Pohnpei, drinking *sakau* is an important cultural experience that is recommended for any visitor who is inclined to try it. However, you should be aware that the rainforests of Pohnpei's interior have been decimated as farmers clear land to grow *sakau*. If possible, try to limit your consumption and to drink *sakau* that has been harvested in the arable coastal areas, not in the interior.

Diving

When diving, it is important to consider the health of the marine environment. Observing the following tips will ensure that those who come after you will be able to experience the magic of the reefs and wrecks of Micronesia and Palau:

- Avoid touching coral and marine life unless you know that doing so is safe both for you and the marine organism.
- Do not touch artifacts that have been left in wrecks.
- Take care not to damage coral or plants inadvertently.
- For more information see the Palau International Coral Reef Center website at www.picrc.org.

Shopping

Bringing home a souvenir is a great way to remember your trip and to support the local economy. You should, however, avoid purchasing jewelry made from turtle shell or black coral. Both animals are threatened and illegal to import to some countries.

Instead, look for environmentally sustainable souvenirs that are produced locally. In the chapters that follow, we have indicated what stores carry locally made goods. Coconut oil, wood carvings, ornaments and jewelry that were not made from coral or turtle shell, grass skirts, fans, wall hangings, or even T-shirts that are sold in locally owned stores are all socially responsible purchases. If you are visiting Palau, consider not purchasing Palauan money beads, which often adorn necklaces. While buying these beads does put money into the local economy, doing so also depletes the country of a limited good that has great cultural and historical significance.

Waste

Garbage is a problem in Palau and the FSM. On most islands, landfills are simply too small for all the trash, so much garbage ends up littering the jungle or polluting the ocean. Palau has recycling capabilities; however, a national effort towards recycling has yet to be enacted. Visitors are encouraged to request the means to recycle products purchased at local businesses as a way to encourage local business owners to commit to the effort. There is also a recycling center on Kosrae. Visitors should ask at their hotel about how to recycle cans and plastic bottles while on the island. In the rest of the FSM, visitors can set a good example by not littering.

SERVICE OPPORTUNITIES

One way to make your trip a meaningful experience is to donate your time or material resources to a local organization. Listed below are just a few of the NGOs and local non-profits in Micronesia and Palau.

Kosrae

Kosrae Conservation and Safety Organization *and* Kosrae Island Resource Management Authority KCSO and KIRMA both work on environmental issues around the island. For instance, they have been instrumental in creating protected water space around the island, such as the Utwe-Walung Biosphere Reserve and the Tafunsak Marine Protected Area. They also organize island clean-ups as well as outreach and education programs in the elementary and high schools. KCSO occasionally teaches a one-semester class at the high school on environmental issues. *KCSO: 370-3673, kcso@mail.fm; KIRMA: PO Box 480, Tofol, Kosrae, FM 96944*

Micronesia Grand Tour Company *and* Kosrae Village Resort Both Micronesia Grand Tour and Kosrae Village Resort offer divers the opportunity to participate in coral monitoring each time they dive. The collected data is given to scientists with a number of coral monitoring projects, including Project AWARE, CoralWatch, Micronesia Conservation Trust, and Reef Check. Kosrae Village Resort, in particular, has won many awards for its environmental projects. *Micronesia Grand Tour: 370-7857, info@micronesiagrandtour.com, www.micronesiagrandtour.com/diving.html; Kosrae Village Resort: 370-3483, info@kosraevillage.com,www.kosraevillage.com/coral.shtml*

Pohnpei

Conservation Society of Pohnpei CSP seeks to preserve the natural environment and biodiversity of Pohnpei through community empowerment and educational programs. Their popular Green Road Show program educates 5th grade students in all of the elementary schools on Pohnpei about the environmental issues facing Pohnpei. *320-5409, csp@mail.fm, www.serehd.org*

Island Food Community of Pohnpei The Island Food Community of Pohnpei seeks to promote the cultivation and consumption of traditional Pohnpeian foods. According to the organization's vision statement, relying on local foods as opposed to imported foods will promote "food security, sustainable development, economic benefits, self-reliance, improved health, cultural preservation, and human dignity." You might be able to help by assisting in the organization's garden or by spreading the word to other travelers, islanders, and local restaurants about the benefits of local food. Island Food could also use your financial support. Become a member for $10. *320-3259, nutrition@mail.fm, pniagriculture@mail.fm, www.islandfood.org*

Chuuk

Chuuk Women's Council Chuuk Women's Council is an umbrella organization for numerous women's groups in Chuuk. The NGO's stated mission is:
"To assist women in becoming productive and self-sufficient members or our
society through comprehensive programs which enhance the social, economic and physical well-being of women and their families in Chuuk." Chuuk
Women's Council offers programs on health issues, women's leadership, and
culture. *330-5263, kfinchuuk@mail.fm, www.cwcfiinchuuk.org*

Habele Outer Island Education Fund Habele is a non-profit organization
based in South Carolina that focuses on improving the educational opportunities for people of the remote islands in Micronesia and beyond. Habele do-
nates school supplies and provides scholarships to students who must move
to attend quality high schools. One of the authors knows several students in
Chuuk who have received Habele scholarships. Without this support, at least
one of the students would not have been able to attend school after the 8th
grade. Habele is run by volunteers, all of whom have taught on outer islands
in Micronesia. *ngm@habele.org, www.habele.org*

Yap

Yap Traditional Navigation Society Yap Traditional Navigation Society is a non-
profit organization incorporated in 2005. The central focus of this group is to ensure
that traditional navigation and canoe-building practices are promoted and preserved. Local men are recruited and trained in the arts of traditional canoe-building
and navigation. This group also hosts the annual Canoe Festival. In 2009, the in-
augural year for this event, all the island's hotels were filled to capacity with outside
visitors. This festival is expected to be quite successful in the future. Donations
from tourists are a major component of funding for the organization. *www.ytns.org*

YAPS, Inc. Yap Animal Protection Society aims to make a difference in the
lives of animals on Yap Island by educating the public about the importance of
spaying and neutering dogs and cats and by raising money to host an annual
veterinary clinic. Because there is no veterinarian on the island, YAPS provides pet owners with an opportunity to get their dogs and cats the immunization shots and other care they require. *www.yapsinc.org*

Palau

International Inspiration International Inspiration is a British school sports
program currently being piloted in Palau. The organization partners with the
local government to promote athletics and physical education. For information
on donations of sports equipment or financial contributions please contact either International Inspiration or the Palau National Olympic Committee. *Palau
National Olympic Committee: 488-6562, pnoc@palaunet.com; International
Inspiration: sport@britishcouncil.org*

Micronesian Shark Foundation The Micronesian Shark Foundation conducts research on sharks in an effort to raise environmental awareness and
protect sharks in Palau. The project is based at the Fish n' Fins dive shop.
Visitors may be able to help the project by recording shark encounters during
their dives. *488-2637, info@msfpalau.org, www.msfpalau.org*

Palau Red Cross Society The Palau Red Cross Society (PRCS) is a non-profit
organization responsible for a variety of community service efforts, including a
blood donor database, disaster relief, aid to fire victims, FA/CPR training, and
military family support projects. The PRCS always needs financial support and
often needs volunteer support for one of their ongoing projects. *488-5780, 488-
5781, prcs@palaunet.com, palredcross@palaunet.com*

Federated States of
Micronesia

Kosrae

Rocking in a small boat on a still, tranquil harbor, you marvel at the intricate perfection of color and shape formed by the dying sun as it plays mischievous games of light and shadow on the broad green canvas of Sleeping Lady Mountain.

You are practically asleep at the wheel of your rental car when an astonishing sight jolts you from your reverie, as your headlamps spotlight...a herd of stampeding crabs.

Toes buried deep in soft, warm sand, you walk through a real-life postcard. To your right, azure water softly caresses the white sands; to your left, stately palms bow reverently to the sea. You pass thatched huts straight out of island lore; their friendly inhabitants welcome you with shouted greetings.

You float, free, weightless, through an underwater wonderland as astonishing as Alice's rabbit-hole, a bizarre, beautiful universe of bright color so fantastic that only Dr. Seuss could have envisaged it. Everything is too perfect to be real.

You leave the main road, walk behind a store, and enter another century. As you tread the cobbles underfoot and gaze in awe at the huge coral walls surrounding you, you strangely feel transported into a wholly different universe, of chiefs and nobles, honor and ritual.

To hear varied accounts of Kosrae is to view the island through a kaleidoscope; no two people see Kosrae exactly the same way. To locals, it is the island of the Sleeping Lady, to the zealous tourist office, "Jewel of Micronesia," to the Protestant missionaries, an "island of angels." To the cynic, this may sound like a fairy tale. However, you can experience all of this and more on the tiny, enigmatic, inviting island of Kosrae.

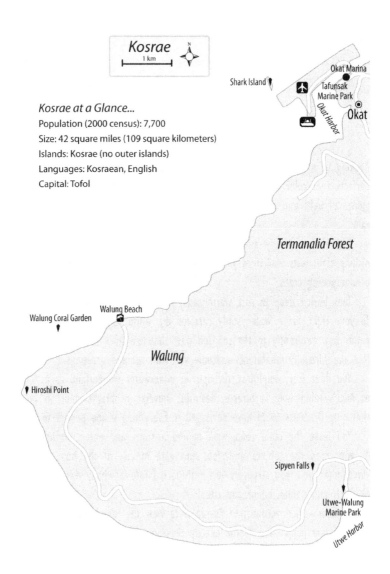

Kosrae

1 km

Kosrae at a Glance...
Population (2000 census): 7,700
Size: 42 square miles (109 square kilometers)
Islands: Kosrae (no outer islands)
Languages: Kosraean, English
Capital: Tofol

Shark Island

Okat Marina

Tafunsak
Marine Park

Okat Harbor

Okat

Termanalia Forest

Walung Beach

Walung Coral Garden

Hiroshi Point

Walung

Sipyen Falls

Utwe-Walung
Marine Park

Utwe Harbor

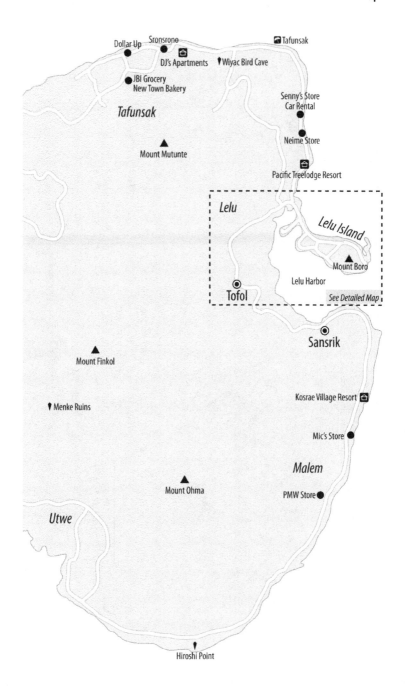

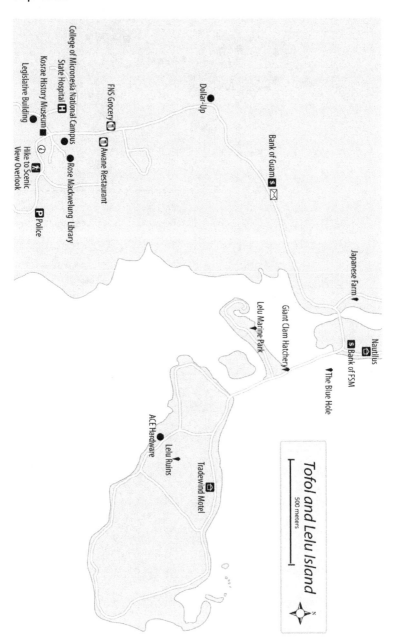

Tofol and Lelu Island

500 meters

N

- Dollar-Up
- College of Micronesia National Campus
- State Hospital
- Kosrae History Museum
- Legislative Building
- Hike to Scenic View Overlook
- FNS Grocery
- Awane Restaurant
- Rose Mackwelung Library
- Police
- Bank of Guam
- Japanese Farm
- Giant Clam Hatchery
- Lelu Marine Park
- Nautilus
- Bank of FSM
- The Blue Hole
- ACE Hardware
- Lelu Ruins
- Tradewind Motel

Geography

Kosrae is as tiny and isolated as it is beautiful. The easternmost landmass in the Caroline chain, Kosrae covers only 42 square miles (109 square kilometers), and it is located nearly 2,000 miles (3,200 kilometers) north of Australia and 2,500 miles (4,000 kilometers) southwest of Honolulu. At only 5.3° north latitude, Kosrae's climate reflects its location. Temperatures remain constant throughout the year, hovering between 82° and 86° Fahrenheit (28° and 30° Celsius). Receiving 200 inches (500 centimeters) of annual rainfall, Kosrae, along with Pohnpei, is one of the wettest places on earth. Though it is a small island, Kosrae has varied topography. Majestic mountains crown its middle, unspoiled white sand beaches ring its perimeter, and a pristine coral reef surrounds the island. Five main rivers irrigate Kosrae, keeping it green all year. Typhoons rarely hit Kosrae, as it lies outside of the typhoon belt.

Kosrae also plays host to a diverse variety of animals and plants, from tusked wild pigs roaming the mountains to hawksbill turtles, blacktip reef sharks, and thousands of colorful tropical fish swimming the seas. Mangrove trees and coconut palms cover the coastal plains, while jungle covers the interior. With such fertile soil, Kosrae could easily be called the "breadfruit basket" of Micronesia. While you are on the island, be sure to sample the delicious local foods, including green, succulent soursop, starchy taro, and tiny bananas that explode with flavor and sweetness.

The beaches, reefs, mangrove swamps, and rainforests invite exploration. Not only does Kosrae shelter sundry plants and animals, it also holds

HIGHLIGHTS OF KOSRAE

Climbing Mt. Ohma: Explore WWII tunnels, dip in stunning triple falls, and gain an astonishing bird's eye view of all Kosrae. pg 68

Exploring Lelu Ruins: Walk the cobbled streets and imagine ancient islanders building and living in the ruins. pg 68

Hiking to Sipyen Falls: Walk into another universe and admire the breath-taking 30-foot high Sipyen Falls. pg 67

Touring the mangroves: Slide through labyrinthine mangrove canals of Utwe-Walung Marine Park on a traditional outrigger canoe piloted by friendly and informative Baba Tadao. pg 73

Cruising in front of the Sleeping Lady at sunset: Take a boat to the middle of a still harbor and enjoy other visitors' company while watching the sun set behind the Sleeping Lady. See pg 75

everything from gorgeous waterfalls to wrecked pirate ships to Japanese-built tunnels from World War II.

Kosrae itself consists of two islands: the large, main island and Lelu Island, home to Lelu Ruins and the island's largest population center. The two islands are connected by a causeway. Kosrae is divided into five municipalities: Lelu, Tafunsak, Malem, Utwe, and Walung.

History

Just as waves and wind once carved Kosrae's stunning physical features from a formless, volcanic mass, so have powerful cultural forces shaped the island's history. From the first Western navigators and whalers to "discover" the island to the well-intentioned Christian missionaries and a succession of imperial overlords, outside forces molded Kosrae into the fascinating place it is today.

Most anthropologists agree that the first settlers arrived on Kosrae during the early 1000s BC and that these pioneers were Malayo-Polynesian maritime people. For over a thousand years, the island flourished as its inhabitants established a highly complex agrarian and fishing society. These early Ko-

> The first settlers of Kosrae probably travelled on large, oceangoing canoes, most likely from Vanuatu or from the Marshall Islands.

sraeans organized their society along matrilineal lines and divided themselves into clans. Family held an important place in their society, a pattern reinforced by the fact that clusters of family members tended to live near each other on family compounds. This tendency for relatives to dwell around a common area still persists on Kosrae today.

Like the medieval Europeans, the early Kosraeans lived according to a strict social hierarchy. According to Elden Buck's *Island of Angels*, citizens fell into four classes: kings, high chiefs, lesser chiefs or land managers, and commoners. In fact, the divisions in early Kosraean society were so

To Be a Commoner

At Lelu kingdom's apex, the Kosraeans lived as a cohesive whole under the rule of one king. All other citizens fell into three classes: high chiefs, lesser chiefs, and commoners.

Only the king and chiefs could come to Lelu Island; common people visited the island only in order to bring food and to offer tribute to the nobles. During these visits, the commoners followed specific protocol. For instance, according to Elden M. Buck's fascinating history of Kosrae, *Island of Angels*, commoners "could not stand upright or talk above a whisper." Rules also barred their entrance to certain areas, which were considered the king's personal domain.

Each day, custom required that a new commoner bring food to the royal family. If that person failed to fulfill this duty, he would receive the death penalty. Thus, according to Buck, these food-bearers travelled cautiously around Lelu "to the specific openings or pass-throughs" where custom demanded that they place the food.

In order to speak with the king himself, Buck writes that "everyone, including nobles, was required to speak with exaggerated slowness," keeping his voice at low whisper. Finally, the king's head had to be higher than that of everyone else in the room, and gazing right at the king's face was strictly taboo.

strong that the kings and high chiefs actually built themselves a separate island on which to live: Lelu. These ancient Kosraeans built a fabulous city of canals, corridors, and over 100 compounds on an island made of fill. Walking Lelu Ruins, it is hard not to imagine fabulous medieval castles in Europe.

Though a Spanish sea captain first sighted the Caroline Islands in 1529, no Westerners actually visited Kosrae until 1824. That June, French Captain Louis Isidore Duperrey landed his ship, *Coquille*, in Okat Harbor. He and his crew spent ten days on the island. Just three years later, the Russian *Senyavin* also landed at Okat; its crew stayed three weeks.

All of the visitors fell in love with Kosrae. The sailors, who exchanged gifts with the islanders, found themselves instantly charmed by the Kosraeans' friendliness. Captain Duperrey described the islanders as "peace-loving people who had no weapons," and the sailors enjoyed the myriad fruits of Kosraean hospitality. During the *Senyavin*'s stay, for instance, the islanders visited the ship every single day, delivering breadfruit and other local foods. In fact, the Kosraeans' curiosity about the outsiders was so great that scores of them flocked to the ship. So many visited, in fact, that, according to Captain Lutke, "there was hardly room to move around."

Unfortunately, not all of the seafaring visitors proved benevolent. Over the next several decades, shipping traffic through Kosrae drastically increased as tales of its beauty, hospitable climate, and friendly people spread throughout the naval community. Suddenly, the Kosraeans found their home inundated by unseemly characters, such as callous whaling crews, slavers, and pirates, such as the notorious Bully Hayes. Even well-intentioned Westerners helped spread disease to Kosrae.

> During this time, captains of slave vessels in the Pacific, known as blackbirders, bargained with local chiefs, trading Western goods in exchange for human traffic.

Thirty years of visits from whalers, blackbirders, and pirates took their toll on Kosrae, dampening the islanders' hospitality and devastating the population with introduced diseases. Over just twenty years, the Kosraean population plummeted from 10,000 to 300. By the time Congregationalist missionaries arrived in Lelu Harbor, hardly any young children or elderly Kosraeans remained. The small, weakened population eagerly welcomed Dr. Benjamin Snow and his fellow missionary workers to their shores on August 20, 1852.

These intrepid missionaries, sent by the American Board of Commissions for Foreign Missions in Boston, ushered in a number of profound changes. The missionaries brought Western-style clothing to the islanders. They also built schools, where, for the first time, the Kosraean language was written. Finally, they quickly converted the islanders; nearly everyone on the island had become Christian by the 1870s.

The church's influence also extended into cultural areas. For instance, church authorities forbade the telling of ancient Kosraean myths, and age-old dances and were outlawed. In addition, the people stopped practicing tattooing, and both alcohol and *seka*, a mild narcotic drink used in spiritual rituals, were prohibited. Finally, the Kosraeans abandoned their matrilineal social structure in exchange for a patrilineal organization.

In 1885, a disagreement erupted between Spain and Germany, as both countries claimed ownership of the Micronesian islands. Though Spain initially won the dispute, the Spanish later sold the Caroline and Marianas Islands to Germany for $4 million. The Germans spearheaded major changes on the island, introducing a cash economy and forcing the Kosraeans to work on coconut farms, thus ending their traditional subsistence lifestyle.

World War I's end drew the curtain on the German Pacific Empire. The Japanese then took control of the Micronesian islands. They would prove to be more involved in Kosraean affairs than either the Spanish or the Germans. The Japanese introduced a number of economic improvements; their policy included initiating the export of sugar and founding an agricultural program. The Japanese did take their toll on Kosrae, though, when they occupied the island during World War II. At this time, most Kosraeans were forced to hide in the mountains as the United States bombed Kosrae.

> The Japanese also created a great deal of infrastructure, including a public school, teachers' residence, hospital, and weather station.

The armistice which ended WWII charged the United States with the care and development of the Trust Territories of the Pacific Islands, which would eventually become the Commonwealth of the Northern Marianas Islands, the Republic of the Marshall Islands, the Republic of Palau, and the

The Notorious Pirate Bully Hayes

During the 19th century, due to the booming whaling industry, scads of nefarious pirates prowled the Pacific, ready to do anything to land a big payday. Yet Bully Hayes's tally of misdeeds far surpassed that of any other evildoer. His crib sheet included fraud, kidnapping, assault, theft, murder, rape, and more. On one occasion, he was charged with 97 crimes. Hayes even drove the island chiefs to seek divine protection. However, Hayes had a gift for evading justice. Miraculously, even when he was arrested, the scallywag always escaped the law's grasp.

By the time he reached Kosrae, Hayes enjoyed notoriety across the Pacific. At that time, he was practically minting money by exploiting the copra market and by trading slaves. Around 1870, Hayes commandeered a ship right out of the Kosrae harbor, leading a U.S. warship right on his heels. However, as usual, Hayes evaded punishment, seeking refuge on yet another island.

Hayes was not so lucky in March 1874. One night, a powerful storm overtook his brig, *Leonora*, in Utwe Harbor. The ship collided with the reef before disappearing under tumultuous seas. Hayes safely made land, though his cargo and many of his shipmates never did. After this, Hayes settled on Kosrae for a while before a British warship drove him away a few years later. Though he left in a hurry, legend has it that Hayes found time to bury his substantial treasure on Kosrae before departing. Once the heat cooled, Hayes returned to Kosrae, only to engage in an argument with his cook, receive a hard hit to the head, and be dumped into Davy Jones's locker. Given the circumstances surrounding his death, Hayes probably never recovered his buried treasure, the whereabouts of which fuel fierce speculation to this day.

Regardless of the grave misdeeds Bully Hayes committed during his lifetime, the pirate did bequeath something special to the island he once called home: a great story, an amazing wreck, and—just maybe—buried treasure.

Federated States of Micronesia. During the 1960s, the United States began to contribute investment and aid to the islands. Originally, the United States governed Kosrae as an outlying administrative district of Pohnpei; some jokingly called Kosrae "Pohnpei's largest outer island." In 1977, however, Kosrae became an independent entity within the Trust Territory. In 1986, the United States signed a Compact of Free Association with Yap, Pohnpei, Kosrae, and Chuuk. Four years later, the newly formed nation, the Federated States of Micronesia, joined the United Nations as an independent member.

During its thirty years of independence, Kosrae has experienced a number of changes. Once the construction of Kosrae International Airport had been completed and Continental Airlines began flying to the island in 1986, a new era of development began. The increased numbers of goods and people flowing to Kosrae precipitated cultural shifts on the island. For example, the newly paved road around the island has allowed more Kosraeans to commute to Tofol to work, and the increased flow of goods to the island has permitted them to buy more imported food. Due to these changes, the Kosraeans have begun farming and fishing less. What is more, modern economic development has, at times, threatened Kosrae's natural environment.

As an incredibly young state—according to 1995 data, the median age of Kosraeans is 19.5 years—Kosrae now faces a cultural dilemma: whether to adapt to modernity or to preserve traditional values and customs. Kosraeans face economic challenges as well. As is common in the FSM, most of the population works in the public sector. However, as U.S. subsidies decrease, many public sector jobs may quickly disappear. Some suggest returning to subsistence fishing and farming, while others advocate an economic shift to focus more on tourism. No one yet knows how Kosrae will deal with these changes.

Culture and People

The differences between Kosrae and everywhere else in the world do not end with the physical. The island's culture—a set of customs infinitely specific and complex that has gradually developed over time—distinguishes Kosrae not only from Western society but also from the rest of the FSM.

First, the island's pace will shock you. Kosraeans never hurry, as evidenced by the 25-mile per hour, island-wide speed limit, which everyone actually follows. Kosraeans value family and human interaction above punctuality. Thus, life on Kosrae moves as quickly as the moseying walkers you will see heading to church on Sunday. Take a deep breath, slip into your sandals, and relax. Nothing here will happen "on time," so enjoy your experience on "island time."

Travelling around the island, you cannot help but notice huge white church spires jutting up out of the jungle. Kosrae is nicknamed "island of angels" for good reason. In 1852, Protestant missionaries arrived on Kosrae. Within the next twenty years, they converted nearly the entire population to Christianity. Christian

> Today, about 90% of Kosraeans are Congregationalists.

mores, traditions, and thinking pervade nearly all aspects of life here. Kosraean culture revolves around the church. It serves as the gathering place, the hub where people meet and socialize; what is more, church positions determine people's social standing on the island.

Kosraeans generally attend church between one and five times weekly. On Sundays, the entire island shuts down, as everyone heads to church for several hours of singing and worship. The Kosraeans are widely renowned for their choral singing. In fact, the carefully attuned listener will recognize numerous melodies as familiar Congregationalist hymns.

Church holidays dot the calendar; they include Gospel Day in August and Arwal in November. Both events focus heavily upon singing. On Arwal, all the churchgoers on the island gather in one church. The youth wear white, and each village's youth choir performs several songs. During each group's final hymn, attendees file up the center aisle, depositing donations in baskets. The churches use these donations for improvements and programming.

Most activities besides prayer, contemplation, and socializing are taboo on Sundays. Strict Christians will not fish, farm, swim, play games, drink, shop, or work on the Sabbath. In fact, since some consider cooking taboo as well, many families prepare a pot of *soup sanri*, or Sunday soup, on Saturday night. They then eat the soup, a delicious combination of coconut milk, copra, rice, salt, fish, crab, and lobster, all day Sunday so that no one needs to cook on the Sabbath.

Due to their religion, the Kosraeans abide by conservative social norms. Hardly anyone drinks or smokes; those who do usually consume in secret. In addition, nearly everyone, women in particular, dresses modestly. Men almost always wear shirts; women cover their shoulders and thighs, usually wearing long dresses or skirts. In addition, male-female interactions follow stringent social mores. Kosraeans also respect strict gender roles at home. Men farm, fish, and assume responsibility for ceremonial tasks, like making *fafa* and cooking pigs. Women preside over the household, cooking and car-

Competitive Church-Building

As do many other cultures, Kosraeans build physical manifestations of hometown pride, but not necessarily the kind that you might expect. Instead of football stadiums or monuments, the Kosraean villages compete to build the biggest church. Driving across the island, it is clear that churches are Kosrae's pride and joy. The citizens spend months, even years, building these monolithic houses of worship.

In a practice that hearkens back to ancient traditions, the Kosraeans work cooperatively to build their churches. When a village decides to build a new church, the villagers collaborate on the church's design as well as the materials and planning for the amount of labor they will need to complete construction. They fundraise for months, soliciting donations to help complete the project. On building day, everyone meets at the work site. They eat a meal together and then begin construction. Around midday, they eat lunch together. Then, the building continues. At the day's end, everyone tells stories over dinner. This collaborative process continues until, finally, the church is complete.

Then, once one village completes its shiny, new church, other villages begin gathering funds in order to build an even newer church. The cycle continues, each village working to outshine the last by building increasingly bigger and better churches.

ing for children and other relatives. Therefore, islanders may be surprised to see visitors break from this accepted framework.

Family holds a primary place in Kosraeans' lives. Extended families tend to live close together, either within a village or on a family compound. Family members take care of each other and share duties, such as looking after young children or sick and elderly relatives. Interestingly, if it is decided that a mother cannot or should not care for her child, that child will be adopted by another family member, often a childless aunt or uncle. Family names are passed down for generations, and most Kosraeans tend to spend leisure time with their families rather than with friends, acquaintances, or co-workers.

Since they value family so highly, Kosraeans spend a great deal of time and energy on family customs, like first birthday parties and funerals. A child's first birthday party celebrates childbirth. Kosraeans spend

> Interestingly, with the parents' permission, anyone can name the infant.

months planning this big event. Intriguingly, the father serves as the chief planner of the day's activities. When the day of the ceremony arrives, the mother awakens early in order to prepare the child. She makes sure that he is clean and well-dressed. During the day, male relatives prepare food and serve the guests, while the women supervise the gift-giving. According to *Some Things of Value: Micronesian Customs and Beliefs* by Gene Ashby,

---

Kosrae Christmas

Kosraeans are absolutely obsessed with Christmas, so obsessed that they have invented a totally unique way to celebrate the day: Christmas marching.

In the United States, the holiday season begins on Black Friday; in Kosrae, it starts on November 1st. Around that time, the islanders begin meeting to practice their Christmas marches. At these rehearsals, each group learns various Christmas hymns, along with accompanying marches, which look something like the choreographed movements of marching bands. When seen from a bird's eye view, the performers form letters and words. Several groups from each village march, including the youth group, the senior citizens, and the women's choir. Each group practices about four hours per night, six nights per week, from early November until Christmas.

Once every four years, the island hosts Kosrae Christmas. For these special Christmas celebrations, the entire Kosraean population meets in one village church on Christmas Day. Every single group then performs for the assembly. Often, Kosraeans who have moved off-island return home for the festivities.

On Christmas Day, the first group begins marching early, around 8 AM; the festivities continue without intermission all day. When I lived on Kosrae, the marching did not end until 11 PM! Eager spectators pack the church, spilling outside onto chairs and bleachers. Outside the church, food abounds, and everyone eats very well. When a group finishes its set, it starts its last hymn, and begins a slow, ceremonious march outside. As they walk, choir members throw candy, gifts, and various household objects into the crowd. Delighted children scramble around the pews for candy while adults fill shopping bags with snacks and goods. When I attended, one group even threw money into the stands!

. If you cannot see the ceremonies in person, the festivities are videotaped and shown on local cable for months before and after Christmas. Marching is even available for purchase on DVD.

fried chicken, soft taro, local fruit, sashimi, pork, breadfruit, and rice are all common first birthday foods. Often, families hire a live band for the party. Each child receives two names at this ceremony: a traditional Kosraean name and a Christian name.

The Kosraeans' intrinsic friendliness will strike you. As you travel around, you will doubtless be greeted by as many luminous smiles as people you see. In addition, Kosraeans love to help others. If they are not too shy, the locals may pepper you with questions. Due to the rarity of outsiders here, Kosraeans are very curious to learn about visitors and their homes.

SOCIAL NORMS

Borrowing

While it might not affect most visitors, Kosraeans live in a collectivist society wherein everyone borrows from one another. Thus, if you leave your sandals outside your door, do not be shocked if someone "borrows" them for several days.

Interacting with Others

Due to social norms, directly addressing an islander of the opposite gender might make that person uncomfortable or be interpreted as a romantic advance. Islanders also never express affection publicly, even by hugging or holding hands; they do not look favorably upon those who do.

Sundays

Although Kosraeans grant some leeway to visitors, strict social regulations govern all Sunday activities. On Sundays, the entire island shuts down, as everyone heads to church for the day. Barring the few Western-owned hotels, almost nothing will be open, so plan accordingly.

Because it is a day of rest, activities like drinking, diving, swimming, fishing, and boating are forbidden. If there is an activity you would like to participate in on Sunday but do not know whether it is socially acceptable, consult with your hotel or tour operator. Or, better yet, attend a church service as it's an interesting, quintessentially Kosraean experience.

Culture of *Muhtactah*

Once upon a time, Aristotle once famously declared that "man is a social animal." In this regard, Kosraeans certainly prove him right.

In keeping with their friendly, family-oriented culture, the Kosraeans have developed their very own particular national pastime: *muhtactah* (muh-day-da).

If you meet any Kosraen, anywhere, at any time of day, and you ask him what he is doing, your query will, time and again, be met with the same standard response: "*nga muhtactah*" ("I am visiting"). Kosraeans love to visit, particularly with their family members. Typically, once the work day ends, an extended family will all gather at one family's house to eat, "talk stories," and maybe even play a little *sakura*—a complex, popular, and addictive four-man card game, imported to the island by the Japanese, which then gained popularity among the islanders.

Kosraens will often *muhtactah* from the time they return from work long into the wee hours of the night.

Visiting

If you are fortunate enough to visit a Kosraean family at home, the family will welcome you with a fresh coconut. They will always offer food. Make sure to eat at least some of the food they offer; refusing food is considered impolite. Also, remember to remove your shoes before entering the house.

Asking Questions

Since they so value social harmony, Kosraeans want to do everything possible to make others happy. In practical terms, this means that the questions which you ask Kosraeans will not always be answered with the true answer; often, a Kosraean will reply to your question with the answer he thinks that you want to hear. Therefore, if you would like to know, for instance, whether it is safe to swim somewhere, do not ask, "Is it safe to swim at this beach?" Ask instead, "Where on the island would it be safe to swim?" If you would like to know whether a restaurant is open on Sunday, ask "What days of the week is the restaurant open?" By phrasing your questions to avoid a direct yes or no answer, you are more likely to obtain an accurate answer.

The Kosraean Funeral

While first birthday parties are culturally significant, in the schema of island life, funerals are the most important cultural ceremonies. Whenever a Kosraean dies, someone rings the church bell in the person's home village to announce the death. The slow, mournful peals last for twenty minutes to announce an adult's death, ten minutes for a child's death. Then, no matter the hour, a messenger travels across the island, since every Kosraean must know the news.

Upon hearing of the death, relatives, friends, and mourners gather. Often, for the initial 24-hour period of the funeral, local schools and businesses shut down completely. While the mourners travel to the funeral site, relatives prepare the body by washing it, dressing it in ceremonial garments, and moving it to a room where mourners can gather around it. Women and family members weep around the body, while others prepare the coffin and grave. Choirs from all of the villages come to sing religious songs throughout the night until dawn. On the following day, the village pastor conducts the funeral. Bible passages are read, and hymns are sung. After that, the coffin is lowered and buried.

Every funeral requires an enormous feast. Guests usually eat roast pig, fried chicken, rice, fish, breadfruit, taro, coconuts, and coffee. Preparing the pig takes longest. The Kosraeans cook the pig in an earth oven, or *uhm*. In order to make the *uhm*, they place black basalt stones on top of firewood and heat the stones thoroughly. Once the firewood is consumed, the stones are spread out over a patch of ground. The cooks then lay the pig on the hot stones and cover the food with layers of banana and taro leaves. Once the pig has roasted for several hours, it is ready to serve. Every guest who attends the funeral, no matter his relation to the deceased, will receive meals as long as he or she remains at the funeral site.

Once the burial has occurred, some close relatives may choose to remain with the bereaved family for a time. For as long as a month after the funeral, relatives and friends gather at the mourners' home to eat food, drink coffee, and give comfort. Thus, while visiting Kosrae, do not be surprised if you notice a house with a big tent outside with scores of people sitting underneath, hanging out. You are probably witness to a funeral.

Travel Information

GETTING THERE AND AWAY

Continental Micronesia is the only airline with services to Kosrae. For more information on flying to Micronesia, see page 27.

If you are a less time-conscious adventure seeker, consider joining one of the field trip ships, which operate among the FSM islands. See page 29 for more information.

HEALTH AND SAFETY

Though Kosrae is generally very safe, visitors should follow a few basic tips to ensure that their trip is uneventful.

For women, it is important to follow Kosraean cultural norms in terms of dress and behavior to avoid unwanted interest. Exposing one's shoulders and thighs invites attention here. It also may not be a good idea to address local men directly.

Though Malem is fine to visit during daylight hours, it should be avoided at night. Other areas of Kosrae are very safe.

Finally, as is common practice when traveling, Kosrae Visitors Bureau recommends that visitors tell their hotel proprietors where they plan to go during the day and approximately how long they will be away. This way, someone knows where you are and how to reach you should you need assistance.

Tap water on Kosrae is unsafe to drink. It is highly recommended that visitors boil their water, drink bottled water, or use water purification tablets. Lelu Water (www.leluwater.com), an on-island company, collects and bottles water. By drinking Lelu Water, you can support the local economy and stay safe.

If, while visiting, you fall victim to a crime, call the **police** emergency line at 911. Should you have any other concerns and need law enforcement assistance, you can call the chief of police (370-3214) or the front desk (370-3333). The police station is located right next to the government building in Tofol.

The healthcare facilities and medicines available on Kosrae are extremely limited. The **Kosrae State Hospital** (370-3012), located in Tofol, across from the legislature building, serves the island. It can provide emergency service and possesses a dispensary, stocked with the most essential medicines. However, the care is basic and the stock of medicines limited.

SERVICES

Kosrae has two banks: the **Bank of the FSM** (9 AM-3 PM; 370-2681) and the **Bank of Guam** (9 AM-3 PM; 370-8720). Bank of Guam has an **ATM** but it will sometimes run out of money, thus rendering it inoperable. Travelers are advised bring cash and travelers cheques. Also, be aware that only the few western-owned hotels on the island accept credit cards.

The **post office** (8:30 AM-4:30 PM; 370-3057) is located in Tofol across from Awane Restaurant.

A public **laundry**, located in Tofol, is due to open in June or July 2010. It will have washers and driers.

Telecomm (8 AM-midnight; 370-3164), located in Tofol across the street from Kosrae High School, offers Internet access and long-distance calling. They can also tell you where to find wireless connectivity on the island.

Getting Around

LAND

Car Rentals

It is strongly advised that you rent a car to explore the island; otherwise you will be dependent upon transportation provided by your hotel, unreliable taxis, and hitchhiking. A few car rental companies are listed here:

DJ's Car Rental This business works with DJ Store. The car can be picked up and dropped off at the airport. *In Tafunsak; Cost: car $49 daily; 370-2308*

Kennedy Car Rental Guests can rent for up to one week; airport drop-off and pick-up can be arranged. Do note that this company speaks very limited English. *In Sansrik; Cost: sedan $36.25 daily, SUV $45 daily; 370-2283*

Senny's Car Rental Like DJ's, Senny's can drop off and pick up the car at the airport for you. Senny's offers discounts for long-term visitors, cutting their rate by 5% for those renting for one week and 10% for those renting more than one week. *At Senny's store in Lelu; Cost: car $50 daily; 370-2524*

Treelodge Car Rental Again, the car can be picked up and dropped off at the airport. *At Treelodge Hotel; Cost: car $55 daily, $45 daily for hotel guests; 370-7856*

The Roadside Stand

No conventional gas stations exist on Kosrae; if you need a fill-up, you will have your gas tank filled by hand from a plastic container (often at very random spots along the road). Gas stations are not the only thing you will find on the roadside, though. As you drive about, you will notice many small stands dotting the roadside, hawking everything from fresh fish to snack foods.

My Educational Bike Ride

A personal experience proved firsthand the benevolent, helpful nature of the Kosraean people. As a Peace Corps volunteer, I traveled the island by bicycle. One night, I was biking home late from the office, all the way from Tofol to my house in Tafunsak. Unfortunately, my bike light had gone out; I could barely see five feet in front of me. About halfway home, I noticed a car behind me. I waited for it to pass, but it never did. As I rode, my tension climbed: *why is this car following me? What do they want? Will they hurt me?* Shaken by the incident, I immediately told my host family what happened upon arriving at my house. After I described the car and driver, they exclaimed, "Oh, that's our cousin! He was just giving you light in order to help you find your way home!" Hearing this, I breathed a sigh of relief, realizing for the first of many times how kind and helpful Kosraeans are.

Taxis

If you plan to use taxis, be aware that taxis on Kosrae are notoriously unreliable. Occasionally, they are quick, but most of the time, they operate on "island time." Sometimes, a taxi you have called will never arrive. It generally costs three or four dollars to take a taxi. Kosrae's two taxi companies are listed here:

Causeway Taxi Company *370-2700*

CB Taxi Company *370-4700*

Hitchhiking

Hitchhiking is commonplace and accepted on Kosrae. If you are not following a strict schedule, hitchhiking can be a fairly easy, pleasant way to get around. In fact, Kosraeans will often drive out of their way to help you.

However, despite Kosrae's relative safety, practice common sense when hitchhiking. It is best to hitchhike with another person; women should never hitchhike alone. Be wary of hitchhiking after dark. Finally, never get into a car if you think the driver has been drinking.

Bike and Scooter Rental

A few hotels rent bikes, scooters, and motorbikes. **Kosrae Village Resort** (pg 65) has, in the past, offered rental bikes for $7-10 per day, depending upon bike condition. While they did not have any working bicycles at the time of this writing, they did plan to have some to rent in the near future. **Pacific Treelodge Resort** (pg 65) offers bike rentals for $15 daily as well as scooter and motorbike rentals for $30 daily.

Kosraean Radio

As you drive or ride around Kosrae, you will get a taste of local Kosraean music on your radio. There is only one radio station on Kosrae; it broadcasts everything from Kosraean music to announcements and Senate sessions.

SEA: BOATS TO WALUNG

It is best to travel to Walung by boat. If you are staying at Nautilus, Kosrae Village Resort, or Treelodge, your hotel can arrange your water transit to Walung. If you prefer to contract independently, fishing boats usually travel from **Okat Marina** (370-9513), in Tafunsak, to Walung every weekday.

Where to Stay

Inexpensive

Tradewind Motel With its mid-Lelu Island location, Tradewind is an easy walk from Mount Boro and Lelu Ruins. Tradewind consists of a cute, neat row of three cottages. *On Lelu Island; Amenities: A/C; Cost: single $42; 370-2308*

DJ's Apartments DJ's Apartments, located in Tafunsak on the inland side of the main road, offer easy beach access as well as privacy. The rooms, found above DJ's Store, feature gorgeous ocean views. Only three rooms are available, so make reservations in advance. *In Tafunsak; Amenities: A/C, beach access; Cost: double $49; 370-3991*

Moderate

 Pacific Treelodge Resort Nestled cozily along a postcard perfect, white sand inlet, Pacific Treelodge Resort commands the best sunrise view on Kosrae. The resort, centrally located between Tafunsak and Lelu, consists of two matching rows of cottages, hewn from local mangrove wood. They offer great views of a large mangrove forest. Friendly, knowledgeable owners Mark Stephens and Maria Grazia are eager to facilitate your trip; they can help you arrange a car rental or organize a snorkeling, diving, kiteboarding, waterskiing, or fishing excursion. Treelodge offers trips all over Kosrae, including day trips to Walung, archeological visits to Lelu and Menke Ruins, and canoe excursions through Utwe-Walung Marine Park.

Even if you do not stay here, Treelodge's excellent restaurant, Bully's, merits a visit. Besides serving great food, Bully's hosts a happy hour and other weekly social events. Last but not least, Treelodge tentatively plans to offer weekend sailing trips around Kosrae, beginning August 2010. *Between Tafunsak and Lelu; Amenities: A/C, TV, kitchenette, mini-bar, porch, kayaks, canoes, scooter and car rental, restaurant; Cost: single $85; double $105; 370-7856, www.divekosrae.com,www.micronesiagrandtour.com*

Expensive

Nautilus Resort Nautilus, located down the street from Treelodge, also has cottages as well as two apartment-style rooms for long-term visitors. Its 18 rooms lie in a lush, beautifully manicured garden, lending a tranquil feel to the hotel. Visitors can relax in one of the many hammocks hanging in the gardens, around the pool, or on the resort's deck. Nautilus Restaurant, which serves everything from creamy milkshakes to tasty local fare and even offers room service, deserves a visit even if you stay elsewhere. Helpful owners Doug and Sally Beitz are happy to organize diving and snorkeling trips, canoe and kayak rentals, or hikes to Mt. Ohma, Menke Ruins, and Lelu Ruins. *Between Tafunsak and Lelu; Amenities: A/C, TV, kitchenette, mini-bar, tea/coffee maker, kayaks, canoes, restaurant; Cost: single $125, double $145; 370-3567, www.kosraenautilus.com*

 Kosrae Village Resort Although Kosrae Village Resort's off-the-beaten-track location between Sansrik and Malem might seem inconvenient, the resort is truly a gem. Step out of your car, cross a wooden footbridge onto the resort's jungle grounds, and enter another world. Suddenly, you are visiting the Kosrae of fifty years ago. The resort's bungalows were built in traditional Micronesian style, under a shady mangrove canopy; sand footpaths connect the cottages, which are lit by torches at night. Situated along the ocean's edge, Kosrae Village Resort also features a gorgeous, secluded beach.

As an eco-resort, Kosrae Village Resort works to fit within its natural environment; fans cool the bungalows, and each room features a garden shower. Each cottage also has a spacious porch, a large bathroom, and two queen beds, complete with mosquito nets. Owners Bruce and Katrina Brandt will gladly make adjustments to meet guests' desires, as well as organize diving trips and other excursions.

Kosrae Village Resort's superb restaurant, Inum, is not to be missed. Also built in traditional Micronesian style, the open-air eatery serves incredible breakfasts, lunches, and dinners. The garlic bread and desserts are to die for. *Between Sansrik and Malem; Amenities: fan, mosquito net, refrigerator, coffee maker, porch, kayaks, canoes; Cost: single $119, double $149, deluxe room or suite $129-169; 370-3483, www.kosraevillage.com*

Where to Eat

Inexpensive

FNS Grocery Though its small size makes it easy to miss, FNS merits a stop. On weekdays, it offers delicious, reasonably priced carryout lunches that are perfect for a picnic. Lunches feature local favorites, usually fried chicken, white rice, and a fruit. *In Tofol, across from JBI; Cost: lunch $4; Hours: Mon-Sat 7 AM-10 PM; 370-2099*

 Awane Restaurant Awane Restaurant offers a variety of moderately priced local, Asian, and American specialties. Situated in a space below Kosrae Conservation and Safety Organization, Awane has a definite hole-in-the-wall feel. However, friendly wait staff and scrumptious, affordable entrées compensate for the atmosphere. Favorite dishes include udon and tempura. *In Tofol, next to JBI; Cost: lunch $5-9, dinner $5-12; Hours: Mon-Fri 7:30 AM-2:30 PM; 370-3345*

Moderate

 Bully's Restaurant Located deep in the mangrove forest at Pacific Treelodge Resort, Bully's Restaurant provides an incredibly relaxing atmosphere. Look over one shoulder into the tangled mangroves; over the other lies the island's rugged interior. Bully's offers reasonably priced and tasty breakfast, lunch, and dinner menus. The burgers, especially the Bullyburger—made from yellowfin tuna—satisfy, as do the fries and breakfast dishes. The tuna sashimi with dipping sauce also impresses. The dinner menu includes sandwiches, chicken dishes, and fresh fish. Bully's also has two special menus: an eggplant menu, which features locally grown eggplant, and an Italian menu, which includes espresso ice cream for dessert. Finally, Treelodge Resort has a full bar with imported beer and liquor. *At Treelodge Resort; Cost: breakfast $3-6, lunch $6, dinner $10-40; Hours 7 AM-9 PM; 370-7856*

Nautilus Restaurant Nautilus Restaurant, which offers both indoor and outdoor porch seating, features a variety of succulent local specialties and favorites from home. Everything on the menu is tasty; however, the thick, creamy homemade milkshakes are particularly good. The fantastic fried rice dishes could feed a family; the sashimi and fish dishes also impress. While the Asian and Pacific dishes, as well as the full bar, keep parents happy, Nautilus also offers a children's menu and an excellent Sunday night pizza special. *At Nautilus Resort; Cost: breakfast $4-9, lunch $4.50-12, dinner $5-15; Hours: 7-9 AM, 11:30 AM-1:30 PM, 5:30-9:30 PM; 370-3567*

Expensive

 Inum Restaurant Kosrae Village Resort's restaurant, Inum, excels not only among restaurants on the island but in all of Micronesia. Just off the beach, the breezy, open-air dining area invites you in; the incredible food bids you to stay. Like Nautilus and Bully's, Inum features both familiar, Western dishes and more adventurous entrées from Kosrae and across the Pacific. Indulge in the mouthwateringly fresh seafood, such as the mangrove crab salad or mahi mahi. Inum also offers local side dishes not found elsewhere, such *ainpat usr*, a tasty combination of banana, coconut milk, soft taro, and breadfruit. The desserts are mind-blowing. Wash everything down with fresh coconut milk, lime juice, or a selection from the full bar. The garlic bread is also good. You can also choose items from any menu whether it's 8 AM or 6 PM. *At Kosrae Village Resort; Cost: breakfast or lunch $8-12, dinner $10-15; Hours: 8 AM-9 PM; 370-3483*

What to Do

SIGHTS

Hiking is as an ideal way to explore the island, and one of Kosrae's most rewarding hikes is **Sipyen Falls**. As you approach Sipyen Falls from Utwe, the distance between houses increases until, almost imperceptibly, civilization falls away behind you. Though the falls

> The hike to Sipyen Falls can easily be done without a guide. The trail begins across the street from Lelu Elementary School.

lie only a ten minute drive from the Menke Ruins entrance, Sipyen Falls might as well be in another universe. To visit, you will hike five minutes up a cool creek under the shade of a nearly impenetrable rainforest canopy before arriving at the massive, 30-foot (9-meter) falls. Below the falls gurgles a serene, tree-shaded pool. Wise, gnarled trees claw the heavens high above your head. Take a seat, close your eyes, and enjoy.

Located in the middle of Lelu Island, **Mt. Boro** offers another great hiking opportunity, boasting all the best of Kosrae and requiring little effort. **WWII tunnels and bunkers** crisscross Boro's summit, providing plenty of adventure for kids, war buffs, and other explorers. What is more, you will enjoy incredible views of the **Sleeping Lady** as you hike.

If you seek a more challenging hike, **Mt. Finkol** is for you. With a summit of 2,064 feet (629 meters) above sea level, Mt. Finkol represents an all-day climbing excursion. However, Finkol rewards those patient enough to reach the summit with amazing views of all Kosrae. If you wish to climb Finkol, Micronesia Grand Tour (pg 70) can provide a guide. Do remember, though, that you can only climb Mt. Finkol during dry season, so check with your hotel about whether a hike is possible during your stay.

Though **Mt. Mutunte** tops out at only 574 feet (175 meters), hiking it also requires a full day, some bushwhacking, and scrambling. However, Mutunte repays the intrepid hiker with both an extensive series of **Japanese tunnels** and fantastic summit views. Matt Rott, of Kosrae Surf Tour Company (pg 72), can guide your hike up Mt. Mutunte.

For a cultural experience in addition to an enjoyable hike, consider

---

Local Legend: *Why Lelu Island Looks Like a Whale*

According to an old legend, a whale once stayed in Yesron with her beautiful daughter. One day, while doing wash, the daughter met two men, who invited her out fishing. After their outing, they went to the men's village, Tukunsru. When the mother whale noticed her daughter's absence, she searched for her and found her in Tukunsru.

When the girl returned again to Tukunsru, the village people killed her whale mother, cooked the meat, and had a party. Missing her mother terribly, the girl found a part of the whale and placed it in a bowl. Soon, that piece grew into a whale.

She and the whale, her mother, canoed to Tukunsru. The townspeople chased them, but the whale smashed the only canoe that came close enough to catch them.

Once they had gotten away, the whale went to Lelu but got caught there. One day, a girl spotted the whale there and tied it with a metal chain. The whale died and remained there, becoming Lelu Island.

climbing **Mt. Ohma**. As soon as you arrive at **Hamilson Phillip's house** at the base of the mountain, you know you are about to depart from the ordinary. Wild pig skulls line the cookhouse walls, bearing testament to the owner's hunting prowess. Hamilson guides visitors on the approximately seven-hour hike to the 1,555-foot (474-meter) summit. From the top, you can see not only the coastal plains of Kosrae but also the harbors and ocean from Utwe to Lelu. However, Ohma offers more than views. It is also full of life; you may catch sight of huge monitor lizards, the *tuhram*, Kosrae's state bird, or fruit bats, which inhabit **caves and tunnels** that the Japanese dug during WWII. Finally, the gorgeous **triple falls** near the base provide a welcome opportunity for a refreshing swim after the hike. In fact, a shorter, easier hike of approximately one hour directly to the falls is available. Upon your return to the base, Hamilson may serve you freshly grown local food or offer a short cultural show, performed by his children. You can set up your Ohma hike with Hamilson through your hotel.

Egypt has the Pyramids, Peru has Machu Picchu, and Kosrae has **Lelu Ruins**. Widely considered a wonder of the ancient world, the massive, basalt-walled city took four centuries to build; the ruins still stand today, a testament to the pinnacle of Kosraean political power and cultural development. Built between 1400 and 1800 as an imperial city designed to house the king, his family, the high chiefs, and their retainers, Lelu consisted of transportation channels, temples, residences, and royal tombs. When you visit, you will marvel at the architecture—some walls still stretch up to 20 feet (6 meters) high!—and the amazingly organized labor it must have required to transport the basalt stones here from Walung. Best of all, Lelu Ruins is not far or difficult to find: it is located in the middle of Lelu village, across the street from ACE Hardware.

If Lelu Ruins appeal to the history buff, **Menke Ruins** beckon the explorer. Although you can reach Menke from the main road in Utwe, the surrounding jungle hides it so effectively that you will feel like Indiana Jones when you discover the ruins in the undergrowth.

> Consisting of over 100 compounds, the Menke Ruins were constructed decades before Lelu.

The Kosraeans have long revered Menke because it houses the temple of Sinlaku, the Goddess of Nature and Breadfruit, according to the island's

---

Ahsit

My family was visiting me on Kosrae, and we were approaching the Lelu Ruins. Suddenly, children's cries rent the air.

"*Ahsit! Ahsit! Ahsit!*" the children shouted jubilantly, pointing at me, my parents, and my brother. My family looked to me confused. Realizing an explanation was in order, I recounted the local legend behind the children's saying.

"You see," I began, "white people have never been very common here. More of them began coming to Kosrae during WWII. Around that time, some Kosraeans saw a group of Americans hammering nails on a construction project. One guy hit his finger, crying out, 'Ah—shit!' Hearing this, the Kosraeans came to believe that white people call themselves *ahsit*."

The name stuck, though now it can refer to any non-Kosraean.

ancient animist religion. Inspired by their awe for Sinlaku's power to procure food during droughts, the ancient Kosraeans frequently made pilgrimages here. According to a local legend, on the night before the missionaries arrived in 1852, Sinlaku's eerie voice resonated throughout the island, as she talked fearfully of a bright light she saw approaching on the horizon. Sinlaku fled to Yap, and the missionaries arrived the next day. However, though some say Sinlaku departed, many locals believe she still resides here at Menke still. Therefore, tourists visiting the temple are encouraged to wear cinnamon-scented garlands to honor Sinlaku.

Ackley Waguk, whom you can contact through your hotel, can guide your hike to Menke. As he leads hikers through to the ruins, Ackley teaches his guests about the wildlife of the rainforest. The three-hour hike does cross the river several times; however, it is not too challenging. At the hike's end, your exertions may be rewarded with fruit from Ackley's own garden. The **Kosrae State History Museum** (Mon-Fri 9 AM to 3 PM; 370-3078), in Tofol, offers free admission to the public. Inside, age-old artifacts and photographs of Kosrae as it once was will deepen your understanding of the island.

Voracious readers and history buffs will enjoy the **Rose Mackwelung Library** (Mon-Fri 8 AM-1:30 PM; 370-3834), housed on the Kosrae High School campus in Tofol. The library offers a collection of photographs and drawings of Micronesia, various reference works about the FSM, and government documents.

Origin of Lelu Ruins

Several different stories attempt to explain Lelu Ruins' origin. According to one legend, Kosrae's king gathered his citizens in Lelu in order to build the walls of a new city. Everyone came from across the island to build—everyone except Sataf, who stayed behind in his village. The people delayed building for several days for Sataf, but when he did not show up, they started work on the walls. This made Sataf so angry that, back in his village, he built an enchanted model of the wall under construction. When he pulled just one stone out of his wall, the walls of Lelu fell to the ground. Since no one understood the reason for the destruction, they worked quickly to rebuild the city walls. Once they had finished, Sataf again used his voodoo wall to destroy all the walls at Lelu. The king sent Sataf a special message summoning him to Lelu. Sataf travelled there by raft, magically drawing giant stones behind him. Once he arrived at Lelu, Sataf began working. He spoke, and the stones placed themselves in a pile. When the building was finished, Sataf returned home.

Thinkers, writers, and travelers have proposed other theories to explain the ruins' origin. Despite overwhelming archaeological evidence that Kosraeans built Lelu, some believe that the Spanish, Japanese, or even pirates built Lelu Ruins.

In 1852, for example, a whaler once asked Kanku, King George's son, who built the old city walls. Kanku explained that, while he did not know why the ruins were constructed or when, he did know that a race of very large men who once inhabited Kosrae built the ruins. In yet another scenario, F.W. Christian suggested that the Japanese built Lelu in the 1890s. He postulated that a group of Japanese sailors who somehow found their way to Lelu built the ruins.

So, as you meander through the ruins of once-mighty Lelu, take a moment to mull the tall tales of their origin.

In Tofol, follow the trailhead next to the Kosrae Island Resource Management Authority (KIRMA) to reach the **scenic view overlook**. This easy ten minute walk leads you through a surreal eucalyptus forest up to an outcropping overlooking Tofol and Lelu.

The **giant clam hatchery**, located on the Lelu causeway, houses protected giant clams. Hatchery personnel tend the clams until they reach a length of up to three meters; they then move the clams to the aquaculture sanctuary in the Walung reefs. Recently, at least 50 giant clams have been released there.

WATER AND OUTDOOR ACTIVITIES

Micronesia Grand Tour (370-7856, www.micronesiagrandtour.com) offers bicycle and Jeep tours. Head to Walung or along the unpaved road into the Termanalia forest in Okat.

The avid **birdwatcher** can keep very busy here. Many birds live on Kosrae, including the endangered Micronesian pigeon. One of the species endemic to Kosrae, the Kosrae Dusky White Eye, a small gray bird, can often be found in coconut trees searching for insects. Another endemic bird, the Micronesian Starling, is particularly skilled at finding ripe fruits and is quite unafraid of people.

> Fifteen resident and nine migratory bird species live on Kosrae.

Yoga

Yoga aficionados can practice even on Kosrae. Anyone interested in practicing yoga here should contact Matt Rott, of Kosrae Surf Tour Company (pg 72). He can schedule a one- or two-hour session any day of the week.

Diving

Several factors contribute Kosrae's excellent reputation among diving enthusiasts. To begin, Kosrae lies outside of the typhoon belt, so major storms rarely hit the island. In addition, Kosrae's unique underwater geography—the coral shelf surrounding the island is ringed by an outer, fringing reef—shelters the reef from those few storms which do arrive. Finally, Kosrae's stringent environmental laws forbid boats from anchoring on the reef. Thus, due to natural and legal protections, Kosrae's coral shelves rank among the most pristine on earth. Moreover, the unreal underwater visibility averages 100 feet (30 meters) or more.

The Kosraean waters also boast an enormous variety of life to observe. Nautilus operator Sally Beitz claims that her guests often surface commenting "that they have never [before] seen such a diversity of healthy hard corals." In addition, Kosrae is home to Christmas tree invertebrates, nudibranchs, octopi, and many other creatures. Finally, wrecks such as WWII planes and whaling ships dot the waters around Kosrae.

Kosrae also suits divers of all ability levels, from the complete novice to the seasoned master diver. Many great dives feature only light current or, sometimes, no current at all. What is more, every resort which offers dive trips also has certification courses, both for those who wish to try diving for the first time and for those who wish to hone their existing skills. Truly, no visit to Kosrae is complete without a dive trip.

Though more than fifty dive sites surround the island, divemasters and enthusiasts alike agree that **Hiroshi Point** surpasses the rest. On this dive, as you approach the wall, you come upon pristine hard coral gardens teeming with diverse sea life, including parrotfish, sea anemones, and swarming fish of all shapes, sizes, and colors. Hiroshi Point also features large white sand patches with coral heads in the middle.

Sleeping Lady Divers Sleeping Lady Divers offers classes, from the open water certification course for novices through advanced courses up to divemaster and assistant instructor. In addition, Sleeping Lady Divers is nitrox-capable. *At Kosrae Village Resort; Cost: one-tank or night dive $69, two-tank dive $99, technical expedition $129; 370-3483, info@kosraevillage.com, www.kosraevillage.com*

Micronesia Eco-Divers Like Sleeping Lady Divers, Treelodge Resort's Micronesia Eco-Divers has PADI certification courses. In fact, they offer all the PADI courses from open water to divemaster level. *At Treelodge Resort; Cost: two dives $125; 370-7856, pacifictreelodge@mail.fm, www.divekosrae.com*

Nautilus For novices who wish to try diving, Nautilus offers the NAUI Introduction to Diving course. As part of this course, after learning theory and completing a short practice dive in the pool, participants go out to one of Kosrae's dive sites, where a guide personally takes them down to about 35 feet. Participants then do another dive. The course costs $175, including lunch and equipment. In addition, Nautilus is the only shop on Kosrae to offer the NAUI instructor certification course. This weeklong course takes place twice each year. Finally, Nautilus offers the NAUI open water, advanced, rescue, and divemaster courses. *At Nautilus Resort; Cost: two dives $125, boat charter $460 daily (includes food, tanks, crew); 370-3567, inquiry@kosraeanautilus.com, www.kosraeanautilus.com*

Fishing

Fishing has always been vital on Kosrae; nearly all Kosraean men, women, and children fish the healthy, teeming reef to supplement their diet.

All three main resorts (see pg 64) offer the opportunity to fish. With **Micronesia Grand Tour** (370-7856, www.micronesiagrandtour.com), visitors can cast or troll from a boat, or try traditional spear fishing with a local guide.

Kayaking and Canoeing

The main resorts also offer kayak and canoe rentals. Kayaks and canoes make it easy to explore the enticing world of the mangrove channels. More adventurous visitors can take the kayaks out to the ocean. If you are up for a challenge, you might even try circumnavigating Kosrae. Nautilus and Kosrae Village Resort also offer guided kayak and canoe trips.

Snorkeling

Hiroshi Point is universally agreed upon as the best dive on Kosrae; it is also a great spot to snorkel. Located at the island's southwest tip at buoy 15, this site offers easy access from the beach. Since the reef lies just over 20 feet (7 meters) below the surface, it is easy to see the mixed sand and coral patches below. The huge coral heads here, which some estimate to be over 2,000 years old, house scores of invertebrates and Christmas tree worms. Many other creatures also live here, including squid, barracuda, eagle rays, and schools of parrotfish and other reef fish. If you venture to the edge of the wall, you will likely catch sight of the sharks that favor the region.

Located alongside the Lelu causeway across from Nautilus, the **Blue Hole** is, unquestionably, Kosrae's most accessible snorkel site. You can reach it either from the Nautilus beach or from the dock on the causeway; once you get close, swim or wade over the reef flat until you reach the site. The Blue Hole, traditionally the royal family's burial grounds, offers excellent snorkeling and diving. Because the outer fringing reef protects the Blue Hole so effectively, the 490 foot (150 meter) wide opening on the reef flat acts like a huge tide pool, trapping a myriad of life forms inside at low tide. What is more, the Blue Hole is accessible under any weather conditions, even when it is too rough to snorkel elsewhere. The Hole itself houses a wide variety of life, including lionfish, pufferfish, sting rays, and scores of young fish. The Blue Hole has also been established as a protected area for giant clams. Best of all, you can explore on your own here and for free!

Surfing

Kosrae surfing features a distinct variety of waves. Many factors, from swell size to winds, work to ensure the presence of quality surf here.

The island possesses two distinct surf seasons. During the low season (April-September), calm winds prevail, creating small east and southeast swells. During this time, surfers of all abilities can safely surf. During the high season (October-March), surfers should have prior experience since swells during this period tend to be much larger.

> Kite-surfing, available through Micronesia Grand Tour (pg 70), occurs on the ocean inlet near Treelodge. The flat water of the inlet offers the perfect setting for this activity.

If you want to surf in Kosrae, it is best to do so through the **Kosrae Surf Tour Company** (370-8906, www.kosraesurftours.com). The grassroots company encourages sustainable, responsible surf tourism on Kosrae. The Company's surfer package offers each participant the following: three meals per day, water, fruit, snacks, airport pick-up and drop-off, all land and water transfers, accommodation at Pacific Treelodge, a personal surf guide, alternate activities for non-surfing days, and a guarantee of un-crowded lineups. The package costs $150 per person per day for double occupancy or $175 per person for single occupancy. Non-surfing guests pay $100 per night.

Swimming

Kosrae offers a number of great swimming spots. **Tafunsak Marine Park**, located along the dirt road just past Okat Marina, features a lovely protected swimming area. It has some great spots to dive into the water, both from the beachside huts and from the bridge across the water, and it lends easy access to the nearby snorkeling at **Okat Channel** and **Shark Island**.

Lelu Marine Park, located in Lelu Harbor along the causeway, also offers a great place to swim. Like Tafunsak Marine Park, it has several local huts, a great place to relax or picnic between swims. Do check with your hotel that the huts are available for use before you go.

Kosrae's beaches also make great places to swim. **Walung** possesses the longest white sand beach on Kosrae. As you walk this beach, make sure to glance inland occasionally, both to admire the local houses along the shoreline and to catch a glimpse of the many terns here. The beach also offers a good view of fishing boats travelling out to sea and lends easy access to snorkeling and diving. At high tide, it is perfect for swimming.

In **Tafunsak**, between the **Wiyac Bird Cave** and the island's northeastern tip, lies another pristine white sand beach. Sometimes ideal for surfing, the area is nice for swimming, too, as long as you are mindful of the reef and rock below. Children's rope swings hang from palm trees along the beach.

Mangrove Tour in Utwe-Walung Marine Park

Although the environmental movement is still fledgling on Kosrae, Kosraeans are beginning to recognize that implementing environmental protections will help preserve the beauty and biodiversity of their island home. The Utwe-Walung Marine Park represents one such effort. In 2005, concerned landowners met to determine how to create sustainable livelihoods. They decided to accomplish this by designating the Utwe-Walung Marine Park a protected biosphere. Future efforts would focus on ecotourism in the area, with an eye to educating visitors and locals about the mangrove and reef ecosystems and their environmental and cultural importance.

Thus, the area, carved out from the shores between Utwe and Walung, has been designated a protected area. The community members chose this area in particular because these mangroves house an incredible amount of biodiversity and provide critical habitat for both adolescent and spawning

The Walung Mystique

A three-mile (five-kilometer) white sand beach, fringed by clear waters lapping upon a pristine reef, stretches its graceful way as far as the eye can see under a golden tropical sun. Although you can see the village from the airport, Walung actually takes its name from the Kosraean word for "country," "hinterland," or a place "on the edge of activity." The name probably derives from Walung's location far removed from Kosrae's traditional capital, Lelu. It is hard, upon visiting Walung, not to feel a pervasive sense of peace here. As a matter of fact, mysterious stone compounds—termed the "Fortress of Solitude" by archaeologists—surround the entire village.

Walung remains a bastion of traditional ways on a rapidly changing island. Connected to the rest of the island by mangroves, Walung is accessible only by a dirt road or by a boat at high tide. Thus, Walung has remained slow-paced and conservative, home to those Kosraeans who eschew the comforts of modernity, in the form of stores and electricity, in favor of a simpler way of life. Walung residents drink rainwater from a catchment system, cook using local ovens, or *uhms*, and earn their livelihoods by selling home-grown produce and fresh fish at markets in Utwe and Tafunsak.

With the prettiest views, the most pristine beach, the friendliest people, the freshest seafood, and the most traditional architecture and culture on the island, Walung is not to be missed.

fish. Therefore, fishing in the area is prohibited. However, educational and recreational activities are encouraged, so come explore this beautiful area by kayak or canoe.

The Utwe-Walung Marine Park resembles no other place on earth, and seeing it by canoe is ideal. Snaking through the mangroves in a canoe helmed by knowledgeable local guide Baba Tadao, visitors can see some of the best-preserved mangroves and coastal forests in all of Micronesia. The careful observer may also notice crabs, fish, birds, and monitor lizards in their natural habitat. Baba Tadao's stories enhance the trip, as he recounts ancient island legends, including the spine-tingling tale of notorious pirate Bully Hayes, whose wrecked brig lies deep at the bottom of Utwe Harbor.

The tour takes several hours, but your time is well spent as you devour the incredible visual feast of the mangroves. By visiting the biosphere, whether independently or on Baba Tadao's outrigger canoe, you will help the Kosraeans generate income in this area. Ideally, this will encourage the Kosraeans to continue preserving it as protected open space. To arrange a trip, you can contact Baba Tadao through your hotel or tour operator.

SHOPPING

Souvenirs

Situated inside a beautiful, traditional-style local hut, the **Kosrae Visitors Bureau** (Mon-Fri 9 AM-3 PM; 370-2228) in Tofol sits across from the Kosrae State History Museum. In addition to offering information about island sights, events, and activities, the Visitors Bureau possesses a good selection of local handicrafts, including woven wall hangings, *fafa* pounders, and wood carvings. This is definitely the best place to buy the products of local artisans.

> Actual store hours may vary dramatically from the stated hours. Ask someone at your hotel to call ahead in the early morning or late afternoon. Also, be aware that businesses may close during or around lunch.

Groceries

JBI Grocery (8 AM-10 PM; 370-2682) has two locations: one in Tafunsak near the elementary school and the other in Tofol next to Awane. JBI has one of the widest selections on Kosrae. Though you will not find much produce here, JBI is a good place to find cereal and other breakfast goods. JBI also stocks a decent variety of canned goods.

Neime Store (9:30 AM-9 PM; 370-3769), located between Senny's and Treelodge, typically stocks the highest quality imported goods available. It carries a variety of snacks and the best liquor on island. It also has a coffee shop.

New Town Bakery (9 AM-5 PM; 370-3398), located next to JBI, sells bread to individual customers as well as to restaurants. Because the loaves are so amazing, you must visit just after they are baked; otherwise, the store will likely be sold out.

Dollar Up (8 AM-8 PM; 370-3378) definitely merits a visit, even if you do not need groceries. The store, which sells a variety of goods, including clothes, food, and household amenities, always amuses. Here you can find products like Reptile Cleaner and the Miraculously Happy Dog. One outlet is in Tafunsak; the other is in Tofol.

DJ's Store (9 AM-8 PM; 370-2381), located in Tafunsak, carries a variety of groceries as well as clothing and general merchandise. It also has rooms for rent and a car rental company.

Senny's/Sronsrono (7:30 AM-9 PM; 370-3188, 370-3311) has one location in Tafunsak and another in Lelu. Aside from Neime, it has the best selection of goods on Kosrae, including fruits and vegetables. It also has a car rental company.

PMW (7:30 AM-11 PM; 370-7748) serves as the Malem-area grocery store. Its ample stock of produce has made it a local favorite.

Midtown Mini-Mart (7 AM-10 PM; 370-3423), located on Lelu Island across from Lelu Ruins and next to ACE, offers a variety of groceries, clothes, and other amenities.

The **Japanese farm** (370-8150), located next to the Lelu Water plant, can be reached from the dirt road just after the bridge leading from Tafunsak and Lelu toward Tofol. The Japanese men who run the farm live here, selling fresh eggplants, cabbage, cucumber, watermelon, tomatoes, okra, tangerines, and corn, depending upon the season. If you enjoy fresh produce, visiting the farm is a must. Note that produce availability depends upon the weather, season, and farming conditions.

Other

Interestingly enough, the stores with the widest selection of goods are actually hardware stores.

ACE Hardware (8 AM-5 PM; 370-2250), with locations in Tafunsak and Lelu, offers an extensive selection of American products.

True Value (7 AM-5 PM; 370-3339), in Tafunsak, features similar goods, mainly imported from Asia.

Nightlife

On Tuesdays, Pacific Treelodge Resort offers **movie night**. At 7 PM, participants gather at Bully's. The movie is projected on a sheet hung across the back of the restaurant. You can even enjoy the film while you dine! Sometimes management will take visitor suggestions on what movie to show.

> There are two bars on Kosrae; one is at Nautilus Resort, and the other is a Treelodge Resort.

Every Thursday, Treelodge organizes a **Lelu Harbor sunset cruise**, which departs from the Lelu dock at 5 PM. As the boat meanders into the harbor, visitors sip beer, mixed drinks, and soft drinks, munch on snacks, and hobnob with ex-pats and fellow travelers. The company is surpassed only by the magnificent view of the sunset over the Sleeping Lady.

Last but not least, Treelodge offers **happy hour** every Friday from 4:30-6:30 PM. Discounted drinks attract a diverse crowd, from locals to ex-pats and fellow travelers. Thus, happy hour provides a great place to get the inside scoop on the happenings about Kosrae and to share travel stories. As the sun sets over the mangrove channel behind Bully's, the view becomes increasingly stunning.

A Kosraean Legend: *The Queen's Snake*

You may notice the peculiar way that the mangrove channels wend in and around Kosrae's coastline. A Kosraean story, retold in Eve Grey's *Legends of Micronesia: Book One*, explains these channels.

Once upon a time, an enormous snake lived in a cave near Tafunsak. This snake had a beautiful human daughter. Each day, the girl ventured to the beach to swim, and each evening, the snake brought her home. No one else knew they existed.

While the king was exploring, he spotted the beautiful girl on the beach. The king, astonished at her beauty, brought her immediately to Lelu and made her his queen. At nightfall, the snake searched for his daughter. He checked the beach and the four different villages. Finally, his sense of smell led him to the king's house. He waited nearby, watching for his daughter.

The next day, while out swimming, the girl saw the snake. She began to bring him food from the king's house each day, all the while keeping his existence secret. One day, when the girl returned from the beach, the king inquired as to her whereabouts.

"I took food to my old father," she said.

The king wanted to see her father, so the girl brought him to see the snake. When she called the snake "father," the king was terrified. The king demanded that the girl return home with him.

"But I belong to my father, too," she protested, though she went home with the king.

The jealous king schemed to separate his queen from her father. One day, he told her that her father should live on Lelu with them. The king summoned all the men of Kosrae to build a house for the snake. Together, they made the largest house on Kosrae, and the snake moved in.

The next day, the king suggested the girl take a trip to Tofol, and she agreed. The king then called his men to the snake's house. He had them place tinder around the house and torch it. Once the house began burning, a bit of ash blew into the air. It travelled all the way to Tofol, where it fell upon the girl. Immediately, she knew something was amiss and hurried back to Lelu as fast as she could.

When the girl and her entourage reached Lelu, the king's servants stood onshore, ready to restrain the queen, should she rush to her father's aid. When the queen jumped from the canoe, the strongest man grabbed her. However, she fought him off, ran to the snake's house, and jumped into the fire to save him. Before anyone could prevent it, the girl burned with her father. After this, the king mourned. He regretted his cruelty to the snake, and he grieved for his queen.

According to this story, the paths through the mangroves mark the snake's journey from Tafunsak to Lelu as he crawled around the island, searching for his missing daughter.

Pohnpei

As you wander through Pohnpei's lush rainforest, gaze through the mist of waterfalls at its soaring mountain peaks, and explore the mysterious ruins of Nan Madol, you may feel as though time has left you behind. Though widely considered to be the most Westernized island in Micronesia, Pohnpei retains a strong connection to the past. Indeed for some, Pohnpei, which means "upon an altar," represents a sacred place beyond time, and when you are sitting around a *sakau* rock, listening to the age-old rhythm of men pounding kava, you might as well be living a thousand years ago.

Pohnpei defies stereotypes; here you will find mangrove forests instead of beaches, farmers instead of fishermen, monumental stone ruins instead of simple huts. Certainly, Pohnpei offers much to satisfy the vacationer, including friendly inhabitants, hiking trails, pristine reefs, and the relative conveniences of Kolonia Town. When you leave, though, you may find Pohnpei haunting your memory as the realization dawns that you only began to experience the deep cultural history of this place while you were here. If you do feel this way, then you will know that you have seen past the stereotypes, that you have seen a piece of the real Pohnpei. While you are here, then, allow yourself to get lost in space, in time, and in the syncopated rhythm of *sakau.*

Geography

Pohnpei, formerly spelled Ponape, is a high island formed by volcanic activity, though there are currently no active volcanoes on the island. Covering 130 square miles (337 square kilometers) and reaching an elevation of over 2,500 feet (760 meters) in the interior, Pohnpei is the largest and tallest island in the Federated States of Micronesia. By contrast, the outer islands of Pohnpei are all coral atolls, formed from rings of coral that have risen around the receding peaks of long-dormant volcanoes.

The eight scattered outer islands of Pohnpei amount to little more than 3 square miles (8 square kilometers) combined and account for a small fraction of Pohnpei state's population.

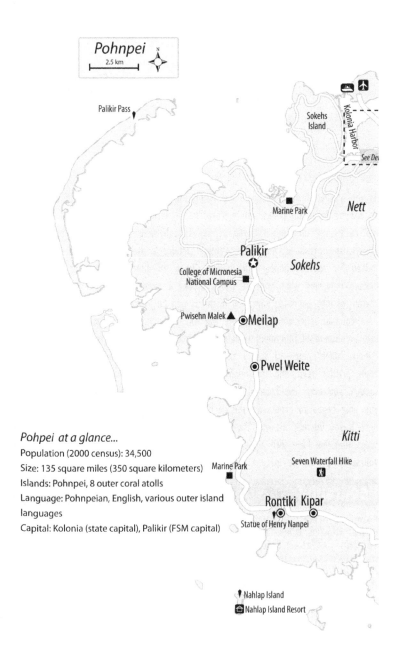

Pohnpei

2.5 km

N

Palikir Pass

Sokehs Island

Kolonia Harbor

See De

Marine Park

Nett

Palikir

Sokehs

College of Micronesia National Campus

Pwisehn Malek ▲ ⊙Meilap

⊙ Pwel Weite

Kitti

Pohpei at a glance...
Population (2000 census): 34,500
Size: 135 square miles (350 square kilometers)
Islands: Pohnpei, 8 outer coral atolls
Language: Pohnpeian, English, various outer island
languages
Capital: Kolonia (state capital), Palikir (FSM capital)

Marine Park

Seven Waterfall Hike

Rontiki Kipar
Statue of Henry Nanpei

Nahlap Island
Nahlap Island Resort

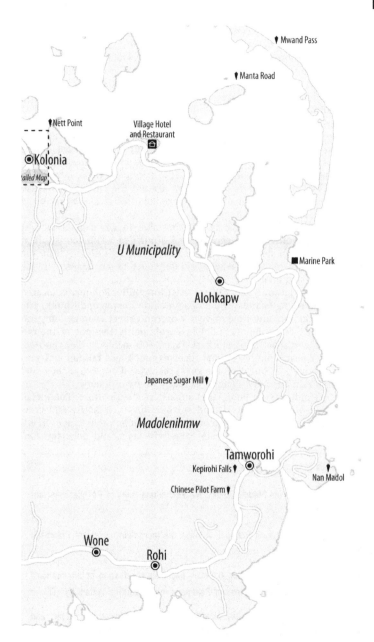

Mwand Pass

Manta Road

Nett Point

Village Hotel
and Restaurant

◉Kolonia

ailed Map

U Municipality

■ Marine Park

◉
Alohkapw

Japanese Sugar Mill

Madolenihmw

Tamworohi
Kepirohi Falls ◉

Nan Madol

Chinese Pilot Farm

Wone
◉

Rohi
◉

Kolonia, Pohnpei's only commercial or population center, is located on a peninsula at the northernmost point of the roughly circular island. The rest of Pohnpei is organized into municipalities, which have traditional significance, though they now each have a municipal government as well. The municipality of Nett consists of Kolonia's immediate surroundings. The other municipalities in clockwise order around the island are U, Madolenihmw, Kitti, and Sokehs. Kolonia is the capital of Pohnpei; the capital of the FSM, Palikir, is located a few miles west of Kolonia in Sokehs.

As visitors fly into Pohnpei International Airport, located on an islet connected to Kolonia by a causeway, they often notice Sokehs Rock before other aspects of the physical landscape. This rock outcropping has a memorable shape and location, but it is typical of Pohnpei's rocky interior. In fact, most of Pohnpei's population clusters around the fringes of the island; a relatively small number of farmers are able to live and work in the mountainous rainforests of the interior.

While flying into Pohnpei, it is also possible to get a good look at Pohnpei's barrier reef, a ring of coral lying 1-3 miles (2-5 kilometers) off of Pohnpei's coast on all sides. This reef protects Pohnpei's shores from the relentless pounding of ocean waves and prevents much damage to the coast even when surf is high.

At 6° 54' north latitude and 158° 14' east longitude, Pohnpei is located in the Eastern Caroline Islands, which also include Kosrae and Chuuk. The climate is tropical, and any time of year, you can expect average temperatures of about 80° Fahrenheit (27° Celsius). Pohnpei is also one of the rainiest places on earth, as the summit averages 400 inches (1,000 centimeters) of rain per year. Pohnpei's coast receives much less rainfall and sees its share of sunny days, but even the coast receives about 200 inches (500 centimeters) of rain annually. Pohnpei is rarely hit by typhoons.

The largest industry on Pohnpei is subsistence agriculture. Pohnpeian families usually occupy a plot of land surrounding their house and grow taro, yams, bananas, breadfruit, coconuts, and various other crops. In addition, many Pohnpeian families raise pigs, chickens, and dogs for con-

---

HIGHLIGHTS OF POHNPEI

Exploring the ruins of Nan Madol: Explore the enchanting ruins of Pohnpei's ancient capital city. pg 98

Snorkeling and diving around Pohnpei: Admire the incredible variety of Pohnpei's marine life. pg 100

Dining at the Village Hotel: Choose from an impressive selection of international dishes and drinks while enjoying one of Pohnpei's most beautiful vistas. pg 97

Relaxing at Ant Atoll: Spend a day strolling the beach, enjoying the water, and exploring an uninhabited coral atoll. pg 105

Participating in a traditional *sakau* circle: Experience the rich traditions of Pohnpei while drinking *sakau*, a local kava-like concoction. pg 87

sumption. It is remarkable that while fishing is important as a livelihood on Pohnpei, it is not nearly as essential or as culturally important on Pohnpei as farming.

Virtually the only cash crops on Pohnpei are *sakau*, pepper, and copra. However, *sakau* is not yet exported in significant quantities, and Pohnpei does not produce nearly enough copra or pepper to balance the goods that it imports. Thus, most currency coming into the country comes in the form of U.S. grants and aid, which support a rather large number of national, state, and municipal government employees.

The rainforests of Pohnpei support a variety of plants and animals. According to The Nature Conservancy, 111 of Pohnpei's more than 700 plant species are found nowhere else on the globe. Animals on Pohnpei include a variety of insects, amphibians, sea and forest birds, and reptiles. The only mammals native to the islands (other than humans) are bats. Pigs, dogs, cats, and rats were introduced by Westerners relatively recently.

> There are no dangerous snakes on Pohnpei, and only a very few species of small critters are poisonous to humans.

Pohnpei's Mangroves

Some visitors to Pohnpei are surprised to learn that Pohnpei has almost no beaches (though its fringing and outer islands do). Instead, mangrove forests surround the island's coast. These forests grow in areas that experience ocean tides and contain salt water. While these swampy forests are perhaps not as appealing as a broad, sandy beach, they constitute a fascinating ecosystem and have a beauty of their own. The best way to experience the mangroves is to kayak or canoe up one of the inlets along Pohnpei's coast and to find a narrow channel that has been cut in the mangrove forest to allow passage.

History

PRE-COLONIAL POHNPEI

Archaeologists estimate that the first people to inhabit Pohnpei arrived as early as 2000 BC. More settlers arrived during the first millennium BC. Little is known about these intrepid voyagers other than that they sailed over the open ocean in canoes, most likely from nearby islands, and built an agricultural society on Pohnpei over several hundred years. Eventually, complicated clan and traditional title systems based on matrilineal descent developed.

One clan, which was to become known as the *Saudeleurs*, gained preeminence during the completion of the city of Nan Madol, which had begun to be constructed many centuries earlier. For several hundred years, the *Saudeleurs* ruled over the rest of Pohnpei from Nan Madol. Eventually, a group led by the mythical figure Isohkelekel overthrew the regime. Control of the island was then handed to the *Nahnmwarkis*, and many of the traditions, titles, and customs that are observed on Pohnpei today were established. For example, as the city of Nan Madol fell into disuse, communities began to meet in feast houses, or *nahs*, which can be seen throughout Pohnpei.

Pedro Fernandez de Quiros was perhaps the first European to see Pohnpei in 1595, although he did not land. Over the next several hundred years, contact with European vessels was sporadic, but this contact began to pick up considerably around the year 1830. Among the first of many beachcombers and whalers to visit Pohnpei was James O'Connell, the "Tattooed Irishman." After being shipwrecked and reaching Pohnpei in a small boat in 1827, O'Connell remained there for five years. He later published an outrageous account of his experiences; he even claimed that the islanders had tried to eat him but that he was able to escape this fate by entertaining the Pohnpeians with a dance. The truth of his account is rightly questioned by most historians. During this time, many diseases were spread to Pohnpei, and the population of the island was decimated.

> By some accounts, as much as 80% of Pohnpei's population died from small pox and other foreign diseases in the 19th century.

COLONIAL POHNPEI

Beginning in the 1870s, whalers began to visit Pohnpei less frequently and missionaries became more common. After a brief dispute between Germany and Spain in 1885, the Spanish took control of Pohnpei as well as other nearby islands. The early years of Spanish governance were fraught with violent conflict as the Spanish attempted to control and convert the islanders while paying little regard to Pohnpeian customs. This conflict was ostensibly a religious dispute between Protestants and Catholics, but in many cases political motives were also at work. Nevertheless, the Spanish succeeded in constructing a fort at Kolonia and converting many Pohnpeians to Catholicism.

In 1899, Germany purchased the islands of modern-day Micronesia and Palau. The Germans sought to develop raw materials on Pohnpei, and to this end, they succeeded in ending warfare among the five *Nahnmwarkis*. For a few years, Pohnpeians and Europeans coexisted peacefully, but armed conflict erupted again in late 1910 and early 1911. This conflict, known as the Sokehs Rebellion, resulted from long-standing Pohnpeian resentment toward foreign occupiers and anger with the policies of the authoritarian German administrator of the time. The rebellion was defeated, but the Pohnpeians did manage to kill the German administrator.

Japan officially gained control over Pohnpei after Germany surrendered in World War I. Japan began the economic development of Pohnpei in earn-

The Book of Luelen

Luelen Bernart, a Pohnpeian educated by missionaries, was the first Micronesian to write a book on the history of an island in Micronesia. Bernart wrote his history, the Book of Luelen, during the twelve years preceding his death in 1946. Bernart includes many Pohnpeian myths, including one story of the creation of Pohnpei. According to the story, a group of settlers from a distant land sailed to the spot where Pohnpei is now located and built the island by piling rocks upon a bit of coral. When waves kept destroying the island, they called for a reef and mangrove to surround and protect the island. This story is the origin of Pohnpei's name, which means "upon a [stone] altar."

est; schools, farms, roads, and commercial outlets were constructed. Japanese rule on Pohnpei became significantly harsher, however, as it became embroiled in conflict with China and the Allied powers. Pohnpei's resources, including its people, were mobilized by the Japanese government for the war effort. Pohnpei did not play a significant role in World War II, however, until early 1944, when the United States unleashed a devastating bombing campaign lasting several months. Amazingly, Pohnpeian casualties were relatively few as the Japanese kept Pohnpeians away from military installations and Pohnpeians learned to anticipate the predictable schedule of bombings.

After Japan surrendered, the United States took control of a huge swath of the Pacific, including Pohnpei. American control guaranteed Pohnpeians certain freedoms and protections, but the immediate post-war period was one of extreme shortages and hardships. Near the end of 1946, the U.S. Navy's administration of Pohnpei began to improve, and schools and democratic institutions began to

> Pohnpei was never invaded during World War II. In fact, the island surrendered one month after World War II ended on the condition that Japanese soldiers stationed on the island be allowed to go free.

be established. In 1947, the United States signed a UN Trusteeship Agreement, which served as the basis for U.S. policy in Micronesia and Palau for over three decades. In 1951, the Navy transferred control of Pohnpei to the U.S. Department of the Interior. The following years saw the development of a number of important institutions and programs in Pohnpei: the Pohnpei Island Congress (which eventually became the Pohnpei State Legislature), the Community College of Micronesia, and the U.S. Peace Corps in Micronesia, among others.

INDEPENDENT POHNPEI

In 1978, the districts of Kosrae, Pohnpei, Chuuk, and Yap voted to form a federation under a new constitution. Pohnpei was the only district to vote against the Constitution of the FSM, although it was bound by the outcome of the vote. From 1979 through 1986, the United States slowly transferred power to the national and state governments of the FSM, and in 1986, the United States and the FSM entered into a Compact of Free Association, an agreement between the FSM and the United States which provides for U.S. grants and aid to the FSM in exchange for freedom of the United States to use islands in the FSM for military purposes.

In the years since 1986, Pohnpei has taken a leading role among the states of the FSM. It is the center of government and business for the nation, and it is certainly the most cosmopolitan of all the islands in the FSM. Like the other states, it has struggled to provide economic opportunity, education, and healthcare to its citizens and especially to its outer island populations. Nevertheless, as Pohnpei moves into the new millennium, there is reason to believe that Pohnpeians will find novel ways to integrate traditional wisdom and modern knowledge in order to improve their health, education, and economic prospects.

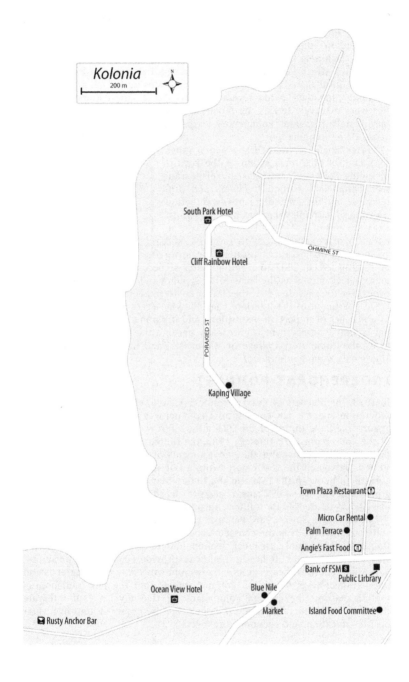

Kolonia

200 m

N

South Park Hotel

Cliff Rainbow Hotel

OHMINE ST

PORAKIED ST

Kaping Village

Town Plaza Restaurant

Micro Car Rental

Palm Terrace

Angie's Fast Food

Bank of FSM

Public Lirbrary

Ocean View Hotel

Blue Nile

Market

Island Food Committee

Rusty Anchor Bar

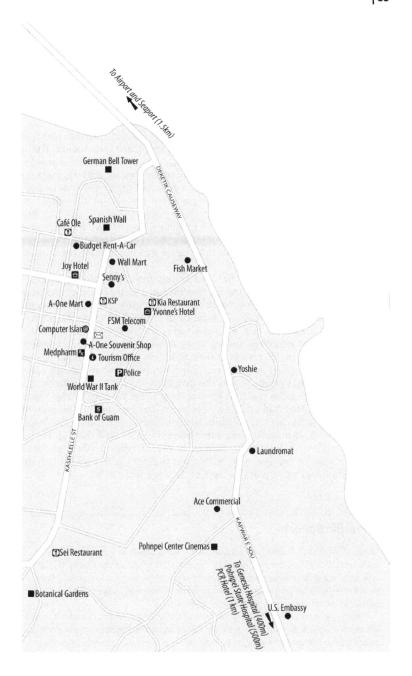

To Airport and Seaport (1.5km)

DEKETIK CAUSEWAY

German Bell Tower ■

Café Ole   Spanish Wall ■

● Budget Rent-A-Car

Joy Hotel   ● Wall Mart
                              Fish Market ●
         Senny's

A-One Mart ●   KSP   Kia Restaurant
                              Yvonne's Hotel

Computer Island   ● FSM Telecom

Medpharm   ● A-One Souvenir Shop
            ❶ Tourism Office

            ❓ Police

World War II Tank ■

Bank of Guam

KASEHLELE ST

                              ● Yoshie

                              ● Laundromat

                    Ace Commercial
                         ●

Pohnpei Center Cinemas ■

KAPWAR E SOU

Sei Restaurant

■ Botanical Gardens

To Genesis Hospital (400m)
Pohnpei State Hospital (500m)
PCR Hotel (1 km)

            U.S. Embassy ●

Culture and People

Although Pohnpei is regarded as the most Westernized and cosmopolitan of the FSM states, it is remarkable for the extent to which traditions have survived, albeit somewhat changed in the face of increasing contact with foreign culture. Pohnpeians observe a traditional system of honorific titles. At the top of the hierarchy are the *Nahnmwarkis*, the chiefs of the municipalities of Pohnpei. Underneath them are various lines of titled individuals, each with a very specific ranking relative to other titled individuals. Titles, which are assigned on the basis of membership in extended family groups, are highly respected by Pohnpeians. While high-titled individuals have no official political power, they receive many gifts and privileges at both public and private functions. Many foreigners are amazed at the extent to which Pohnepeians will defer to their *Nahnmwarki* and village chief, but for Pohnpeians, the title system is a customary way of life, an important expression of their culture, and a means for social advancement, as people who play by the rules can expect to advance in rank themselves as they age.

High-titled individuals are honored at important periodic ceremonies called *kamadipws*, or feasts. On most occasions, each family attending a *kamadipw* ceremoniously gives food, both locally grown and store-bought, to a chief, who in turn distributes most of the food back to the attendees. Foods such as breadfruit, pig, dog, and turtle are cooked onsite in a traditional oven, called an *uhmw*, before being divided up. The *uhmw* consists of a bed of heated rocks, on which fruit and meat is laid and then covered with banana leaves. A *kamadipw* is an opportunity for Pohnpeians to show off their agricultural produce, and the man bringing the largest pig or the biggest yams, which can reach five feet in length and take ten or more men to carry, is respected and envied by his peers. Despite the introduction of new foods, such as pigs, dogs, and imported packaged foods, the traditions associated with feasts have survived remarkably well through centuries of contact with foreigners, though in recent years a few high-titled leaders have asked for money to be brought to feasts in lieu of food, diluting the communal and traditional aspects of the *kamadipw*.

Honorific Speech

Respect for high-titled individuals is embedded in every aspect of Pohnpeian life, especially language. The Pohnpeian language includes certain sets of vocabulary that are reserved for highly ranking members of the traditional hierarchy. For example, Pohnpeians use special variants of many common words, such as *eat, shower, head*, or *hand*, to refer to the actions or body parts of the *Nahnmwarki*.

While older Pohnpeians and linguists lament that younger generations do not master these vocabularies and some honorific words are being forgotten, there is still a strong tradition of speech-making on Pohnpei. At feasts and other occasions, Pohnpeian men can earn the respect of their peers by displaying eloquence in honoring their superiors and, sometimes, debasing themselves through the use of these special words.

Yams

Pohnpeian yams are not to be mistaken for sweet potatoes, which are commonly called yams in North America. Yams, in contrast to sweet potatoes, are very starchy and fairly tasteless.

Farmers on Pohnpei are very jealous of their yams, the most prestigious agricultural product on the island. Although a Pohnpeian man will proudly point out his other crops, his yams are always tucked out of sight, hidden from everyone until they are uprooted for a feast.

The *sakau* circle is an essential fixture at traditional Pohnpeian feasts as well as smaller social gatherings. *Sakau en Pohnpei*, a type of kava, is a locally anesthetic and mildly narcotic drink made from the crushed roots of a certain pepper plant, which are mixed with water and squeezed through fibrous strips of hibiscus bark. In the late afternoon, it is not unusual to see Pohnpeians gather around large, flat stones selected for their acoustic properties and to hear the hypnotic, rhythmic echoes of *sakau* being pounded. Many vendors sell bottles of watery *sakau* beside the road, but it is a poor substitute for the real stuff, which is consumed fresh from a coconut shell cup passed among drinkers according to strict rules of traditional rank. Though the drink looks and tastes like mud, Pohnpeians love the feeling associated with *sakau*, and sure enough, those who drink *sakau* invariably grow silent and feel a sense of peace come over them as the drug takes effect, numbing their mouths and gradually lulling them to sleep. The few studies on *sakau* have found no ill effects associated with consuming small amounts, though the water used to make *sakau* can carry pathogens, but habitual use over many years has reportedly contributed to liver problems.

> *Sakau* is less intoxicating than alcohol, but combining alcohol and *sakau* is not recommended, as it can make both drugs dangerously potent.

Feast Houses (*nahs*)

Undoubtedly the most important architectural element in any Pohnpeian community is the *nahs*, or feast house, an open pavilion-like structure with a raised floor along three walls and a wide opening in the fourth wall. On most days, it is not unusual to see people relaxing, working, or sleeping in a *nahs*, but its true function only emerges during a feast. At this time, the platform along the back wall is reserved strictly for the chiefs, their wives, and their honored guests. Women usually sit along the sides facing the front, when they are not busy organizing and distributing baskets of food. Meanwhile, men sit in *sakau* circles in the center of the *nahs* or remain outside the *nahs* cooking pig, dog, yams, or breadfruit.

Many Pohnpeians own a *nahs*, which they use as an addition to their house except on feast days. Other *nahs*, however, are owned and maintained by the communities that use them. With the permission of the landowner, you should feel free to seek respite from the tropical sun in the shade of a *nahs*. You must, however, remember not to use the two small doors at the back of every *nahs*. These are for the exclusive use of the *Nahnmwarki* and his senior adviser, the *Nahnken*.

Sakau and Deforestation

Sakau has been an important part of Pohnpeian culture for hundreds of years. Unfortunately, the increasing population of the island and, presumably, the increasing frequency with which Pohnpeians drink *sakau* have had a detrimental impact on Pohnpei's jungles, as large areas of Pohnpei's interior rainforests are being cleared to make room for *sakau* cultivation. Deforestation in the interior is a major concern as it can contribute to droughts, landslides, and loss of biodiversity. According to The Nature Conservancy, forest cover on Pohnpei dropped from 43% to 12% in the period from 1975 to 2002. The Nature Conservancy as well as the Conservation Society of Pohnpei are working to change this trend.

Despite the endurance of particular Pohnpeian traditions, imported goods and ideas have greatly changed life on Pohnpei. Many families on Pohnpei own a television and spend several hours per day watching movies or TV shows. Having grown accustomed to foreign food, Pohnpeians often prefer a bag of chips to a mango as an afternoon snack. An educated Pohnpeian can earn more money by accepting a post in a government office, but he no longer has the time or inclination to grow his own food.

Still, in spite of the threats posed to Pohnpeians' livelihood by foreign influence, there is reason to be optimistic. There are increasingly strong movements to return to local food and preserve the natural environment. Moreover, modernization has improved some aspects of life on Pohnpei; nearly all Pohnpeian children have access to decent schools, and Pohnpei now has an inclusive democratic government. In addition, traditional knowledge of many matters, such as food preparation and local construction, is still widespread if no longer universal. In light of the extreme degradation of local culture occurring elsewhere in the Pacific, such as Majuro or Guam, one should not take for granted the rich traditions that are still alive on Pohnpei.

In Pohnpei, social change comes at a leisurely pace. Scan the front page of the *Kaselehlie Press*. You will not find columns about dynamic or controversial political figures. Instead, you will find stories on school field trips, NGO fundraisers, government initiatives, and possibly the death of a Micronesian in the U.S. Army. Nevertheless, these stories show how life in Micronesia is becoming more modern in both negative and positive ways.

Pohnpeian Dances

If you are lucky, you may have the opportunity to observe a traditional Pohnpeian dance while you are on Pohnpei. As on many of the islands in the FSM and Palau, traditional Pohnpeian dances are a distinct and highly developed art form. Pohnpeian dances were traditionally performed on a platform supported over a series of canoes on the water. Both men and women would dance topless wearing grass skirts, although now it is common to see women wearing coconut or grass bras while dancing. Dancing on Pohnpei is an evolving art form, and although many Pohnpeian dances share similar movements, innovation is also very common and even encouraged in some cases.

SOCIAL NORMS

Although Pohnpeian social norms are changing rapidly, many still observe some of the
ancient customs. No visitor could or should
attempt to master the nuances of Pohnpeian
social norms. Often, all that is needed is the
good sense to follow the lead of others. Still,
it is good to be aware of Pohnpeian customs
that you may observe, and learning just a few of the following norms can
go a long way toward earning the respect of locals.

> You will see Pohnpeians
> beckon one another by
> holding their arm out and
> moving their wrist down as if
> they were patting someone's
> head.

Alcohol

Responsible consumption of alcohol is generally accepted on Pohnpei,
although some conservative Pohnpeians look down upon it. You should be
aware that alcohol is illegal in the district of Madolenihmw and on most
outer islands of Pohnpei.

Ceremonies

In a Pohnpeian feast house, known as a *nahs*, the elevated area at the back
of the structure and the doors there are reserved for high-titled individuals. During a feast, it is appropriate for a foreign visitor to sit on the platforms near the entrance while facing the front with his or her legs pulled
up on the platform. Do not sit with your legs dangling from the ledge when
a feast is in session. Men may also stand outside the *nahs* near the local
oven, or *uhmw*, located a short distance from the *nahs*.

Dress

To avoid offending Pohnpeians, visitors should dress very modestly. Wom-
en should ensure that their thighs are always covered, even when swimming. Tightly fitting clothing, spaghetti straps, and exposed undergar-
ments should be avoided. Most Pohnpeian women wear long skirts with a
T-shirt or blouse. Men usually wear pants or shorts with a T-shirt or Hawaiian shirt. Flip-flops are appropriate footwear for both sexes at all times.

Traditional Medicine on Pohnpei

Pohnpei has a rich history of traditional medicine. As in many cultures throughout the
Pacific, Pohnpeians believed that a person's health was intimately related to spiritual
matters. Upon becoming ill, Pohnpeians might have sought the help of a traditional
healer, a sorcerer, or both. Although the introduction of Western medicine has changed
the beliefs of many Pohnpeians about health and healing, it is not unusual to hear Pohnpeians blame an accident or illness on evil magic.

Knowledge of healing through the use of plants is still passed from one generation
to the next, usually within one's own family. Pohnpeians are very reluctant to discuss
traditional methods of healing with anyone outside of their family, much less with foreigners. If you take ill and are offered any traditional Pohnpeian remedy, it is recommended that you consult common sense before ingesting anything. Do not assume that
traditional healing methods are effective or advisable.

Eye Contact

You may find that Pohnpeians are reluctant to make direct eye contact; this is often perceived as rudeness by Westerners while Pohnpeians see it as a sign of modesty and respect. Also, when passing between or in front of other adults, it is polite to bend down slightly and avoid lingering.

Saving Face

Pohnpeians are much more concerned than most Westerners with saving face. One manifestation of this desire to avoid embarrassment is Pohnpeians' tendency to answer questions indirectly or in the way that they believe the hearer wants the question to be answered. For example, if you ask a Pohnpeian person, "Is it safe to walk this way at night?" he or she may be ashamed to answer that it is not. You can learn more by rephrasing the question: "What is the safest way to get to my hotel?"

Sakau

If you are invited to participate in a traditional *sakau* circle, you should sit where indicated by your hosts. After any high-titled individuals present have had a drink, the cup of *sakau* is passed around the circle without skipping anyone. It is rude to refuse the cup of *sakau* on its first few passes. Even if you do not wish to drink, you should take the cup and touch the liquid to your lips before passing it on.

Visiting

Pohnpeians generally welcome both expected and unexpected visitors to their homes. It is appropriate to bring a small gift of food when visiting. When going inside someone's house, one should always remove one's shoes.

Travel Information

GETTING THERE AND AWAY

Air

The only viable option for most travelers is to fly. On Mondays, Wednesdays, and Fridays, Continental Airlines offers an eastbound flight from Guam to Pohnpei, which then continues from Pohnpei to Hawaii with several

> Most hotels will pick you up or drop you off at the airport for less than $10 if you notify them ahead of time.

stops along the way. On Tuesdays, Thursdays, and Saturdays, the flight travels in the opposite direction, landing in Pohnpei on its way from Hawaii to Guam.

Sea

If you are travelling from another state in the FSM, it is possible to join one of the national government's ships on a field trip. While these trips are a great way to discover the outer islands, they are very irregular. It is not recommended that you plan an itinerary around one of these field trips unless you are staying in Micronesia for several months. See page 29 for more information about joining a field trip ship.

HEALTH AND SAFETY

In general, Pohnpei is an extremely safe place for travelers. The simplest precautions will virtually ensure that your trip is safe and enjoyable.

Both women and men may safely travel alone during the day, but at night, it is recommended that you stay in well-lit areas, travel with a group, or ask a hotel or restaurant employee for the safest route to your destination. Women who are traveling alone may have to endure some cat calls and stares, especially in Kolonia. There is very rarely any threat of real violence behind these behaviors, and the most effective response is usually to ignore the offending individuals.

Visitors are almost never pick-pocketed, robbed, or assaulted. As in nearly any place, if you leave valuables unsecured, they are liable to be stolen. Your risk of encountering crime on Pohnpei is further reduced if you avoid bars where young men are imbibing a combination of *sakau* and alcohol.

While driving, riding a taxi, or hitchhiking, always keep an eye out for drunk drivers. If you suspect that your taxi driver is drunk, get out of the car immediately and find another way to reach your destination. Also, keep an eye out for pedestrians and dogs, both of which tend to view the road as their domain. The paved road circling the island, recently completed with money from the embassy of Japan, is in decent shape in most places, though there are some very rough patches. The roads branching off the main road are sometimes extremely rutted, and one should exercise caution when driving these roads, especially after a rain.

If you are the victim of a crime during your stay on Pohnpei, contact the police (320-2221).

The **tap water** on Pohnpei is not safe to drink, and it can make visitors who are not accustomed to it very ill. Bottled water is readily available in convenience stores and restaurants. Food served in restaurants, especially if it is served hot, is nearly always safe, though the same cannot be said for the local dishes that are cooked and sold in roadside stands. See page 37 for detailed information on diseases and illnesses in Micronesia.

There are two **hospitals** on Pohnpei. Both the **Pohnpei State Hospital** (320-2215) and the smaller, private **Genesis Clinic** (320-3381) are located on the road to Madolenihmw just outside of Kolonia. Of the two, Genesis offers slightly better care. Services at both hospitals are limited, however, and for serious health issues, you will probably want to fly to Hawaii or Guam. In addition to the pharmacies at the two hospitals, there is one pharmacy in Kolonia, **Medpharm** (320-3314), which carries some over-the-counter medications.

There are dispensaries in the rural areas of Pohnpei and on the outer islands. By and large, these facilities do not receive adequate support from the national government, and the few medications that they have in stock are likely to be expired.

SERVICES

The **FSM Telecommunications Corporation** (24 hours daily; 320-2740), known commonly as **Telecom**, located near the center of Kolonia, sells phone cards and cell phones. There also a few unreliable computers available to the public. A phone card allows you to browse the internet on these computers fairly cheaply.

Across the street from Telecom is **Computer Island** (320-4942), a small internet café with slightly easier-to-use, but still unreliable, computers.

The **post office** (Mon-Fri 8 AM-3 PM; 320-2313) is located near Telecom on Kolonia's main road. If the post office runs out of stamps, as often happens, you can also purchase stamps in the **Philatelic Bureau** next door.

The **Bank of Guam** (Mon-Fri 8 AM-3 PM; 320-2446) and the island's only **ATM** are located near the southern end of Kolonia's main road. The ATM is open 24 hours, but it often breaks down or runs out of cash. The **Bank of the FSM** (Mon-Fri 8 AM-3 PM; 320-2838) is located a short distance further south near Palm Terrace.

Pohnpei boasts a single movie theater, **Pohnpei Center Cinemas** (320-3456) on the road out of Kolonia toward U. The small but well-kept theater shows new releases on three screens.

There is a coin-operated **laundry** in the ground floor of the green, two-story building on the road to U and Madolenihmw near Ace Commercial Center.

Getting Around

AIR

Caroline Islands Airlines (320-8406), also known as CIA, is the only carrier to the outer islands of Pohnpei and Chuuk. The owner, operator, and pilot, Alex Trettnoff, flies a couple of very small prop planes to Pingelap, Mwoakilloa, Sapwuahfik, and the Mortlocks in Chuuk a few times a month. Though the charges for tickets and luggage are onerous and some find Alex's personality abrasive, flying to the outer islands is relatively painless and affords some nice aerial views of the islands. Tickets start at $100 one-way.

LAND

Taxis

If you are not planning to rent a car, taxis will be your main form of transportation around Pohnpei. Taxis usually run until 10 PM, and it is almost always easier to call rather than to

> Be prepared to share a taxi with others headed in your direction.

flag a taxi down. If you need help calling a taxi, any hotel or store employee will be willing to call for you. Taxi drivers are fairly reliable, but you may have to give them a landmark to find less frequented locations. Taxi rides within Kolonia are $1 per person, to or from Sokehs or U $2-3 per person, and to remote areas $5-$15 per person.

Capital Taxi Service Capital Taxi Service offers reliable service in and around Kolonia. *320-5485*

D's and A's Taxi Service D's and A's is the most reliable taxi company for rides to and from Sokehs. *320-1291*

Triple R Taxi This is the only taxi company to offer regular service to Kitti. *320-3096*

Waido Taxi Service Offers taxi service to and from Madolenihmw as well as within Kolonia. *320-7248*

Car Rental

Although it is possible to reach all of Pohnpei by taxi, the only way to be in complete control of your itinerary is to rent a car. There are several car rental companies operating in Kolonia, and some hotels also rent cars.

Budget Rent-A-Car Cost: sedan $55, SUV $65; 320-8705

Micro Car Rental Cost: car $50; 320-2122

Hitchhiking

Another way to get around the remote areas of Pohnpei, especially Kitti and Madolenihmw, is to hitch rides. If you are walking along the main road in one of these areas or waiting in one of the covered "bus stops" near the road, before long a friendly local will pull over and offer to take you to your

> Though most Pohnpeians will refuse to accept money for rides, offering a few dollars for gas is a polite gesture.

destination or as far as they are going. Hitchhiking on Pohnpei is generally safe, but it is best not to hitchhike alone and only to hitchhike in daylight hours.

At the beginning or end of the workday, you may be able to catch a ride with an unmarked "taxi." These carpools carry people to and from their jobs in Kolonia Town and may be willing to take you along for $3-$5 per person.

SEA

It is relatively easy to arrange a trip to the islands near Pohnpei. Some resorts or tour operators offer trips to Ant Atoll or Pakin. Small boats frequently travel between Pohnpei and Pakin, the closest inhabited outer island of Pohnpei, or you may be able to

> The Village Hotel (pg 97) and Pohnpei Surf Club (pg 102) both arrange trips to nearby islands.

secure transportation to Pakin by asking around. Prices vary depending on whether transportation is included as part of a diving or tour package. Trips to Ant start at $60 and up, and trips to Pakin are usually $100 or more.

Field Trips to Outer Islands

A great way to see the outer islands of Pohnpei is to accompany one of the FSM passenger or cargo ships on a field trip. A few times a year, the FSM national government will send these ships on a round trip to the islands east or south of Pohnpei or on an extended trip to Chuuk and Yap. The ships usually travel at night and spend the days anchored near small atolls, giving passengers an opportunity to spend a day at each stop. If you can secure a place to stay, it may even be possible to spend a week on one of the islands and catch the ship on its way back to Pohnpei. See pg 29 for more information about field trip ships.

Where to Stay

It can be hard to predict when certain hotels will fill up for a national or regional conference. Thus, if you have a strong preference as to where you will stay, it is a good idea to book in advance.

Inexpensive

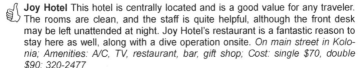 **Nahlap Island Resort** This resort, located on a small island off Pohnpei's southwestern coast, is a favorite escape among locals. After a short boat ride to the island, one can explore Nahlap Island, relax in a hammock, play volleyball, basketball, or billiards, swim, snorkel, kayak, or enjoy some of Pohnpei's few beaches. Accommodations are very basic, and those not prepared to rough it should consider a day trip to the island rather than an overnight stay. Moreover, Nahlap is not close to any other sights, restaurants, or sizable stores. It is good destination for a weekend stay rather than as a base for other activities. The tiny cabins and huts are furnished with foam sleeping pads, clean sheets, and small electric fans. The staff is very helpful, though they tend to operate on a relaxed, "island time" schedule. Call several days ahead to make reservations and arrange transportation. *Nahlap Island in Kitti; Amenities: fans, kayaks, snack shop; Cost: hut $20, cabin $30; 320-5009 (ask for John David or Marcia Kind)*

Yvonne's Hotel This is a comfortable hotel for travelers on a budget. The rooms are spacious and fully furnished, and the towels and linens are clean. The staff is proficient, but they are not the most helpful. Many rooms have a kitchenette or balcony; be sure to ask if this is important to you. *Behind Telecom in Kolonia; Amenities: A/C, TV, kitchenette; Cost: single $55, double $75; 320-1248*

Moderate

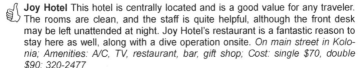 **Joy Hotel** This hotel is centrally located and is a good value for any traveler. The rooms are clean, and the staff is quite helpful, although the front desk may be left unattended at night. Joy Hotel's restaurant is a fantastic reason to stay here as well, along with a dive operation onsite. *On main street in Kolonia; Amenities: A/C, TV, restaurant, bar, gift shop; Cost: single $70, double $90; 320-2477*

Cliff Rainbow Hotel Cliff Rainbow Hotel, located on a hill away from Kolonia's busy main road, aspires to greatness. The charmingly decorated lobby and exterior offer the visitor a place to relax and visit with other travelers. The rooms are clean, and the staff is proficient. *On side street in Kolonia; Amenities: A/C, TV, restaurant; Cost: single $95, double $106; 320-2415*

South Park Hotel Across the street from Cliff Rainbow Hotel, South Park Hotel is a bit more functional and less ornamented. It caters mostly to Japanese visitors, but the staff is very helpful to English-speakers as well. Many of the rooms feature a wonderful view over Sokehs Harbor, and the hotel boasts an excellent restaurant. *On side street in Kolonia; Amenities: A/C, TV, restaurant; Cost: room $50-120, cottage $70; 320-2255, southparkhotel@mail.fm, http://southparkhotel.info*

Ocean View Plaza Hotel This hotel occupies a hill overlooking Kolonia Harbor, and the rooms, which are comfortably furnished, all have a great view of the water. The apartment-style rooms include a kitchenette with a refrigerator, oven, stove, counter, sink, and dishes. The restaurant and bar on the first floor are both great, and the lobby has a small gift shop selling handicrafts. The hotel also rents cars. The staff is very good about helping guests arrange tours, transportation, or airport pick-up and drop-off. *On road to Sokehs in Kolonia; Amenities: A/C, TV, kitchenette, restaurant, bar, gift shop; Cost: single $80-85, double $85-130; 320-7879, rumorsinc@mail.fm, www.fm/oceanview*

PCR Hotel This is a small, reasonably priced resort in a quiet waterfront location. All the rooms have a balcony overlooking one of Pohnpei's inlets, and the hotel has a dock out back, where the Pohnpei Surf Club hires boats for surfing, fishing, and tours of Nan Madol, Ant Atoll, and elsewhere. The restaurant downstairs serves decent, all-you-can-eat sushi at lunch for $6.50. Discounts are available for guests who book for a week or longer. *Off road to Madolenihmw; Amenities: A/C, TV, mini-fridge, wireless internet, restaurant; Cost: single $75, double $85; 320-4982, pcrhotel@gmail.com, www.pcrhotelpohnpei.com*

Expensive

The Village Hotel This resort is the premier resort on the island, yet it remains relatively unknown to visitors from outside of Micronesia. The rooms are open air, treetop bungalows (shielded by mosquito screens) offering phenomenal views of Pohnpei's lush coast. Owners Bob and Patti Arthur are friendly and happy to facilitate a water-borne excursion to Ant Atoll, Nan Madol, or elsewhere. The restaurant has easily the most magnificent view anywhere on Pohnpei and possibly the best food on the island as well. A small beach is a short walk down the hill from the bungalows. Staying at the Village is well worth the minor inconveniences of staying outside of Kolonia. *In Awak, U; Amenities: fans, restaurant, bar, tours, boats, kayaks, gift shop; Cost: bungalow $105-130; 320-2797, thevillage@mail.fm, www.thevillagehotel.com*

Where to Eat

Most restaurants serve American or Japanese dishes rather than Micronesian cuisine, but just about every restaurant offers fresh tuna sashimi, a must-eat for any visitor to Pohnpei.

Inexpensive

Angie's Fast Food This fast-food joint serves fried chicken, hot dogs, burgers, and a few other dishes. A popular spot among locals, Angie's does not offer much in the way of variety or healthy options, but the chicken is tasty, the service is good, and the plates are very reasonably priced for their size. *Next to Palm Terrace; Cost: meals $2-6; Hours: Mon-Sat 9 AM-10 PM; 320-1480*

Café Ole This diner is one of the few restaurants on Pohnpei that serves breakfast. The menu features a good variety of American breakfast and lunch dishes. The pancakes and grilled tuna burger are very good, and most other items on the menu are decent, if not spectacular. *Near Spanish Wall; Cost: meals $5-10; Hours: Tues-Sun open for breakfast and lunch*

Joy Hotel Restaurant This restaurant is a favorite spot for lunch and dinner among both locals and visitors. The Joy Lunch–a Japanese plate with fried tuna, sashimi, miso soup, rice, and a small salad–is by far the most popular item on the menu, which includes a variety of Japanese and American favorites. The fish burger is also very tasty. Be sure to enjoy the free local snacks set out just inside the door. *At Joy Hotel; Cost: meals $5-14; Hours: 7 AM-3 PM, 5-9 PM; 320-2447*

Kia Restaurant This relatively new restaurant offers a few American and Japanese dishes. There is nothing too special here. The food, however, is decent, and the staff is very helpful and accommodating. The restaurant also has a TV, so it is a good place to catch a sports game, assuming the game is televised during business hours. *Behind Telecom, in parking lot of Yvonne's Hotel; Cost: meals $5-12; Hours: Mon-Sat 7AM-2 PM, 5:30-9 PM; 320-5130*

KSP This restaurant opened relatively recently. KSP offers a buffet serving a few Pohnpeian dishes. It is one of very few restaurants that serve anything resembling traditional, local foods. However, the buffet is a bit overpriced, and the few local dishes served do not do justice to traditional Pohnpeian cuisine. *On main street in Kolonia, next to Telecom; Cost: meals $4-7; Hours: Mon-Sat open for lunch*

Moderate

Cliff Rainbow Restaurant This restaurant has a decent selection of American dishes, including pizza. The décor is beautiful and the staff is very helpful, but the food is a little disappointing. *At Cliff Rainbow Hotel; Cost: meals $7-12; Hours: 7 AM-9:30 PM; 320-2416, cliffrainbow@mail.fm*

 Ocean View Orchid Restaurant This restaurant is not conveniently located unless you are staying at the hotel of the same name, but it is worth a short taxi ride to sit on the patio out back while enjoying a beer and one of the restaurant's tasty sandwiches (the crab and cheese sandwich is recommended). Aside from the sandwiches, the restaurant's food is very good, though it tends to be a little expensive. The staff is very friendly and helpful. *At Ocean View Plaza Hotel; Cost: sandwiches $5-8, meals $9-30; Hours: 6:30 AM-10 PM; 320-7879, rumorsinc@mail.fm, www.fm/oceanview*

 Sei Restaurant This restaurant offers an all-you-can-eat buffet at lunch and dinner for reasonable prices in a peaceful atmosphere. The Japanese dishes are tasty, and the sashimi is great. The restaurant is located in a beautiful, wooden building tucked away in a quiet corner of Kolonia. *Off main road in Kolonia; Cost: lunch $7.50, dinner $9.50; Hours: Mon-Sat 11 AM-2 PM, 6-8:30 PM; 320-4266*

Town Plaza Restaurant This restaurant has undoubtedly the widest selection of dishes at any restaurant on Pohnpei. This lesser-known restaurant essentially has three full menus, including American, Japanese, and "island" dishes. The food is generally good, and the atmosphere is quiet and a bit more formal than most establishments on Pohnpei, though not so formal as to preclude dining in a T-shirt. The restaurant is open for dinner daily. *On side street in Kolonia; Cost: meals $7-15; Hours vary*

Breadfruit

Western visitors are often unfamiliar with breadfruit, an enormously important food on Pohnpei. The name is an apt description of the fruit, which is starchy, somewhat fibrous, and only a little sweet. It is never consumed raw, but it is boiled or baked by itself or with other ingredients. Breadfruit is very nutritious, and it is an excellent source of fiber.

The breadfruit tree is used for a variety of purposes. Micronesian canoes are invariably carved from the strong and durable wood. It is also used for medicinal purposes, to make glue, and to create handicrafts.

Expensive

South Park Restaurant This restaurant boasts perhaps the best view of Kolonia Harbor on Pohnpei. The enclosed patio looks out toward Sokehs Rock, and dining here at sunset is truly awe-inspiring. The restaurant serves mostly Japanese dishes, which are very good, if a little expensive. *At South Park Hotel; Cost: meals $10-25; Hours: 7-10 AM, 11:30 AM-2 PM, 5:30-9 PM; 320-2255, southparkhotel@mail.fm, southparkhotel.info*

The Village Hotel Restaurant Dining here is truly a magnificent experience. Serving breakfast, brunch, lunch, and dinner, the restaurant looks out over a beautiful section of Pohnpei's coast in Awak. Even if you do not stay at the Village, it is worthwhile to have brunch at the hotel while connecting to the free wireless internet or disconnecting from the outside world completely. The Village Hotel is also home to the Tattooed Irishman bar (pg 104). *At Village Hotel; Cost: breakfast $6.50-12, lunch $9.50-12, dinner $12-20; Hours: 7 AM-9 PM daily; 320-2797, thevillage@mail.fm, www.thevillagehotel.com*

What to Do

SIGHTS

Kolonia Town, the largest population center and only town on Pohnpei, sits on a peninsula in the north of Pohnpei. It is hard to romanticize Kolonia, a sprawling, somewhat

> Prior to 1989, the capital of the FSM was in Kolonia.

dirty town. When Oliver Sacks visited Pohnpei in 1994, he described Kolonia as "charming" and "sleepy," but development has continued apace, and on weekdays the town can seem a bustling boom town compared to the rest of quiet Pohnpei.

Kolonia's History

The town dates to the late 19th century, when the Spanish built a fort and a few administrative buildings. When the Germans took control of Pohnpei, the town remained relatively small until it was destroyed by a typhoon in 1905. The Japanese later rebuilt and greatly expanded the town, but Kolonia was again destroyed during World War II by American bombardment. Since then, the town has been rebuilt again, and gradually Kolonia has grown into the bustling population and commercial center it is today.

First-time visitors to Pohnpei are often surprised by the mixture of old and new found in Kolonia Town. On Kolonia's main road, small stalls where vendors sell local food sit in the shadow of the FSM Telecommunications Corporation's huge satellite dishes. On the waterfront, one can see fishermen paddling canoes through the mangroves while commercial jetliners thunder overhead several times every day. These juxtapositions are a defining part of the Pohnpei experience.

Streets in town are marked, but the street names will do little to help you orient yourself. No one refers to streets by their names but rather to neighborhoods and landmarks. The **Spanish Wall**, one of very few remnants from the days of Spanish control, is located at the north end of the main road. The wall now serves as the outfield wall for a baseball field, but the wall is interesting as perhaps the oldest relic of colonialism in Pohnpei. Nearby is a **German bell tower**, part of a church constructed in the early 20th century. From the top of the tower, you can get a good view of sprawling Kolonia Town.

The **Pohnpei Botanical Gardens** are located at the opposite end of the main road from the Spanish wall. Here it is possible to see various plants found on Pohnpei including bananas, breadfruit, and taro. The office of the **Island Food Committee**, a non-profit organization promoting the cultivation and consumption of local food, is located in the gardens. The **public library** just outside the entrance to the gardens is small but nevertheless impressive considering how little reading is valued on Pohnpei.

> For information about the Island Food Committee of Pohnpei and other NGOs, see page 44.

Scattered throughout Pohnpei are many **relics of World War II**, including a **large gun** on Sokehs ridge and the **Japanese sugar mill**, clearly visible at the top of a hill along the main road in Madolenihmw. Almost all of these Japanese relics are covered in rust and lack any markers or signposts whatsoever, but a **Japanese tank** parked near the tourism office in Kolonia is in reasonably good condition and is worth seeing.

Follow the road out of town to west, and you will reach Sokehs municipality, which includes both **Sokehs Island** and the northwest sector of Pohnpei. Sokehs Island sits across Kolonia Harbor from town and is topped by the distinctive **Sokehs Rock**, one of the most memorable features of Pohnpei's physical landscape and the first that most visitors to Pohnpei see. This mountain is emblazoned on many souvenir T-shirts and coffee mugs sold in town.

Further into Sokehs is Palikir, the **capital of the Federated States of Micronesia**. The national government is housed in several modest buildings on a well-kept campus, which was completed in 1989. Nearby is the **College of Micronesia, National Campus**. The college offers associates' degrees, certificates, and vocational education to students from around the FSM. The campus itself is attractive, and the school's library, located near the center of the campus, houses a fantastic collection of literature on Micronesia and the Pacific (Wed 8 AM-9 PM, other weekdays 8 AM-5 PM; 320-2480). The librarian for the Pacific collection, Iris Falcam, is a great resource for anyone interested in learning about Micronesia.

Continuing on the road from Kolonia will lead into Kitti. Soon after entering Kitti, one passes **Pwisehn Malek**, a steep mountain resembling its namesake (for a laugh, ask a tour guide or cab driver to translate *pwisehn malek*). Further south, a road splits off toward the dock for **Nahlap Island Resort**. Beside the road to the dock is a **statue of Henry Nanpei**, an extremely wealthy and influential Pohnpeian businessman. As the main road continues toward Madolenihmw, it passes a truly magnificent section of Pohnpei's mangrove forest and coast.

The road passes next into Madolenihmw, the poorest section of Pohnpei but also the highest ranking in traditional hierarchies. Madolenihmw is also important on Pohnpei as the location of **Nan Madol**, an absolute must-see for any visitor to Pohnpei. A collection of impressive stone structures resembling log cabins linked by a network of canals, Nan Madol is believed to have been the cultural and political center of Pohnpei from the 12th to the 17th century AD. The highest chief in Pohnpei's traditional title system still resides nearby. Locals treat the ruins with a kind of reverential awe and say that magic brought the unique basalt stones from around Pohnpei to the site of the ruins. A short trail leads from the road to Nan Madol; the owners of the intervening land usually charge $3 per visitor to pass through to the ruins. Take a taxi from Kolonia to the trailhead or hire a boat to approach the ruins at high tide.

Near Nan Madol is **Kepirohi Falls**, perhaps the most popular and distinctive of Pohnpei's many beautiful waterfalls. The waterfall can be accessed via a short trail off of the main road in southern Madolenihmw. Local children and visitors enjoy swimming in the pool at the base. If you choose to swim at the waterfall, you should be aware of the danger of water-borne diseases and flash floods, which can descend from upstream even when it is not raining at the waterfall.

Not far from Kepirohi falls is the **Chinese pilot farm**, reached via a dirt road beside Madolenihmw High School. The farm was established by the Chinese embassy ostensibly to demonstrate the cultivation of indigenous and imported crops to Pohnpeian farmers. In reality, the farm exists largely to sell produce to Chinese and other ex-patriots. Still, it is possible to see numerous varieties of banana and taro here, some of which are labeled. The operators of the farm, when they are present, are nice enough and will show you around if you ask them.

The main road around Pohnpei finally passes through U, the smallest of Pohnpei's five municipalities. Along the road you will see numerous *sakau* bars and many of Pohnpei's most beautiful vistas, especially in the village of **Awak**, before arriving back in Kolonia.

For a guided tour of Nan Madol or any area of Pohnpei, contact the **Village Hotel** (pg 97), **Micro Tours** (320-2888), or **Iet Ehu Tours** (320-2959). All three will organize almost any activity.

Henry Nanpei

Henry Nanpei, the son of a high-ranking member of Kitti's traditional title system, earned a fortune as a trader and merchant. Using wealth that he had inherited from his father, he established a business trading with the foreign vessels that were becoming increasingly common in Pohnpei's waters in the late 19th and early 20th centuries. Eventually, he came to control a huge percentage of the privately-owned land on Pohnpei, as he traded the goods he obtained from foreign merchants to Pohnpeians in exchange of their land.

Nanpei is a controversial figure among historians. He opposed the colonial governments of Spain, Germany, and Japan and became a leader among Protestants on Pohnpei, although many believe that he did so in an effort to increase his own power. In any case, Nanpei is an enigmatic and highly compelling figure in Pohnpeian history.

WATER AND OUTDOOR ACTIVITIES

Diving

The islands of Micronesia are known as some of the world's premier places to dive, and Pohnpei is no exception. The pristine state of Pohnpei's reef, the beauty of its marine life, and the clarity of its waters rival that of Australia's Great Barrier Reef. Because Pohnpei is often passed over by divers in favor of Palau and Chuuk, it is likely that you will be the only diver at a particular dive site on a given day.

Pohnpei once had a number of dive shops, but a few of these have stopped offering services to divers in recent years. The dive shop at the Village Hotel, however, is still in operation and is highly recommended.

Village Hotel Tours The Village Hotel's dive shop caters primarily to English-speaking guests, and the staff and divemasters at the Village are the friendliest, most knowledgeable, and most professional on the island. Diving trips include a boat, driver, divemaster, air tanks, and weights. Trips cost $95-200 per person depending on the number of divers, but these prices are subject to change with rising gasoline prices. The Village also rents equipment and offers PADI courses, but it is a good idea to contact the hotel ahead of time if you are interested in these services. *At Village Hotel; Cost: $95-200 depending on number of divers; 320-2797, thevillage@mail.fm, www.thevillagehotel.com*

Nan Madol

Nan Madol has impressed visitors to Pohnpei for centuries. The earliest visitors to Pohnpei suspected that the ruins were as old as the Egyptian pyramids. Indeed, the construction of the approximately 100 artificial islets of the ancient city with huge basalt logs quarried on the opposite side of the island is a feat rivaling the construction of the pyramids. It is so incredible that most locals believe only magic could have transported the stones to the site of the ruins.

It is possible to construct a history of Nan Madol based on traditional stories and archaeological evidence. Nan Madol was completed by a dynasty of rulers called the *Saudeleurs* in the 11th or 12th century. The *Saudeleurs*, who imposed a harsh tribute on the rest of Pohnpei, wished to keep a close eye on the activities of local chieftains, and thus they invited all the chiefs of the island to live with them at Nan Madol. Eventually, the *Saudeleurs'* rule became too harsh, and Isohkelekel, a legendary figure some say was descended from a god on the island of Kosrae, led the Pohnpeians in revolt. Defeated, the *Saudeleurs* acquiesced to a new political organization for Pohnpei based on rule by the *Nahnmwarkis*. For a time, the *Nahnmwarkis* resided at Nan Madol, but due to a famine, typhoon, or other unknown cause, the city was abandoned about 400 years ago.

The compound's most important building and the best preserved is Nan Douwas. Due to the awe in which Nan Madol is held by Pohnpeians and the relatively small amount of archaeological excavation that has been done here, the structure appears as it might have to the first Europeans to land on Pohnpei. To reach Nan Douwas from the mainland, one must wade across a small canal and climb up into the structure between 10-foot high walls on either side that are overgrown with jungle and mangroves. In the center of the structure is a small, underground alcove, where archaeologists believe that *Saudeleurs* and *Nahnmwarkis* were buried.

Fishing

Pohnpei is a fantastic place to catch both reef and pelagic fish. Most dive shops and tour operators, as well the Pohnpei Surf Club (pg 102) organize fishing trips. For an even more memorable fishing trip, try to find a trusted local to take you. Not only will you have an unforgettable cultural experience, you may pick up a few tips from someone whose family has been fishing these waters for centuries.

> When you are spear fishing, it is best to keep the dying fish you have caught in a canoe or cooler floating on the surface rather than in the water, where they might attract sharks.

Pohnpeians often go fishing at night or spear fishing. There are both risks and thrills associated with these types of fishing, but if you follow the lead of an experienced Pohnpeian fisherman, you should be perfectly safe.

Hiking

You can hike to the top of **Sokehs Rock** via a fairly steep trail from the road around Sokehs Island. The hike includes a short climb up a rusty, makeshift ladder. If you are deterred from the hike up Sokehs Rock, consider hiking up **Sokehs Ridge**. Coming from Kolonia take the road straight after crossing the bridge to Sokehs Island. The rather steep road leads up to a lush ridge affording views both toward and away from Kolonia as impressive as those to be found on the Rock. A **small Japanese bunker** can be found on the ridge facing away from Kolonia.

There are many trails through Pohnpei's jungle for those who are interested in finding them. One trail in the Kitti district, popularly known as the **"seven waterfall hike,"** affords ample opportunity to see some of Pohnpei's waterfalls. The all-day hike winds through secluded jungle and supposedly passes by seven waterfalls, though some hikers count only six. You will, however, want to find a guide rather than attempt to hike through the jungle on your own. See pg 99 for information about tour operators.

Private Property

Most land on Pohnpei is privately owned. Even in what looks like the densest jungle to Western eyes, Pohnpeians strictly respect the land and agricultural produce of others. It is best to ask permission or go with a guide when hiking in the jungle, picking fruit, or choosing a spot for a picnic.

Snorkeling

If you are not interested in diving, you can still see some fantastic marine life while snorkeling. In most spots the water is crystal clear, so snorkeling at the ocean's surface will allow you to see nearly as much marine life as diving under the water.

Surfing

Pohnpei is famous among surfers as the location of **Palikir Pass** or **P-Pass**, the site of one of the best, most consistent breaks in the world. A steady stream of the world's best surfers passes through Pohnpei from September through May to surf at P-Pass and other sites on the island's barrier reef. However, surfing on Pohnpei is not for beginners. Even relatively strong surfers can be swept off their board, slammed into a reef, and buried under several tons of water in a matter of seconds on a high surf day.

If you are interested in surfing, contact the **Pohnpei Surf Club** (920-7343, pscsurfclub@yahoo.com, www.pohnpeisurfclub.com), a tour operator, or one of the dive shops to hire a boat.

Dive Spots on Pohnpei

Pohnpei has over 30 dive sites, but here are a few of the best:

Manta Road is so named for the frequency with which manta rays pass through the 50-feet (15-meter) deep channel here. The current is often strong, and the visibility varies. Yet, even on relatively murky days, you can see quite a lot: the author once saw a manta ray with a 10-foot (3-meter) wingspan while snorkeling along the surface. The mantas are fairly shy, and they may leave if you come too close. Instead, try to wait, remaining as still as possible, and then follow a short distance behind the mantas as they pass. Your chances of seeing a manta are greatest December through May. Other sea life frequently spotted in Manta Road includes eagle rays, garden eels, reef sharks, and a variety of coral and anemones fed by the sediment carried by the current.

Mwand Pass is a pass in Pohnpei's reef under 2 miles (3 kilometers) from Manta Road. Visibility in the channel, which is about 160 feet (50 meters) deep, is usually quite good. The variety and volume of coral here is truly incredible. Tubastrea, gorgonians, and various soft coral trees line the walls of the pass, the interior walls of the adjoining reef, and the exterior walls, which can be reached when conditions permit. Butterflyfish and Napoleon wrasses are among the brilliant and varied fish that can be found at Mwand Pass.

Nan Madol should not be missed by any visitor to Pohnpei, but divers can experience an entirely different aspect of the ruins. Coral covers the basalt columns near the edge of Nan Madol, and though visibility is often poor here, it is possible to view a variety of sea life among the ruins and at a nearby Japanese World War II wreck.

Pakin, one of Pohnpei's outer islands, is also one of its best spots for diving. Although it is some distance away from Pohnpei and the surf can be quite high, it can usually be reached during the summer and early fall. A variety of large and small fish, sharks, coral, and dolphins have been spotted here.

Ant Atoll, a neighboring island of Pohnpei, is touted by some as the best place to dive in Pohnpei. One can dive in the atoll's only entrance or in a few other spots inside and outside the lagoon. Like at Pakin, the visibility varies, but it can be as far as 160 feet (50 meters). The colors of various hard and soft corals, small fish, and various other sea creatures are stunning. One can also see large sea life, such as eagle rays, manta rays, various reef sharks, and schooling fish as well as occasionally turtles and dolphins.

Since reaching Ant Atoll and Pakin requires crossing open ocean, surf conditions may delay a scheduled trip to these islands for a few hours or a few days.

Swimming

While mangroves surround most of Pohnpei's coast and few beaches can be found, there are many places to swim on the island. A number of **marine parks** dot Pohnpei's coast, and it is possible to spend a day in the sun at any of these for a very small fee. **Nett Point**, on the end of the peninsula to the east of Kolonia, is another good spot for swimming.

Visitors are encouraged not to swim around Kolonia or Sokehs Island, as pollution renders doing so unsafe and unsavory, and not to swim amongst the mangroves, as doing so could be hazardous to both the swimmer and this fragile ecosystem. Many visitors to Pohnpei choose to swim in various freshwater streams, but before doing so, you should be aware of the risk of waterborne diseases and flash floods.

SHOPPING

The most visible sign of Westernization on Pohnpei is the explosion of shops and stores around the island. For better or worse, large grocery, hardware, and convenience stores are constantly opening in Kolonia, and many families, even in remote parts of the island, are running small convenience stores. While this does mean that visitors to Pohnpei will find a decent selection of local and imported goods, many of these stores are extremely similar to one another. Below is information on a few of the best stores.

Souvenirs

A-One Souvenir Shop (hours vary; 320-5995), on the main road in Kolonia, is highly recommended as one of the best places to find Pohnpeian handicrafts. Here you will find a wide selection of locally made, traditional handicrafts, beautiful wood carvings, and other souvenirs for a third of what you would pay at a similar store in the United States or Europe.

Kapinga village, a neighborhood in Kolonia named for the outer island of Kapingamarangi from which many of its residents come, has many small shops selling handmade crafts for bargain prices. Even if you do not intend to buy anything, walking through Kapinga village, which feels very different from the rest of Kolonia, is a worthwhile diversion.

> The Kapingamarangi people are renowned for their handicrafts, including small carvings of animals and canoes.

You can also find a small selection of handicrafts at other establishments, such as Palm Terrace (see below) and Joy Hotel (see pg 94).

The **Office of Tourism** (Mon-Fri 8 AM-3 PM; 320-2421) in Kolonia is rather disappointing, but it does offer a few maps and brochures and is perhaps the only place to purchase Pohnpei postcards.

Groceries

Most foreign visitors to Pohnpei find the grocery stores extremely limited. Nevertheless, it is possible to find all the essentials: dairy products, a variety of canned and dried goods, freshly baked bread, and even fresh fruits and vegetables. **Palm Terrace** (7:30 AM-9 PM; 320-2882) has the widest selection of groceries on the island. It also carries many souvenirs, household goods, and clothes.

Ace Commercial (Mon-Sat 7:30 AM-10 PM, Sun 9 AM-9 PM; 320-2518), on the road to Madolenihmw, also has a decent selection of groceries for slightly less than at Palm Terrace.

A-One Mart (8 AM-midnight; 320-2537) carries a variety of canned goods and pastas and is conveniently located on the main road.

Pohnpei has a couple of good markets for local food. The **"fish market,"** a short distance inland on the road from the airport, is the best place to find fresh fish. There are also a few stalls selling local fruits and occasionally mangrove crab. If you do not want to clean and prepare fish yourself, visit the **market across from Blue Nile,** where the venders will fillet the fish or prepare sashimi for you. Here you can also find a variety of local fruits, vegetables, and dishes.

> You can also find stalls or individuals selling local produce around town or beside the road very cheaply.

Convenience Stores

Wall Mart (8 AM-10 PM), named for the neighboring Spanish Wall, not Sam Walton, carries groceries and household goods. There is also a small fast-food joint in the front of the store.

Next door is **Senny's** (7 AM-9 PM; 320-1008), another convenience store with sundry goods.

Yoshie (9 AM-8 PM; 320-2412) undoubtedly has the widest selection of household goods, electronics, and other miscellaneous goods to be found on the island.

Blue Nile (9 AM-10:30 PM; 320-7476), on the road to Sokehs, sells many items in bulk.

Nightlife

To experience authentic Pohnpeian nightlife, one must visit one of countless *sakau* **bars** in Kolonia, along the main road around Pohnpei, and in secluded spots throughout the jungle. Usually located in small bungalows or in open lots, *sakau* bars serve bottled or freshly pounded *sakau*, a mildly intoxicating drink made from the roots of a local pepper plant, to Pohnpeians every day from about four in the afternoon until around midnight. Since *sakau* is a mild narcotic, these bars are almost always very serene places to spend an evening, although things get rowdier when patrons imbibe alcohol with their *sakau*. Pohnpeians are usually very welcoming to foreign visitors to these bars, but it can be helpful to be invited by a Pohnpeian friend who can initiate you in the drinking of *sakau*.

Rusty Anchor Bar This bar, located in the basement of an unmarked warehouse, is the watering hole of choice for many of Pohnpei's American, Australian, and European ex-patriats. Boasting a pool table, a beautiful view of Sokehs Island, occasional live music, and one of the best selections of beer available on Pohnpei, the "Rusty" hosts friendly English-speakers and locals in a relaxed, though decidedly un-Pohnpeian, atmosphere. When you find your way to the building, enter the door on the left and walk down the steps to find the bar. *On road to Sokehs; Cost: drinks $2-5; Hours: opens 4 PM, closes after midnight most nights; 320-8601*

The Tattooed Irishman This bar, located at the Village Hotel, is certainly the most beautiful on Pohnpei. The only thing Irish about the Tattooed Irishman is the sign greeting visitors as they enter. Nevertheless, the cocktails, beer and wine selections, and service are all excellent, and the view of the ocean off the Awak coast is magnificent. *At Village Hotel; Cost: drinks $2.50-10; Hours: 4:30 PM-midnight daily; 320-2797, thevillage@mail.fm, www.thevillagehotel.com*

Outer Islands

The outer islands of Pohnpei are a fantastic place to get off the proverbial beaten track. Unfortunately, this also makes them some of the world's most inaccessible places. Traveling to nearby islands, such as Ant Atoll and Pakin, is relatively easy; most tour operators and dive shops as well as some hotels routinely arrange day trips to these places. Traveling to any of the other islands, however, requires a sublime combination of luck, determination, and an adventurous disposition, and having a local contact or two can help. Still, anyone who makes it to these outer islands will be rewarded with a truly once-in-a-lifetime experience of picturesque island landscapes and distinct languages and cultures.

ANT ATOLL

Ant Atoll, also spelled Ahnd Atoll, the closest "outer" island to Pohnpei, is a small, uninhabited coral atoll just west of Pohnpei. Where Pohnpei's physical landscape defies traditional stereotypes of Pacific island, Ant Atoll meets most people's expectations for sandy beaches, lagoons, and plenty of coconut trees. This atoll is a very popular spot among visitors for snorkeling, bird watching, or simply enjoying a picnic on the beach. It is also one of Pohnpei's best dive sites (see box on pg 102 for information about diving at Ant Atoll).

PAKIN

Pakin, a small atoll 20 miles (30 kilometers) northwest of Pohnpei, is about two and one half hours from Pohnpei by boat, though reaching the atoll is very dependent on surf conditions. The inhabitants of Pakin are Mortlockese (from the Mortlocks island group in Chuuk state) rather than Pohnpeian. The atoll is a superb spot for diving. See box on pg 105 for information about diving at Pakin.

Staying on Outer Islands

If you plan on staying overnight on an outer island in Pohnpei, it is best to radio ahead to ask for permission from the mayor or chief. You will not be refused permission, but observing this formality is appreciated by the locals. Moreover, if the islanders know when and for what purpose you are coming, they will arrange a place for you to stay.

Bringing a few modest gifts for your hosts is always a good idea. If it has been several months since a ship has been to the island, locals will be running short on rice, flour, and sugar. Otherwise, instant coffee or any food not readily available on the island will be appreciated.

MWOAKILLOA

Mwoakilloa, also spelled Mokil, is a tiny coral atoll about 100 miles (160 kilometers) east of Pohnpei. The Mwoakillese, like many outer islanders, are culturally distinct from the inhabitants of nearby islands, and as caring for one's possessions is an important value for the Mwoakillese, Mwoakilloa features perhaps the most beautiful and meticulous landscaping on any comparable island.

Funeral rites, important on Pohnpei and other nearby islands, are even more central to life on Mwoakilloa, and funerals traditionally last 40 days. Mwoakillese families will delay burial for months and raise great sums of money to ensure that their departed loved ones are laid to rest in the proper manner and correct location. About 150 people live on the largest of Mwoakilloa's three islands.

Alcohol

Alcohol is prohibited on most outer islands of Pohnpei. Rather than import beer or liquor, many outer islanders drink liquors based on fermented coconuts. These concoctions, often called tuba, are similar to palm wine. Tuba is also illegal on most islands, so if you decide to partake, do so in private and avoid becoming intoxicated.

PINGELAP

Another small atoll east of Pohnpei, Pingelap is remarkable for the warmth and openness of its approximately 300 inhabitants. The atoll, which consists of three islands, is well-known among geneticists due to the unusually high occurrence of achromatopsia, a rare form of color blindness. After a 1775 typhoon reduced the island's population to less than 20 individuals, the recessive genetic disorder began to crop up more and more often in the island's limited gene pool, and about 8% of Pingelapese have the disorder today. Oliver Sacks' riveting book *The Island of the Colorblind* recounts his visit to Pingelap and study of the psychological and social implications of achromatopsia.

Pingelap is also notable as the site of *kahlek*, or nighttime flying-fish fishing. Nearly every night from January to April, Pingelapese fishermen participate in *kahlek*, using torches to attract the flying fish and nets mounted on long poles to snag them from the air. *Kahlek* is truly a specta-

Dwindling Population

Though the outer islands of Pohnpei are stunning and their inhabitants are kind, they are not what they once were. The population of many outer islands throughout Micronesia has dwindled since the 1970s to no more than 400 on most islands. Mwoakilloa, for example, is estimated to have once supported over 700 residents. Now, only 150 Mwoakillese live on the island, though several thousand now reside on Pohnpei, in the United States, and elsewhere.

Though many of outer islanders have moved in search of economic opportunities, they maintain strong ties to their home island. Some still own land or houses that are being cared for by relatives and periodically return to their island to visit family.

cular sight for visitors to the island. It is also a highly ritualized form of fishing, and women are strictly prohibited from observing or participating in *kahlek*, except from afar.

SAPWUAHFIK

Sapwuahfik, which is sometimes called by the name of its largest island, Ngatik, is an atoll of about 500 people 100 miles (160 kilometers) southwest of Pohnpei. The island is famous as the location of a brutal massacre in 1837. Captain C. H. Hart had tried to take a number of tortoise shells from the island in the previous year only to be driven away by the islanders. He returned in 1837 intent on revenge and led his crew in a massacre of all the male inhabitants of the island. Then, Hart left one member of his crew and a few Pohnpeians to govern the island. In the following years, Sapwuahfik was repopulated from the women and children who survived the massacre and the men left in charge by Captain Hart.

One fascinating result of the Ngatik massacre was the development of a new language. Ngatik Men's Creole, an amalgamation of English and Sapwuahfikese, is spoken only by the adult males of the island, though women and children understand it. All inhabitants of the island also speak Sapwuahfikese, a language closely related to Pohnpeian.

NUKUORO AND KAPINGAMARANGI

These two tiny atolls are far south of Pohnpei and can only be reached via a field trip ship since both islands lack airstrips. Culturally and linguistically these islands are much closer to Polynesian islands such as Tahiti and Samoa than to the rest of Micronesia. Even physically, the inhabitants of these islands bear a greater resemblance to the tall, broad-shouldered Polynesians than smaller Micronesians.

According to Nukuoro legend, the island was settled by a Samoan prince who was forced to leave the island Samoa by his brother who wished to be the sole heir to the kingship of the island. The defeated brother, along with his family and followers, sailed over 2,000 miles (3,200 kilometers) to Nukuoro where he became the island's first king. The atoll, which consists of over 40 small islands around a small, circular lagoon, now has a population of about 350.

Kapingamarangi is notable for the extent to which local construction techniques are still utilized. Whereas concrete and tin-roofing has become the norm on most other outer islands, as these materials are much less labor-intensive, most structures on Kapingamarangi are thatch-roof huts made in the traditional style. Of the atoll's 33 islands, most of its 500 inhabitants live on two of these islands connected by a bridge.

Outer Island Offices on Pohnpei

	Mwoakilloa	Pingelap	Sapwuahfik	Nukuoro
Office phone	320-2360	320-6145	320-8679	320-3599

Building Canoes

Although some of Pohnpei's outer islands now rely completely on fiberglass boats with outboard motors, most have retained the knowledge of building canoes. On Pingelap, building a canoe is often a communal activity, and at times, an entire section of the island will turn out to help fell a breadfruit tree, measure and shape the tree, and carve the body and accessory parts of a canoe.

On one such occasion, I offered to help a group of Pingelapese men move a partially carved canoe from the spot in the jungle where the breadfruit tree had been chopped down to a more accessible location where work could be completed. I knew that only two or three people could lift a finished canoe without difficulty, so I thought that moving this unfinished body would be a simple job. As ropes, poles, and more and more men were assembled, however, I began to realize that I had underestimated the task. All in all, it took 30 men over three hours to move the canoe a quarter of a mile by pulling on a rope tied to the bow in short, energetic bursts. Everyone enjoyed the thrill of hauling the canoe, but perhaps none enjoyed it more than the older men yelling instructions as they sat and watched the canoe pass by.

Opposite: Men carving out a traditional canoe on Ta Island, Chuuk
Below: Two Pingelapese canoes on Pohnpei

Above: Kosreans at a local festival
Below: Fisherman launching boat, Kosrae
Opposite: Fisherman on Kosrae casting net

Above: Visitors at the ruins of Nan Madol
Below: Kepirohi falls, Pohnpei

Chuuk

A paradise of countless pristine islands, a myriad of coral reefs teeming with life, and a living underwater museum, Chuuk is many things. Unfortunately, Chuuk is also afflicted with poverty so grim that it intimidates many potential visitors. Those who do venture here are amazed both by the awe-inspiring natural beauty and by the incredible hardships that are an integral part of everyday life in these islands.

If you journey to Chuuk, you will be rewarded with a one-of-a-kind experience. Scuba diving here is an experience so intense that history seems to become palpable. In Chuuk, you can swim through gigantic World War II wrecks that serve as tombs for the servicemen who perished in them, snorkel with thousands of vibrant fish, savor the freshest seafood on earth, and learn about the beautiful and complex ways of the Chuukese people. Despite Chuuk's poverty, many foreigners and FSM citizens will admit grudgingly that the Chuukese are the most welcoming, friendly, and outgoing people in the FSM. Indeed, Chuuk may be the best kept secret in the Pacific, and because most travelers neglect it, its environment and culture have remained relatively intact. Certainly, Chuuk is a special place; many who come find themselves forever changed by the majesty of the islands and people.

HIGHLIGHTS OF CHUUK

Wreck diving: Whether you are a novice or experienced diver, dive at one of dozens of amazing wrecks in Chuuk. pg 134

Picnicking on a small island: Escape to your own private island for an afternoon or several nights. pg 134

Visiting the Japanese Wartime Communications Center: Visit this historically significant building on the picturesque campus of Xavier High School. pg 133

Admiring Sapuk Lighthouse: Hike to this gorgeous historical monument. pg. 136

Hiking Tonachau Mountain: Hike up the quick and relatively painless path for magnificent views of the lagoon. pg 136

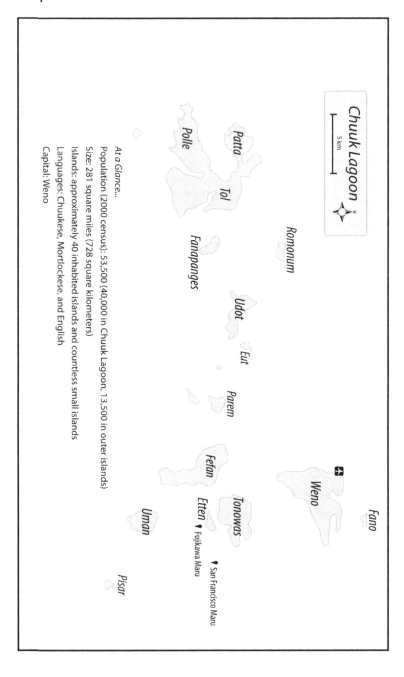

Chuuk Lagoon

5 km

N

Patta

Polle

Tol

Romonum

Fanapanges

Udot

Eut

Parem

Fefan

Uman

Etten ◆ Fujikawa Maru

Tonowas

◆ San Francisco Maru

Weno

Fano

Pisar

At a Glance...

Population (2000 census): 53,500 (40,000 in Chuuk Lagoon, 13,500 in outer islands)

Size: 281 square miles (728 square kilometers)

Islands: approximately 40 inhabited islands and countless small islands

Languages: Chuukese, Mortlockese, and English

Capital: Weno

Geography

Chuuk, formally known as and still often referred to as Truk, is the largest state in the FSM with approximately 53,000 people living on about 40 islands speckled across the 1300 miles (2,100 kilometers) of Pacific between Pohnpei and Yap. Chuuk state is just over seven degrees north of the equator giving the islands tropical weather all year.

> The word *chuuk* means "large mountains," and although now it is the name of the entire state, previously it referred to the high islands in Chuuk Lagoon.

As one flies into Chuuk, the beauty is striking. There are numerous islands with abundant plant life, mountainous terrain, and mangrove forests resting on an ocean of kaleidoscopic blue colors, coral heads, dazzling sea creatures, and historical artifacts. Truly, Chuuk Lagoon is one of the most beautiful locals in Micronesia.

Most of the Chuukese reside in Chuuk Lagoon on islands near the capital of Weno. There are many outer island atolls in the state, but they account for only about twenty percent of the state's population. Some of these islands are separated from the capital by nearly 200 miles (320 kilometers) of ocean.

The capital of Chuuk is Weno or, as it is sometimes called by foreigners, Moen. It is located in the eastern section of Chuuk Lagoon.

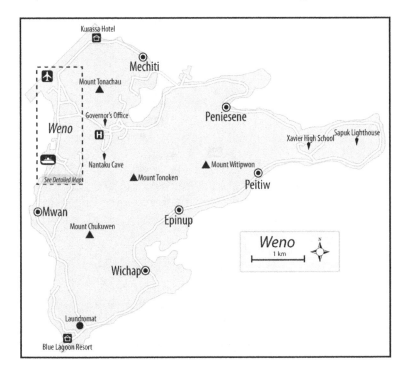

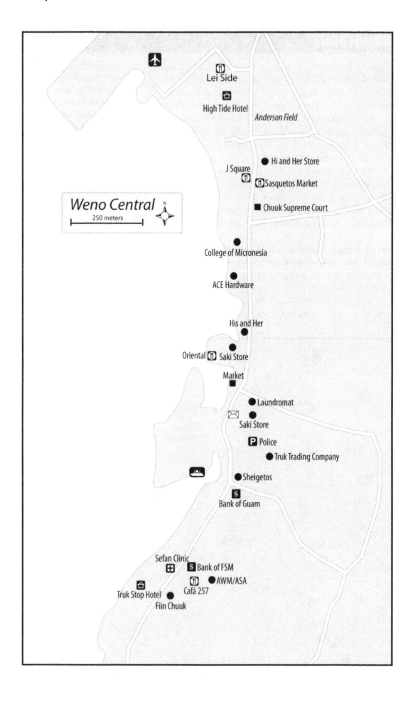

Lei Side

High Tide Hotel

Anderson Field

Hi and Her Store

J Square

Sasquetos Market

Chuuk Supreme Court

Weno Central

250 meters

College of Micronesia

ACE Hardware

His and Her

Oriental Saki Store

Market

Laundromat

Saki Store

Police

Truk Trading Company

Sheigetos

Bank of Guam

Sefan Clinic

Bank of FSM

AWM/ASA

Café 257

Truk Stop Hotel

Fiin Chuuk

South of Weno there are several large islands, including Tonoas, Fefan, and Uman. To the southwest of Weno is the Lagoon's largest island, Tol. Weno has a greater population than Tol, but the latter is greater in size. Though it is not the only island with a large population, Weno is the only one with basic infrastructure, and even on Weno it is inadequate.

Chuuk's outer island atolls include the Mortlocks, the Halls, and the Western Islands. The Mortlocks are southeast of Weno and are named after James Mortlock, captain of the *Young William*, a British ship that noticed them while journeying from Australia to China in 1795. The Hall Islands are 60 miles (100 kilometers) north of Chuuk, while the Western Islands, as the name implies, are about 60 miles (100 kilometers) due west.

> The extreme remoteness and the irregular boat and plane schedules make a visit to the outer islands extremely difficult, but still very rewarding.

The outer islands are less populated and more austere, and their cultures have been less affected by outsiders.

Although the islands across Chuuk have many geographical similarities, you will find that each island is physically unique. Caves, huge black volcanic rocks, mangrove forests, fields, and beaches are just a few of the features that may characterize any given island. The plant life on most islands consists of breadfruit, coconut, banana, and taro. Some islands are known for growing foreign foods such as pineapples, pumpkins, cucumbers, and lettuce. One such island, Fefan, is known as the "farming island," and most of the fresh local produce available at the markets on Weno is brought in daily by boat from Fefan.

As a visitor to Chuuk, you will have opportunities to visit and explore several caves used as wartime bunkers, to dive or snorkel among wondrous marine life and preserved ships of World War II, and to stay on one of the tiny "picnic islands." Whatever reason you have for visiting Chuuk, make time to appreciate the rare natural beauty of the land, water, and sky that makes Chuuk one of the most breathtaking spots on the planet.

History

Archaeological evidence indicates that people started inhabiting the islands of Chuuk during the first millennium BC. Both linguistic evidence and local folklore suggest that the first inhabitants journeyed to Chuuk from Kosrae. Although few specifics are known about the early settlers, the people living in Chuuk in prehistoric times were amazing sailors. They

Chuuk Lagoon

A 130-mile (210-kilometer) long barrier reef with sporadic atoll islands creates the border of Chuuk Lagoon, one of the largest lagoons of its kind in the world. The reef has several passes for large ships and serves as a large natural harbor. This geographical fact has made Chuuk a target for occupation by foreign naval fleets and has had an incalculable affect on Chuuk's development over the past 100 years. Inside Chuuk Lagoon are Weno and the other high volcanic islands, all covered by the bountiful vegetation that is characteristic of the state.

used the sky, tides, and sea life to navigate extremely long distances. Daily life probably centered on collecting breadfruit, taro, coconuts, and bananas and hunting for fish and other sea creatures. It is clear that these early Chuukese were successful because by 1556, when the first documented European ship arrived, the population had grown in number and spread throughout the numerous islands and atolls that are now Chuuk state.

> Unfortunately, the early settlers of Chuuk had no written language, but the Chuukese do have a rich and abundant collection of oral histories and stories that have been passed down for generations.

As early as the 16th century, Chuuk began to be visited by European ships. Chuuk was the last area in Micronesia to receive Europeans for trading. One of the earliest ships visiting Chuuk was the Spanish *San Lucas*. The ship and crew not only ran into some rough weather but also became entangled in hostile exchanges with people on an atoll west of Chuuk Lagoon named Pulap; at least two crew members are recorded to have died in an altercation with the local residents.

It was not till the late 19th century that Europeans had regular contact with the islanders in Chuuk Lagoon, and their notes indicated that they were hospitable, friendly, but reserved. The Mortlocks were visited earlier and more frequently than Chuuk Lagoon as they were found to be consistently peaceful toward European visitors. Altogether, accounts of interactions between Chuukese and outsiders throughout the 19th century range from peaceful, helpful interactions to horror stories. Regardless of whether the Chuukese were any more hostile to foreigners than their counterparts in Palau or Pohnpei, their constant warfare amongst each other earned them a reputation as a violent people; this, in turn, may have led early copra traders and whalers to avoid them as much as possible.

Many Chuukese from the lagoon and Mortlocks were known to travel to Guam in large canoes to trade for iron tools and other practical items that they could not furnish themselves. Aside from the use of modern tools and a few limited contacts with whalers, Chuuk and its people remained insulated from outside culture and influence.

Western contact picked up in 1873 when the first missionaries arrived in the Mortlocks. The religion and new economic institutions were quickly adopted by the friendly Mortlockese, and only a few years later, there were churches on eight Mortlock islands and plans to bring Christianity to Chuuk Lagoon. In 1879, missionaries from Pohnpei arrived on the Lagoon island of Uman at the request of a local chief. When American missionaries arrived in 1884, they found that four islands already had churches and chiefs of other islands were requesting them. Traders also came more frequently, exposing Chuuk to more Western goods.

One Tree Hill

The most recognizable of Weno's three mountains is the smallest, Tonachau. It is on the northwest side of the island across from the airport runway. Atop the summit of Tonachau stands a single wind-bent tree making the mountain a unique and useful landmark. Tonachau is sometimes referred to by outsiders as One Tree Hill.

In Francis X. Hezel's essay, *The Beginnings of Foreign Contact in Truk*, he explains that the presence of missionaries opened the Chuukese to Western ways and material desires while the traders who brought new technologies challenged their traditional beliefs and customs. Although they were not collaborating, missionaries and traders together brought about immense changes to the cultures and ways of the Chuukese people.

In 1886, Chuuk was formerly ruled for the first time in history by foreigners, the Spanish. The area would change hands three more times over the next 100 years before Chuuk would have its independence. Germany bought Chuuk from Spain in 1898. In turn, the Japanese acquired the islands after World War I.

As early as the 1880s, the Japanese started traveling to Chuuk and investing people and time into the agricultural development of the islands. As Japanese influence grew, the Japanese began to attempt to assimilate the local people and also began seizing their land. Japan's administration immediately following World War I is considered a prosperous time due to the growth of the sugar, mining, and fishing industries. Unfortunately, the start of World War II ended the relatively peaceful occupation of the island. As Japan's imperialist aspirations grew and the war progressed, Japanese rule become more oppressive and, at times, inhumane. During World War II, Chuuk caught global attention because Chuuk Lagoon served as a base of the Imperial Japanese Navy's Combined Fleet. Chuuk Lagoon was an ideal harbor for ships, and its few passes made it easily protected.

> By 1942 there were approximately 96,000 Japanese in Micronesia, though the local population was only 50,000.

In 1947, after the conclusion of WWII, Chuuk joined with Pohnpei, Kosrae, the Marshall Islands, and Northern Mariana Islands to form the Trust Territory of Pacific Islands (TTPI). The United States was the trustee of the TTPI and was tasked with overseeing development of the islands. In 1990,

Operation Hailstone

February 17th and 18th, 1944 changed the tide of the war and set events in motion for the FSM's current political situation. On these days, the U.S. Navy attacked the Imperial Japanese Navy's airstrips, bunkers, and radio positions in a plan named Operation Hailstone. Over the two-day period, over 400 aircraft were destroyed along with more than 50 ships. It is calculated that 150 Chuukese civilians, 30 U.S. serviceman, and as many as 2000 Japanese died. It said that when the Chuukese realized there were U.S. planes coming, they cheered in anticipation of their liberation, but when the bombs started to drop, everyone was terrified and ran for cover. Many ships, airplanes, and artifacts of the battle still remain at the bottom of Chuuk Lagoon, and many visitors from Japan and across the world visit them every year. On February 17th, 2009, representatives from Chuuk, Japan, and the U.S. gathered on Weno in honor of the 65th anniversary of Operation Hailstone. Chuuk's governor gave a moving speech indicating his thankfulness for the freedom of his people but also deep sadness at the loss of the life during the battle. He also wished for the hatred and misunderstandings that lead to such devastation to end. Both Chuuk and Japan have done much to facilitate reconciliation. Japanese are welcomed guests in Chuuk, and some travel there every year to pay their respects to lost relatives. There are also several monuments in honor of lost Japanese serviceman.

the Federated States of Micronesia joined the United Nations. Since the early 1990s, there has been a steady economic decline in Chuuk. The education system, water, sewers, radio station, roads, and power plant have fallen into disrepair. There are several main causes for this including reductions in U.S. aid and cultural practices that make governing at the state level difficult, but perhaps the most significant reason is a lack of quality political leadership. Throughout Micronesia, Chuuk is now known for its problems rather than its strengths. Chuuk offers a relatively low level of formal education, it is "dirtier" than the other places, the economy is stagnant, and it is infamous for its violence. Whether rates of violent crime are actually higher in Chuuk as compared with other places in the FSM is difficult to say, but the perception that they are is widespread.

Chuuk is also home to some of the most passionate people that I have ever met, people who continue to spend their lives improving their communities and trying to push Chuuk to its collective potential. As for the present, Chuuk is just that, potential waiting for something to change the momentum that has been pulling it down for nearly twenty years.

Culture and People

Although there are many daily chores in Chuukese life, the pace of life is predictable and slow. Someone visiting Chuuk and only witnessing downtown Weno on a busy day would get a wrong impression of the Chuukese lifestyle. Nevertheless, life is far from simple; the emphasis on family creates complicated social structures within family compounds, villages, and islands. To understand Chuukese culture, one must understand the intricate social networks and relationships that determine how things are run from the level of a single family all the way to the state government.

The extended family is at the center of Chuukese life. Chuukese gain a great sense of identity and pride through their families. Children are cared for by extended families and whole communities. Children usually have more space and freedom to explore than in the Western world. As children grow, they are taught the housework and chores that make up much of the daily work on an island in Chuuk.

> Cousins refer to each other as brothers and sisters, and frequently aunts, uncles, or grandparents will take on the main caretaking responsibilities for relatives' children.

As children grow older and become teenagers, the family will rely on them for maintaining the household and gathering and preparing food. It is not uncommon for children to stop going to school altogether at age 14 or 15. While families value education, they also find value in having a few children focus on homestead activities. There are only a few high schools in Chuuk; most islands do not have one. Thus, if a family wants their children to have a high school education, they may need to send them to an island that has a high school. Most people have family on Weno or other islands with high schools; in the best cases, children attending high schools stay with family on these islands. Sometimes families pick and choose only the best students from their family to continue with their education. One issue that arises from the fact that many teenage boys, who are not in school nor are subject to supervision, have many hours of free time, which they sometimes use to abuse alcohol and drugs or cause mischief.

As people reach early adulthood, they begin to think about marriage. Often, husbands and wives meet in high school. Since islands can be small and nearly everyone is related, leaving the island for high school is an opportunity to meet people who are not relations. It is also common for an older man to seek a younger wife. To marry a woman, a man must formally ask the woman's mother and father and also numerous other relations. It is also appropriate for him to give gifts of fish, firewood, and coconuts. If the family does not like the man or has a problem with his family, they will deny the request. At times, two individuals who love each other would not be allowed to marry because the two families have other conflicts. This exemplifies the importance of family in Chuukese life, as the family's interests and honor are valued above the individual's. It may also be that a child is arranged to be married to someone else and has little to no input in that decision. Arranged marriages were the norm two generations ago, but now most people do have a say regarding the choice of their spouse.

Chuukese Language

Chuukese is the language spoken in Chuuk Lagoon, the Western Islands, and the Halls. There are around 45,000 Chuukese language speakers. The language has far fewer words than the English language. Mortlockese is spoken in the Mortlocks and parts of Pohnpei. The language is closely related to Chuukese, although it is distinct. One clear difference is there is no letter "L" in Chuukese while it is prominent in Mortlockese.

Love Stick

The Chuukese love stick is part of a traditional courtship custom that is unique to say the least. It is often culturally inappropriate for a male and female to be with each other in public. If a man and woman were caught together, even if they were only talking, it could bring serious shame on the woman's family and fuel the wrath of her male relatives toward the man. The love stick was a socially acceptable method for young men and women to get around this taboo. Males would carve pieces of wood into broad spear-shaped sticks. The sticks were of varying lengths and had unique notches and designs. Some say the male would make two sticks: one perhaps a yard long and a duplicate stick just long enough to display in his hair. After dark, the man would sneak to the woman's hut, put his love stick through the grass hut, and tap the woman's head attempting to wake her. She would then feel the stick and could tell from the designs if it was a man she was interested in. To invite the male into the hut, the woman would pull on the stick. To tell him she was coming out, she would shake the stick. To reject the invitation, she would push the stick out.

Some view the custom as romantic, given that the young man ventures off into the woods with only moonlight to guide him in hopes that his beloved accepts him. Nevertheless, it is a custom that must have been ripe for awkward situations and funny stories.

It is still not unusual for man to sneak up to a woman's room and whisper for her to come outside. These days, however, it seems it is done most frequently by drunks.

With no written language until relatively recently, Chuukese used stories to form oral histories, teach lessons, and entertain. These stories incorporate legendary chiefs, tragic events, and proud moments and allow Chuukese to connect to and appreciate their ancestors and customs. The stories also tell of the wars, grudges, and compromises that happened between islands or villages.

When you have the opportunity to chat with locals, ask them about the island they are from. Although not everyone is willing to share stories from his or her island, most people are willing to talk about their islands' past. Ask around and try to hear all the stories you can because every story is a significant piece of art and culture.

> Island stories and legends are considered precious and important forms of cultural heritage by the Chuukese.

Some of these stories are turned into artwork known as storyboards. Carved boards of breadfruit wood depict some of the ancient stories of Chuuk. This artwork is an expression of creativity, skill, and respect for ancestry. You may find these boards in a hotel gift shop, at a few stores around Weno, or perhaps with individuals selling them on the street. Other common pieces of art include hand carved masks, love sticks, and sea creatures. Most of these crafts are handmade from people living on the island of Fefan.

The majority of people in Chuuk occupy themselves with subsistence fishing and agriculture. This includes farming taro, fishing, collecting bananas, climbing for breadfruit, and raising chickens and pigs. There are numerous other daily chores that must be done in a household, such as washing clothes, car-

> Work is shared between males and females, and though men and women have distinct roles, their duties do overlap at times.

ing for children, cleaning, gathering firewood, washing dishes, and cooking. Families are large and all the work is done by hand, making every chore laborious. Although daily life in Chuuk involves hard work, there are many hours for sitting, drinking coffee, and talking. Indeed, the Chuukese are experts on doing nothing at all. Individuals who have a strong work ethic are appreciated, but it is not the most significant quality for which people are respected.

Chuuk's government is by far the largest employer in the state. The U.S. government is the main source of funding to Chuuk state. There are

Turtles

Storyboards, loves sticks, and weaved fans are all fantastic locally made products you can purchase and take home with you. Turtle shell jewelry is popular in Chuukese fashion and can be found many places. The jewelry usually takes the form of rings, earrings, or beautiful hair combs. Turtles have long been a part of Chuukese diet and wearing turtle shell jewelry is an important tradition; unfortunately due to loss of habitat and global warming, the turtles are at risk of extinction. Because of this, it is illegal to transport any turtle shell products to the United States or Guam. Turtles play an important role in Chuukese culture, but most likely they do not play such a role in yours. Please, help protect the turtles and abstain from purchasing turtle shell products.

many teachers in the state, and it is one of the few viable careers available to individuals on every island. Serving in the U.S. military is considered a lucrative option by many in Chuuk. Religious ministry is also extremely common. A religious position brings respect and honor to a person's family along with increasing the person's influence in the community.

> As of 2008, the FSM had more Army recruits per capita and the higher casualty rate per capita than any state in the United States.

Families usually have enough food and, often times, more than anyone can eat. There are times, however, during droughts or storm surges, for example, when people run out of food and go hungry. In the outer islands, due to climate change and rising sea levels, the taro patches sometimes get saturated with saltwater, which kills the crop. At these times, people depend on their families on bigger islands or in the United States to send money for rice. Sometimes help is forthcoming, and sometimes it is not. I lived on an island that was in need of food, and it is worrisome how much weight people lose when there are taro and rice shortages. The Chuukese and Mortlockese are strong, resilient, and generous people, and there were numerous times during my stay in Chuuk when people served food to me while going hungry. Their concern for my health over their own is just a small example of how caring the Chuukese can be.

Local foods include ripe or young bananas, which are often boiled and covered with coconut cream. Breadfruit is a seasonal fruit and is served boiled or pounded into a stiff substance called *kon*. *Kon* is usually topped with sweet coconut milk. Taro is a root that grows year round; it is also boiled, shredded, pounded into *kon*, and covered in coconut milk. Fish is eaten raw with salt and lemon, barbequed, boiled in coconut milk, or salted and preserved for weeks or months. Other sea life that is eaten includes crab, octopus, turtle, and snail. Pigs and chickens are raised on the islands and are eaten during celebrations and important events.

Despite the wide variety of local foods, canned meats such as Spam, corned beef, mackerel, and luncheon meat as well as rice are the foods of choice for many Chuukese. These foods lack nutritional value and are extremely high in fat and sodium. The widespread consumption of these foods has made diabetes an epidemic in Chuuk and throughout the Pacific.

SOCIAL NORMS

Although it would be extremely difficult for a visitor to learn all the customs of Chuuk, becoming familiar with a few practices can earn the respect of locals.

Borrowing

When an individual in Chuuk asks to "borrow" something from a friend, family member, or stranger, it is understood that the individual will not necessarily get back what they give. Within the family there is also an assumption that when someone asks for something, it will be given. It is not customary to refuse food or water to anyone, especially a relative.

Dress

Men dress according to activity or profession. Men in government or school usually wear dress pants, shoes, and Hawaiian style shirts. Among the young males in Weno, baggy jeans and T-shirts are popular.

Chuukese women wear local skirts with flower designs or long muu-muus. Dress is conservative, and skirts or dresses often extend to the ankles. Women from the outer islands tend to dress more conservatively, but again, younger people are likely to try more modern styles. Regardless, sandals are worn by both men and women for both style and practical reasons. People always remove their footwear before entering a home, and having shoes can make this practice a real pain if you are coming and going all day.

Paying Respect

Traditionally, it is customary for a woman to be physically lower than the men in the room. If men are in chairs, women sit on the floor or bend at the waist when they walk. If men are sitting on the floor, women crawl to serve the males or move about. This practice is still followed in traditional settings and homes, especially on the outer islands. Even in schools and places of business, this social custom is sometimes still followed.

For a woman, it is still customary in all settings to bow her head when walking in front of a seated man and to say "*tiro*," or "excuse me." I recommend that all visitors to the islands follow this custom when passing in front of a seated man or woman.

Female Leadership

Men hold the most respected and powerful positions in Chuukese society. The highest positions in churches, traditional hierarchies, families, and political institutions are held by men. Although some women do reach positions of power and influence, it is far too rare.

Women are respected within the household and make many important domestic decisions. It is also increasingly common for women to go to college. Nevertheless, a very real glass ceiling still exists in Chuuk, making it hard for women to obtain higher positions in government or the workplace. Many men do not respect female leaders; they find a woman who is giving instructions to be against cultural norms and extremely disrespectful. Chuuk's failure to promote female leadership and to support women in important positions of government is perhaps its greatest fail-

Funerals

Funerals are extremely important in Chuukese culture. Funerals can include as much as a week of mourning. It is important for the families that the funerals are done properly to show respect for the deceased relative. This sometimes involves delaying the service for weeks to ensure distant family members or the body itself arrives back on the deceased's home island. Funerals can also be extremely costly, and it requires family and friends near and far to contribute labor and resources to ensure a proper funeral. The ceremony involves days of crying, speechmaking, singing, and praying.

ing. Change is occurring very slowly in Chuuk, and women are slowly becoming more respected, though there still is great opposition to women's rights and privileges.

Travel Information

GETTING THERE AND AWAY

Air

Continental Airlines, typically called Mic Air in Chuuk state, flies to Chuuk on a daily basis and is the only way to get to Chuuk from outside the FSM. You can fly to Chuuk through Honolulu or Guam. If you come through Hawaii, your flight time will be about 12 hours including your stops in Majuro, Kwajalein, Kosrae, and Pohnpei. A flight from Guam to Chuuk is about two hours, but you will most likely have to spend a night in Guam before your flight. See pg 27 for more information about flying to Micronesia.

Sea

Periodically, one of the FSM's field trip ships comes to Chuuk from Pohnpei. Taking a field trip ship is long because the ships stop on every island along the way. It is important to take quality food, drinking water, and a good jacket or tarp, since you may be on the boat for as many as four days before reaching your destination. The ships depart and arrive in Weno at the Trans Co. docks, which are located opposite the Chuuk State Police Station. At the Trans Co. office, you can find information on ship schedules and shipping rates. See pg 29 for more information about joining a field trip ship.

HEALTH AND SAFETY

Chuuk has a reputation throughout Micronesia for being a rough and even violent place. In spite of this reputation, Chuuk is a safe place to visit, and although violent crimes take place in Chuuk, tourists are practically never involved in violent incidents. Violence in Chuuk usually happens in areas that visitors do not go. The only exceptions, which are rare, are those occasions when violent altercations occur downtown, putting bystanders in danger. Most people visiting Weno, however, will never experience this side of the island. The biggest threats to visitors are the drunk or high young men that frequent the side of the roads throughout the day and night. I would suggest being polite but also brief with people you think may be intoxicated.

The **police** station is located just off the main drag in downtown Weno on a small road just north of Truk Trading Company and next to an old warehouse. The prison is also located there and overlooks TTC's driveway. (Prisoners looking over the fence may ask for change or make small talk as you walk out of TTC.) The Chuukese police do not have the best reputation, and I have even witnessed officers making inappropriate comments and gestures to both Chuukese and visiting women. The police do have a fleet of vehicles, but due to periodic gas shortages, they may not be operable. As a result, response time to a distress call may be slow. To contact the police you may call 911 on a local phone or press 0 to speak with a Telecom Operator who will connect you to them. I always advise calling the police when a situation arises; there are some quality officers who will do their best to help you. It is certainly better than doing nothing.

Tap water in Chuuk is absolutely unsafe. Restaurants and hotels can provide filtered or boiled water to drink. You can assume water served at restaurants to be safe. Aqua Serve is a water filtering plant in Chuuk, and many stores carry it as well as imported bottled water. Usually, tap water in hotels is safe for brushing your teeth.

The **Chuuk State Hospital** (330-2444) is near the Governor's Office in Nataku. It is a 10-minute drive from downtown Weno. The hospital has a poor reputation, and it is not recommended except in emergency cases. For minor issues, the hospital may also mean waiting a long time before seeing a doctor. There is a **pharmacy** in the complex across from the hospital if you need medications, although you should always travel with any medications you are already taking because there is no guarantee they will have what you need in stock.

Sefan Clinic (330-6167) is located in the complex next to Truk Stop Hotel and is small and extremely clean. There is typically little or no wait, and the doctors are professional and helpful. There is a **pharmacy** (Mon-Fri 9 AM-12 PM, 1-5 PM, open irregularly on Saturdays) and lab inside Sefan clinic. I would recommend going to Sefan Clinic for all medical needs other than emergencies. You will need to pay the cost for a consultation, but the fee is small.

Diving Safety

If you are coming to Chuuk to dive, make sure you are certified for the depths you will be diving. Although there are wrecks at shallow depths, many are deep even for experienced divers. Know how deep you can go and set your own limits.

There is one operational decompression chamber in Chuuk. In case of an emergency this chamber is available, but it is extremely costly. It is wise to have dive insurance that covers the dive chamber. Although it is unlikely you will need to go to the dive chamber, things do go wrong, and

---

Safety Tips on Chuuk

It is important for everyone to heed these tips, but women are the targets of most of the harassment. Women visiting Chuuk will likely be verbally harassed on the streets by men. Although dressing modestly is helpful, you will be the subject of unwanted attention. You will always feel and be safer if you travel with a companion.

- Do not go out in Weno at night and *never* walk around at night
- Always travel with at least one other person, especially when walking
- Do not get in a taxi or car if the driver is intoxicated
- Always be considerate in public by not being rowdy in the street or stores, as this may attract unwanted attention and may also be viewed as rude in general
- If traveling to any place not on the main road, get a local tour guide, ask permission from land owners, and let the hotel in which you are staying know where you are going

the $25 DAN insurance is a cheap way to protect yourself. See pg 37 for more information on diving safety.

SERVICES

The **post office** (Mon-Fri 9 AM-3:30 PM) in Chuuk is a small orange building on the main road just north of TTC. Get there in the morning to avoid the lunchtime rush. The building does not have air-conditioning and is a sauna on a hot day.

There are two banks in Chuuk. The **Bank of Guam** (Mon-Thurs 9 AM-3 PM, Fri 9 AM-5 PM; 330-2377) is located next to Sheigetos store in downtown Weno, and the **Bank of the FSM** (Mon-Thurs 9 AM-3 PM, Fri 9 AM-5 PM; 330-2331) is across from The Truk Stop and Sefan Clinic. When coming to Chuuk you should bring with you enough cash or traveler's checks to get you through your visit. There are **no functioning ATMs**, and the only businesses that accept credit cards are Kurassa, High Tide, Truk Stop, and Blue Lagoon. Also, there is no foreign currency exchange, so get U.S. dollars before arriving.

Getting Around

AIR

Air travel within the state of Chuuk is possible through **Carolina Islands Airlines** (320-8406), also known as CIA. The plane, which seats about seven passengers, travels to the Mortlocks and the Halls. The pilot is skilled at flying the small plane and landing on the tiny runways on the outer atolls. It takes about an hour to reach the Mortlocks from Weno. The difficulty of traveling with CIA arises from the inconsistency of flights. Although CIA has a schedule, it is routinely changed at the last second. Frequently passengers will show up for a morning flight and begin checking in only to learn that the flight is cancelled. On a positive note, the plane is kept in good condition and is not the reason for the cancellations. A one-way ticket costs about $120. Chartering the plane is also an option although an expensive one.

LAND

Car Rental

Rentals are available at Truk Stop, Blue Lagoon, High Tide, and Kurassa. You may find having a car unnecessary if you are staying in town and do not have plans to explore outside central Weno. If, however, you are staying at Blue Lagoon, renting a car may be more convenient than having to wait for the hotel bus or a taxi every time you go into town.

> It is helpful to know that sometimes car rentals are referred to as "U-Drives."

Blue Lagoon Resort *Cost: sedan $55, moped $25; 330-2727, 330-2438, blresort@mail.fm, www.bluelagoondiveresort.com, www.truk-lagoon-dive.com*

High Tide Hotel Rentals are only available to hotel guests. *Cost: car $40; 330-4646, hightidehotel@gmail.com*

Kurassa Hotel *Cost: car $30-35 (hotel guest), $55 (others); 330-4415, kurassahotel@yahoo.com*

Truk Stop Hotel *Rentals are only available to hotel guests. Cost: sedan $55, compact SUV $65; 330-7990, trukstop@mail.fm, info@dive-truklagoon.com, www.dive-truklagoon.com*

Driving in Chuuk

The roads in Chuuk are horrendous, and there is an art to driving on them without ruining your vehicle. In general, drive extremely slowly, follow the person in front of you, and avoid driving in the middle of puddles, which can swallow the car completely. Also make sure your rental has a spare tire, especially if you are driving away from town toward the area of Xavier High School.

Buses

Tour buses are available through the hotels, and these seem to be the most comfortable option if you just want to check out the island. For about $15, they will take you all the way to Xavier High School and back. The best part about taking a bus is that if there is a flat tire, you will not have to fix it.

Moped Rentals

Mopeds are available at Blue Lagoon Resort for $25 per day, but I could think of cheaper and less uncomfortable ways to humiliate yourself in Chuuk. Given Weno's puddles, pot holes, and mud, you may want to explore the island from a tour bus or rental car instead. On a several occasions, I observed tourists on tiny rented mopeds forging into a foot or more of mud in stopped traffic. Though they would try to balance the bike in the puddle, inevitably, they would lose balance and put their foot knee-deep in muddy water. Mopeds may be fun, but they are not practical in Weno. I would only recommend renting a moped if it has been unusually dry on the island for several days.

Mind the Holes

The roads in Chuuk have been in complete disrepair for many years. If walking in Chuuk, be sure to wear shoes that you don't mind getting dirty or ideally a pair of sandals with a thick rubber sole and straps around the ankle as well as foot. Puddles may appear to be a few inches deep, yet are actually a foot or more in depth. Old sometimes jagged pieces of re-bar also hide in the puddles along with other sharp scraps.

Taxis

Taxis cruise around town from about 7:30 AM until sunset. Taxis are usually marked with small, white signs made from Styrofoam. In Chuuk, anyone who wants to operate a taxi throws a taxi sign on the windshield and starts picking people up. The cost to go nearly

> Most taxis do not travel to the area of Xavier High School on the northeast side of the island.

everywhere is one dollar per person, and it is usually marked on the taxi sign. The cost to go to Blue Lagoon from town or back may be two or three dollars a person. Keep in mind that the farther you get from downtown, the fewer taxis there will be. As soon as it starts to get dark, taxis are very hard to find, so make sure you get back to your hotel before nightfall. Drivers in Chuuk have been known to drive under the influence; before getting in a taxi, make sure you feel comfortable with your driver's state of mind.

SEA

Boat Hires

If you desire to take a cruise around Chuuk Lagoon or visit some of the other islands, hiring a fiberglass boat and a driver is an option. Although there is small port near the main market in town with numerous boats and drivers who would be happy to rent their services to you, I would recommend against going with anyone you do not know. You can, however, make arrangements through many of the hotels for day trips within the Lagoon. If you would like to visit a particular island, it is better still to go with a local guide who has family there. In the event that your hotel does not have these services available, it is likely that a hotel staff member could connect you with a friend or relative who is familiar with the island. Hotel rates for day trips vary. If you go through someone else, you may have to pay as much as $50 per day plus the cost of gasoline, which can be eight or nine dollars per gallon. You can try to negotiate a better price, but be sure to settle on a price before leaving.

> Always keep in mind basic water safety and, if possible, obtain a life jacket from your hotel. Most boats in Chuuk have no life jackets.

Supply Boats

If you are considering journeying to the outer islands, there are supply boats that make the trip every month or so. Boats going to the outer islands are completely unreliable and have no schedule whatsoever, so there is no way to plan a trip around them. These voyages, which depart from the Trans Co. docks located opposite of the Bank of Guam, typically take between 20 and 48 hours. When traveling on these ships, be prepared to be packed in with many other people and livestock; you may also be hit by a strong storm, which can be quite nerve wracking. The trips can also become most uncomfortable if you suffer at all from seasickness.

All in all, these boats are unreliable, unsafe, and only for the adventurous. Other than volunteers, foreigners do not take these boats, and I would not recommend them. Passage on these boats is about $20.

Taking the Supply Boats

I had the pleasure of riding two of Chuuk's supply boats: the *Pukiel*, nicknamed by some the *Puke*, and the *Miss Chi Yung*. On one trip, I spent most of the night vomiting over the side while a storm sent waves crashing over me before going to sleep between a pregnant woman who took pity on me and a pig. Another trip went much more smoothly, and when I disembarked, an ambulance was waiting to pick up a woman who, to my surprise, had given birth during the trip.

Where to Stay

All hotels listed come with air-conditioning units. Keep in mind that power outages in Chuuk are common, but the hotels are pretty quick to start their backup generators.

Inexpensive

 Kurassa Hotel Kurassa is located on the northwest side of the island on a waterfront property. This hotel is popular among Micronesians because it offers good rates for locals and the rooms come with a stove, refrigerator, oven, and even some cookware. The furnishings are older and more worn than those of the other hotels, but the rooms are larger and include a TV and DVD player. The hotel staff is extremely kind, and they will go out of their way to accommodate your needs. There is a small convenience store located below the hotel building that has snacks and beverages. The hotel is about a 25-minute walk into town, but one can find a taxi fairly easily. The Rose Garden restaurant across the street has been closed for months, and it can be difficult to go into town at night. You may choose instead to cook your own dinners at the hotel.

Kurassa is by far the best deal in town, especially for those traveling on a budget. The hotel also has an unbelievable rental car deal: only $30 daily for hotel guests. Kurassa does accept credit cards, but they add an additional fee for all credit card charges. *Northwest Weno; Amenities: A/C, TV, kitchenette; Cost: single $60, double $70; 330-4415, kurassahotel@yahoo.com*

Moderate

 High Tide Hotel High Tide is located immediately south of the airport and is across from Anderson Field. High Tide's rooms, which include TVs and DVD players, are the newest on Weno and are kept consistently clean. Although the rooms can accommodate two people, they are a little small, and the beds are twin size. Taller guests might consider staying in one of the suites, which have queen beds. The Presidential Suite, which has one king bed and several couches, may be the nicest room on Weno. The hotel offers internet access in their main lobby, but you will have to buy a phone card from the front desk. The hotel has a great location, as it is close to stores and restaurants without being in the middle of downtown Weno. High Tide restaurant and Lei Side store and restaurant are within easy walking distance.

High Tide is not on the water and does not offer any services to divers. It is recommended for travelers on shorter stays. *Near airport; Amenities: A/C, TV, internet access, snack shop, restaurant; Cost: single $63, double $68, suite $80-110; 330-4646, hightidehotel@gmail.com*

Expensive

Truk Stop Hotel Truk Stop is located on the water along the west side of the island near downtown Weno, a short walk away from many businesses. The view from Truk Stop's dock at sunset is truly awe-inspiring. The Truk Stop's rooms are spacious, though older than most, and they include a TV. It is the only hotel in town where the showers are consistently hot. Truk Stop has a restaurant downstairs as well as a small internet café with free wireless internet for hotel guests. Truk Lagoon Dive Center offers expert local dive guides, rental equipment, and all-in-all excellent service for divers. The resort's masseuse is considered to be the best on the island, the gift shop is well stocked with local handicrafts, and the hotel rents DVDs. Next to the hotel is Hard Wreck Café and Bar, a great place to unwind at night or play pool. Truk Stop is a family-owned and family-run business, and owners Bill and Kiki Stinnett are very friendly and helpful.

Truk Stop's services and location make it a great hotel for divers as well as those coming in for short stays. Truk Stop accepts credit cards and even offers cash advances on credit cards for a very reasonable fee. *Near downtown Weno; Amenities: A/C, TV, wireless internet, gift shop, restaurant; Cost: single $110, double $120, suite $160; 330-7990, trukstop@mail.fm, info@dive-truklagoon.com, www.dive-truklagoon.com*

Blue Lagoon Resort Blue Lagoon's location is by far the most beautiful and tranquil on the island. The hotel, which is approximately 20 minutes by car from the airport or downtown Weno, overlooks Chuuk Lagoon and the islands to the south and west. The hotel consists of a number of large, cabin-like buildings on several acres of a grassy peninsula shaded by coconut palms. A sandy beach invites guests to the water for kayaking, snorkeling, swimming, or relaxing. The rooms are not the newest, but they are adequate in size and have comfortable beds.

The resort seems to be constantly improving one or another aspect of its property. The resort includes a restaurant, lounge bar with karaoke, outside bar with a miniature billiards table, masseuse, and gift shop. The gift shop also sells some snacks, but the prices are better at a store next to the dive shop. Blue Lagoon Dive Shop has been in business over 35 years and has the most experienced divemaster on the island. In addition, the resort can organize excursions to surrounding islands for a picnic or fishing trip. There is a computer available for guests to use for a fee.

Blue Lagoon is a great choice for those who want to enjoy a relaxing stay away from crowded Weno, but it is not convenient if you want to go into town, in which case you will probably want to rent a car from the resort. Even if you are staying somewhere else in Chuuk, it is worthwhile to spend a peaceful afternoon at Blue Lagoon. The resort is expensive and may not be an ideal place for those on short trips to Chuuk. *South Weno; Amenities: A/C, internet access, restaurant, bar, gift shop, beach access, tours, car and moped rental; Cost: single $120-125, double $135-140, suite $190; 330-2727, 330-2438, blresort@mail.fm, www.bluelagoondiveresort.com, www.truk-lagoon-dive.com*

LIVEABOARDS

Visitors to Chuuk who are primarily interested in diving should consider a liveaboard. The **SS Thorfinn** and the **Odyssey** are both fine diving vessels that offer an alternative way for divers to experience Chuuk. Each vessel has single and double occupancy guest rooms, kitchens, dining rooms, lounges with TVs, sun decks, and dive launch areas. Guests pay for a seven-day stay, which includes all meals, non-alcoholic beverages, and up to five dives per day. Both ships carry about 16 guests. Trips cost anywhere from $2,195 to $4,495 per person. Visit the websites listed below for up-to-date, detailed information on the ships.

SS Thorfinn *330-3040, 930-1276, thorfinn@seawave.net, www.thorfinn.net*

Odyssey *(800) 757-5396, (904) 346-3766, info@trukodyssey.com, www.trukodyssey.com*

Where to Eat

Inexpensive

Sasqueto's Market /J Square J Square and Sasqueto's Market are two out-door, carry-out options on the road just north of the FSM Supreme Court. They are open for breakfast and lunch, and both are good for a quick bite on the run. For breakfast, there is usually some combination of pancakes, hot dogs, and eggs. For lunch, you can find fried fish, sashimi, tapioca, breadfruit, bananas, or *kon*. They also serve a few American choices such as spaghetti, barbeque chicken, teriyaki chicken, salad, and cheeseburgers. The food is excellent for the price. Get there before 1:30 PM for the best selection. *Near FSM Supreme Court; Cost: breakfast or lunch $2-5; Hours: 7 AM-2 PM*

 Café 527 Café 527 is located in the same complex as the AWM grocery store and the Bank of the FSM. The restaurant serves local food, fried chicken, pork stir-fry, and other dishes. Several vegetable options are also available. The variety and quality of the food varies from one day to the next. The restaurant has a comfortable dining area, and it is open for lunch. *Next to AWM grocery; Cost: lunch $6; Hours: 11 AM-3 PM; 330-2874*

Moderate

Oriental Restaurant Oriental Restaurant, located just off the main road be-hind a gas station, specializes in Korean food. The restaurant is usually not crowded and has small, private air-conditioned dining rooms with great views over a bustling harbor. The restaurant offers a great five-dollar breakfast that comes with some unique options, and every meal includes spicy kimchi and a peppery cucumber salad. For lunch, try a three-dollar cheeseburger to go or order from the dine-in menu. *Side road in Weno; Cost: meal $5-18; Hours 6:30 AM-9 PM*

 Lei Side Lei Side is located in a complex between the airport and High Tide Hotel. The restaurant is air-conditioned, clean, and engagingly decorated ac-cording to the season. Lei Side has a respectable breakfast and lunch menu. Their breakfast sandwiches are delicious, and their pizza, though a bit expen-sive, is easily the best in the FSM. The restaurant also serves some first rate ramen dishes that taste as good as they look. Lei Side is a great place to wait before boarding your flight. *Near airport; Cost: meal $10-12; Hours: 7 AM-2 PM, 6-9 PM; 330-6727*

Expensive

High Tide Restaurant High Tide Restaurant, located next to the hotel of the same name, is more spacious than the other restaurants on Weno, and it is simply decorated with photos of Chuuk from years past. The restaurant's large variety of dishes includes sandwiches, stir fry, local meals, and some good vegetarian options. The restaurant has a casual feel and is a popular spot for lunch. Try the Local Moco, a huge helping of spaghetti, or the High Tide Cheeseburger, the best burger in Chuuk. Staff members at the restaurant are extremely helpful and willing to go out of their way to make you feel wel-come. The restaurant is quiet in the morning, making it a good spot to sip cof-fee and get some work done. *At High Tide Hotel; Cost: meal $7-15; Hours: 6:30 AM-2 PM, 6-9 PM; 330-6644, hightidehotel@gmail.com*

 Blue Lagoon Restaurant Blue Lagoon Restaurant, located at the resort of the same name, is a comfortable, air-conditioned dining room open for break-fast, lunch, and dinner. The restaurant's excellent menu has the most variety of any on the island. The sashimi side dish comes with plenty of tuna and is a particularly good deal. The Divers Club is highly recommended as is the surprisingly flavorful and thick chicken curry. The service at Blue Lagoon is very professional and prompt, but it lacks the friendliness found at High Tide or Truk Stop. Nevertheless, Blue Lagoon Restaurant is the best on Weno, and even if you are not staying at Blue Lagoon, it is nice to stop by at lunch to enjoy the food and atmosphere. *At Blue Lagoon Resort; Cost: meal $10-25; Hours: 6:30 AM-9 PM; 330-2727, 330-2438, blresort@mail.fm www.bluelagoondiveresort.com, www.truk-lagoon-dive.com*

Truk Stop Restaurant Truk Stop has outdoor seating on a waterside patio as well as indoor seating in an air-conditioned dining room decorated with interesting local handicrafts. The restaurant serves breakfast, lunch, and dinner. The menu offers a wide range of foods including stir fry, a hot roast beef sandwich, a chicken melt, taco salad, and a variety of well prepared seafood dishes. The banana pancakes are a specialty. The Sunday lunch buffet is also very good, and though it varies week to week, it often includes fresh sashimi, breadfruit, fried fish, popcorn shrimp, and sweet and sour pork. Truk Stop also sells some of the most mouthwatering baked goods in Micronesia; their cheese bread and cinnamon rolls are to die for. The staff at the restaurant is extremely friendly but less professional than elsewhere. There can be long waits for food, and I have walked out of the restaurant several times after waiting over 20 minutes for a server to approach my table. Other times, food was undercooked or the bill was incorrect. Still, if you have a large reservoir of patience, the food is good enough to keep you coming back. Truk Stop has wireless internet, but if you are not staying at the hotel, you will have to pay a fee to use it. *At Truk Stop Hotel; Cost: meal $10-25; Hours: 6:30 AM-9 PM; 330-7990, trukstop@mail.fm, info@dive-truklagoon.com, www.dive-truklagoon.com*

What to Do

SIGHTS

Weno does not make a good first impression on visitors. The roads are rife with pot holes and mud, litter is strewn around the town, and there is widespread impoverishment. Weno also feels crowded because many people commute there on a daily basis. Weno's commercial center becomes abuzz around 3 PM every other Friday when government checks are issued. Numerous boats and people can be seen coming and going from Weno carrying sacks of rice, cases of chicken, and canned goods. Despite the disrepair of the roads and buildings, Weno and the Chuukese living there have much beauty, culture, and kindness to share with visitors. Central Weno has two main roads. The airport, hotels, and many shops are located on the first, while the second leads up a hill to the government buildings and two of the island's high schools.

The **Japanese Communication Center** is in the village of Penia in the northeast section of Weno. The Communication Center is a dense fortress with cement walls four feet thick and huge metal blast doors. It is now the main building of **Xavier High School**. The Communication Center did not receive much damage during WWII, and is one of just a few buildings from this era still standing intact. The Catholic Church owned the property before WWII and was able to reclaim it after the Japanese surrendered. The Japanese government has recently painted the building and built a windmill as a memorial. The Jesuits currently run the school, which accepts students from all across Micronesia and is widely regarded as the best high school in the FSM; many state and national leaders are alumni of Xavier. The views from near the chapel and from the roof of the main building are beautiful. The school appreciates any donations left by visitors. To reach the Japanese Communication Center, follow the road from town about forty minutes until it turns into a dirt path. Then, take a right up a steep, muddy road. If you decide to take a rental car up this road, make sure you have the tools to replace a flat tire. Alternatively, consider taking a guided tour here.

Nantaku Cave is located up the long hill in Nantaku. Follow the road up the hill past a Sammy Store and Chuuk State Hospital. After a quarter mile, you will see a water tank and the **governor's house**. The path to the cave starts below the governor's house on the opposite side of the road. The hike is steep, and the path is muddy; be sure to wear proper shoes. Also, you should attempt this hike with a guide or a local friend and ask for permission from the land owners, who may charge five dollars per person to see the cave. A group of young men may also ask for money. The caves are a striking black color and are cooled by a breeze. On the end facing west, there is a **large gun** used by the Japanese during World War II. The cave is a unique and interesting piece of history, but litter and graffiti signify that it is now used as a hangout for local youth. The cave also offers a rare and breathtaking view of Weno and Chuuk Lagoon.

Pisar is a tiny "picnic island" only a quarter mile around. This secluded, peaceful island is the perfect escape from the dirty, crowded roads of Weno, and visitors consider it a rare opportunity to stay in such a pristine

> Pisar is the perfect spot for either a day trip, barbeque, or an overnight stay.

and secluded spot. The island itself is about an hour fiberglass boat ride away from Weno. It sits on the reef at the southernmost point in Chuuk Lagoon. The island is sandy and has plenty of coconut trees, a retreat house, and several rooms with beds. Nearby is some of the best **snorkeling** to be found in Chuuk. If you want to arrange a trip to Pisar, contact Dickenson Doice (330-6990 or 330-7779) for prices and information. Remember to bring your own food, water, and lanterns, since there are no facilities or inhabitants on the island. A favorite spot among Peace Corps volunteers and locals alike, planning a trip to Pisar is well worth the effort, and for those who do not mind living a little on the rugged side, spending a night on the island is highly recommended.

Tonoas Island is just over two miles due south of Weno. The island has many interesting sites including several **Japanese guns** located in the northeast corner of the island. You can also explore a number of **caves** once used as coverage during typhoons.

> Tonoas Island was the capital of Chuuk during the occupation of Japan.

WATER AND OUTDOOR ACTIVITIES

Diving

Chuuk is home to the greatest wreck diving in the world. The **Japanese Underwater Fleet** at the bottom of Chuuk Lagoon is by far the greatest tourist attraction in the state. The lagoon offers an astounding 48 possible wrecks to dive, enough dives to keep both divers and history buffs enthralled for weeks. The wrecks also create unique habitats for coral and other sea creatures. Chuuk Lagoon is truly an underwater monument to those who fought and died in WWII. For those coming to Chuuk for other reasons, it would be well worth getting dive certified in order to dive in Chuuk, a place that attracts divers from all over the globe.

Fujikawa Maru is the must-see wreck; it was built in 1938 as a passenger and cargo ship. The *Fujikawa* transported silk, cotton, and other material in India and South America. In 1940, it was requisitioned by the Imperial Japanese Navy and converted into an aircraft transport vessel. The ship is currently south of Weno between the islands of Eten and Uman resting 122 feet (37 meters) below

> Please, keep in mind the health of the lagoon and dive sites. Chuuk Lagoon is an underwater museum; please, do not take anything from the sites and treat the coral and sea creatures with respect.

sea level at its deepest point. Beautiful coral has grown all over the ship, making it an attraction for both divers and sea creatures alike. Dive into the cargo holds to find rare WWII artifacts and five Japanese Zero fighters in excellent condition. For those seeking spectacular wreck diving photographs, this is the dive for you.

The San Francisco Maru is referred to as the "Million Dollar Wreck" for its abundance of cargo both on the deck and in the cargo holds. The *San Francisco* is a deep wreck, and only experienced divers should attempt this dive. Parts of the ship are as much as 200 feet (60 meters) below the surface. The deck is decorated with numerous tanks and trucks, while the cargo holds are filled with WWII torpedoes, bombs, aircraft engines, and much more.

Two of the best dive shops in Chuuk are the Blue Lagoon Dive Shop, which is located next to Blue Lagoon Hotel, and the Truk Lagoon Dive Shop, which is located at Truk Stop Hotel. Both operate their own boat fleets, rent all necessary equipment, mix nitrox, and offer technical dives.

Blue Lagoon Dive Shop Blue Lagoon Dive Shop has been in operation since 1973 and has an excellent reputation. *Cost: one-tank dive $70, two-tank dive $105, night dive $75, outer reef dive $125; 330-2796, bluelagoon@truk-dive.com*

Truk Lagoon Dive Shop *Cost: two-tank dive $95, night dive $50; 330-7990, trukstop@mail.fm, info@dive-truklagoon.com*

Shark Diving

Though the focus of diving in Chuuk is on the wrecks, every dive also offers the chance to observe majestic sea creatures. There are walls of coral off the island of Fayu that plunge deep into the ocean, and sea life of all forms converges there to create an ocean expressway. One spot in particular is known as a cleaning station for sharks. Here, it is possible to see blacktip and gray reef sharks in extremely intimate proximity. This is a rare treat for anyone who has the courage to dive here. If you are not dive certified, you can also snorkel at this site, as it is shallow.

Hiking

The Japanese built the **Sapuk Lighthouse** in the early 1930s. Today, it is a magnificent structure with an aura of nostalgia. The lighthouse sits near the abandoned homes of its previous operators. There are also several **large guns** at the base of this historical monument that were used to protect the lagoon from U.S. ships entering from the north. This site is a bit off the beaten path and requires a hike. The land it sits on is private, and going with a local guide is highly recommended. Also, be sure to ask permission from the landowners. You may be asked to pay five dollars or so to look around and take pictures.

Tonachau Mountain, also known as **One Tree Hill**, which rises 750 feet (230 meters) above sea level, sits across from the runway on the northwest portion of the island. To reach the summit, follow the main road north past the airport runaway and continue as the road turns right. Take the steep dirt road on your right. This road is used to access a telephone tower near the apex of the mountain. There are houses on either side of the road, and it is polite to say hello to those you pass. At the telephone tower, another extremely steep and densely overgrown path leads to the summit; this path is not recommended. At the top is a nice view looking west over the airport and out into the lagoon. If you time your walk just right, you can watch an airplane take off or land from the summit. This is fun little outing and gives visitors a chance to see some more of the island without needing to rent a vehicle. Going with a local friend is never a bad idea, but in general this is a safe and well-traveled path during the day. Be sure to bring comfortable shoes and water.

> This mountain is a traditional site held to be the home of the god Souwoniras and his son.

SHOPPING

No stores accept credit cards. Store selections always depend on when ships come in, and shortages of all products are typical. Most the stores in Chuuk carry a similar selection of groceries, basic canned foods, sandals, and clothing. Chuuk is not really known as an excellent shopping locale, but good deals and some random items of interest (mint condition Michael Bolton concert T-shirts, for example) make shopping fun and interesting.

Souvenirs

Fiin Chuuk is across from Truk Stop Hotel in small, fenced lot. The store is run by Chuuk Women's Council and sells locally made handicrafts. The selection here is usually a bit different from that of the other gift shops, and the vendor tends to pay the artisans more. If it is closed, see if the staff at the Truk Stop Hotel can open it for you or tell you when it will be open.

Groceries

Markets are scattered along the side of the road throughout downtown. They mostly sell betel nut, canned meat, *kon*, fish, and bananas. The bananas are cheap, delicious, and always in season. Every once in a while, there will be amazing pineapples in town; be sure to sample these if you find them.

AWM/ASA (Mon-Sat 8 AM-7 PM, Sun 10 AM-5 PM; 330-5875) grocery and department store is located in the same the plaza as Café 527 and the Bank of the FSM. At first, the grocery store may feel like a warehouse because the posterior half is a hardware store. The store's prices are competitive, and its selection is better than most places in the FSM. AWM has a wide selection of canned foods along with a few fruits and vegetables. AWM does usually have the best selection of sweet snacks including some chocolates. The department store attached has cheap clothes, sandals, and swimsuits, and some T-shirts are only one dollar. A selection of sports equipment is in the back. The department store usually has a number of bootleg DVDs from China for five dollars. AWM has a small selection of shells and local handicrafts, but the selection and quality are not as good as can be found some other places. They also sell cold beer and boxed wine.

Sheigetos (Mon-Sat 8 AM-8 PM, Sun 10 AM-5 PM; 330-2584) is between the Bank of Guam and Saramon Chuuk Academy. Sheigetos is clean and air-conditioned and has the feel of a Western grocery store. They have a great selection of chips as well as some frozen treats. Sheigetos's fruit and vegetable selection is as sparse as other places, but sometimes you can find something fresh. In the freezer section, they sometimes have frozen pizzas, which you can ask the staff to cook in the front. They also carry many brand name toiletries. The attached department store is nothing to speak of.

Truk Trading Company (Mon-Sat 8 AM-7 PM; 330-2700), known as TTC, is opposite Saramon Chuuk and Sheigetos and sits back from the main road. The quality of its food is usually worse than that of the other stores, and it is not as clean. They do offer some good deals, and the store carries a few fruits and vegetables, beer, and wine. They also have a small ice cream parlor inside as well as a barbershop.

> TTC is filled with many random products, and it is a fun place to look around. Also, if you cannot find what you need at other stores, TTC may have it.

Convenience Stores

Saki Store (9 AM-5 PM) has two locations; one is behind the post office, and the other is a large blue building on the main road near Oriental Restaurant. Saki has many electronics, DVDs, sandals, and trendy clothing. It is a fun store, and if you see something you like you can try to barter with the salesmen—I think they enjoy it.

His and Her (9 AM-5 PM; 330-5125) has a smaller location across from Saki store on the main road as well as a larger location between High Tide Hotel and J Square. As you will discover, His and Her is where fashionable Chuukese people shop. The store focuses mostly on modern clothing and styles but also carries a range of products. His and Her tends to be more expensive than the other stores, but the goods are of a higher quality.

Lei Side Store (8 AM-9 PM; 330-3727) is in the same complex as Lei Side restaurant near the airport parking lot. This is a clean store with a nice selection of cold beverages and snacks. They carry mostly brand name products and sell some electronics. On occasion, they sell baked goods including tasty cupcakes.

Sammy Stores (Mon-Sat 9 AM-5 PM; 330-4227) are located all around Weno, but the main location is in Nataku. This store is a favorite of those living on the island. Sammy Stores have a good selection of cold beverages and juices. There is a Sammy Fabrics Store on the main road near ACE Hardware where you can see and buy the fabrics that are used in Chuukese muumuus and dress shirts. You can even have a garment made for you.

Other

ACE Hardware and Office Stores (8 AM-5 PM; 330-4167) are located just south of the College of Micronesia. They have the highest quality hardware and office supplies available on the island.

Sammy's Fabrics (9 AM-5 PM) is located in between ACE and COM. This store has the largest selection of fabrics on islands. Many of the local skirts, dresses, muumuus, and shirts are made from fabrics available here. Choose a fabric and have a shirt or skirt made for you.

Nightlife

Weno does not have much nightlife, and frequently visitors are so busy running around during the day that they prefer to relax in the evening. For those wanting a nightcap or a few cold beers, there are really only two options available.

Blue Lagoon Resort Blue Lagoon Resort has both a lounge and an outdoor bar. The bar has a peaceful, relaxed "island" atmosphere, though it gets rowdy every once in a while. Above the bar hangs a fairly large set of shark jaws that makes one question how safe the diving really is. There is a pool table near the bar as well. The lounge is not usually open, but they do have equipment for karaoke. *At Blue Lagoon Resort; Hours: 4-11 PM; 330-2727, 330-2438, blresort@mail.fm, www.bluelagoondiveresort.com, www.truk-lagoon-dive.com*

Hard Wreck Café The Hard Wreck Café, located next to Truk Stop Hotel, is a more traditional bar. There is usually a good mix of locals and tourists there, and if you are looking to meet a few friends over a beer or find that government employee that has been missing from work all week, try the Hard Wreck. Sign and decorate a dollar and hang it above the bar; you will be forever memorialized as one of the few lucky individuals to experience Chuuk. *Next to Truk Stop Hotel; Hours: 6-10 PM; 330-7990, trukstop@mail.fm, info@dive-truklagoon.com, www.dive-truklagoon.com*

Outer Islands

The outer islands are known for their more traditional cultures and people. Although day-to-day activities on every island generally center around doing chores, preparing food, attending church functions, and socializing, life on these islands is slow. The outer islands, with a few exceptions, do not have island-wide electricity, running water, phones, internet, or reliable transportation. Buildings made from local wood and coconut fronds are as prevalent as concrete homes. Depending on the island and the time of year, the flies and mosquitoes can be quite thick. Few foreigners visit these islands, and those that do usually come to do research or volunteer.

If you want to visit an outer island, make arrangements through the **Chuuk Visitors Bureau** (330-4480 or 330-4133) so they may introduce you to someone in Weno who has family on the island to which you are going. The people of these islands are extremely hospitable and care for guests well, but arrangements should always be made in advance. The outer islands tend to be less affluent than those in Chuuk Lagoon. Thus, if you are planning a long stay, you will need to bring food such as rice and canned meat. Instant coffee is a great gift to show your appreciation. Cigarettes can also be given as gifts and are appreciated a great deal by some.

MORTLOCKS

The Mortlocks are southwest of Chuuk. They are divided into the Upper Mortlocks, Mid-Mortlocks, and Lower Mortlocks. The Upper Mortlocks consist of Nama Island and Losap Atoll, which are about 60 miles (100 kilome-

> The Lukunoch dialect has been compared to Mortlockese with a Bronx accent.

ters) from Weno. Namaluk Atoll, Etal, Kuttu, and Moch make up the Mid-Mortlocks, with Moch being 160 miles (260 kilometers) from Chuuk Lagoon. The Lower Mortlocks consist of Satawan, Ta, Lukunoch, and Oneop and are as far as 175 miles (280 kilometers) southwest of Chuuk. Ta, Kuttu, and Moch are actually in the Satawan atoll, while Lukunoch and Oneop are on a separate atoll east of Satawan. Each island has its own unique feel, atmosphere, and reputation. People from Lukunoch, for example, are known for how they speak while Kuttu is understood to be the most religious; Kuttu is divided into two villages: one Protestant and one Catholic. Moch is known for its fishing and strong junior high school, while Satawan is heavily populated.

The runway is located on the western portion of Ta. Ta and Satawan are neighbors and one can walk from one to the other during low tide in about 3 hours. Ta is five miles long, but only a few hundred yards wide, and it has a population of a few hundred people. Satawan, on the other hand, is usually a bustling place; students from the other islands live here as well as permanent residents. Satawan also has several tanks from WWII that are next to the main road; these are easy to locate and are a favorite spot among the occasional visitors. Two decomposing planes can be found on the island. To get to one of them, you must travel through several properties, so make sure you have a local guide to help you find your way. The beach on the northwest side of the island is scattered with old stone lookout posts. There is a rumor you can walk from Satawan to Moch during low tide, but this is really only possible in theory. The water is nearly always too deep, and the islands are at least 15 miles (24 kilometers) apart.

WESTERN ISLANDS

The Western Islands consist of the atolls of Puluwat, Pulap, and Namonuito and the island of Houk. These islands have cultures that reflect their Yapese neighbors to the west. Namonuito has an airstrip and a more modern feel than the other islands. Houk, on the other hand, is known as one of the most traditional islands in the Micronesia. Those in the Western Islands still produce sailing canoes and teach traditional navigational techniques that use the stars and sea life. Unfortunately, much of this traditional knowledge has never been recorded, and there is a danger that traditional navigators in Chuuk will become extinct.

HALL ISLANDS

The Hall Islands consist of the Nomwin and Murilo atolls, which lie 75 miles (120 kilometers) north of Weno. These islands do not differ culturally in many ways from the islands in Chuuk Lagoon. Their location makes trips into Weno common, but they receive few foreign visitors.

Yap

Strolling lazily down the roads of Yap, you cannot help but be struck by the fluorescent blues, yellows, and pinks surrounding you. Colors picked from the screens of Technicolor movies fill your view. Every shade of green imaginable is displayed on flora of all textures and shapes. Massive banana trees loom over the roadway, creating canopies of shade. Smells of hibiscus, honeysuckle, and plumeria overwhelm your nose just as the beauty of the trees, sea, and people overwhelms your eyes.

Tropical beauty abounds here in Yap, but beneath the amazing sights and smells is an incredible culture. Yap is widely renowned as the most traditional island in the Western Pacific, a place where a visitor can see life as it has been lived for thousands of years. Most Yapese live in traditional thatch roof houses made of local wood and subsist mainly on locally grown foods and the day's catch. Still, modernity is beginning to encroach upon Yap, and it is not uncommon to see Yapese and neighboring island women wearing traditional garments while shopping in modern grocery stores or having conversations on cell phones. Nevertheless, traditional dances, ceremonies, and tribal rules still guide the lives of the Yapese people. It is this mix of contemporary and traditional that makes any visit to Yap a truly unique experience.

HIGHLIGHTS OF YAP

Diving with manta rays: Swim alongside gentle manta rays at several of Yap's famous manta cleaning stations. pg 157

Experiencing an authentic cultural tour: Learn about Yapese stone money, traditional navigation, weaving, and handicrafts. pg 156

Fishing: Fish the waters as islanders have done for millennia. pg 158

Visiting the outer islands: Experience some of the most traditional and remote places in the world. pg 162

Viewing and riding local canoes: Admire the ancient Yapese traditions of building and navigating sailing canoes. pg 159

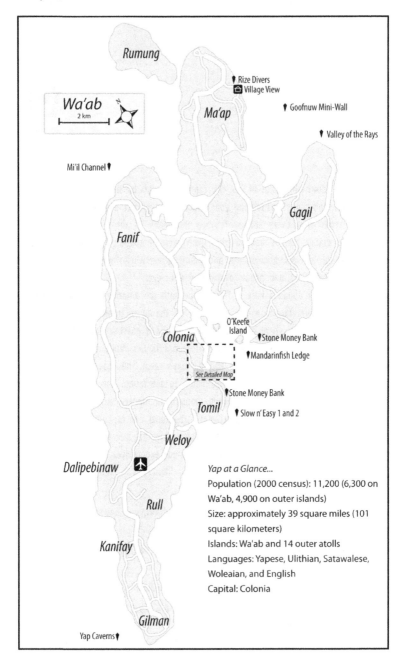

Wa'ab

2 km

Rumung

Ma'ap

♦ Rize Divers
🏠 Village View

♦ Goofnuw Mini-Wall

♦ Valley of the Rays

Mi'il Channel ♦

Gagil

Fanif

O'Keefe
Island

Colonia

♦ Stone Money Bank

♦ Mandarinfish Ledge

See Detailed Map

♦ Stone Money Bank

Tomil

♦ Slow n' Easy 1 and 2

Weloy

Dalipebinaw ✈

Yap at a Glance...
Population (2000 census): 11,200 (6,300 on
Wa'ab, 4,900 on outer islands)
Size: approximately 39 square miles (101
square kilometers)
Islands: Wa'ab and 14 outer atolls
Languages: Yapese, Ulithian, Satawalese,
Woleaian, and English
Capital: Colonia

Rull

Kanifay

Gilman

Yap Caverns ♦

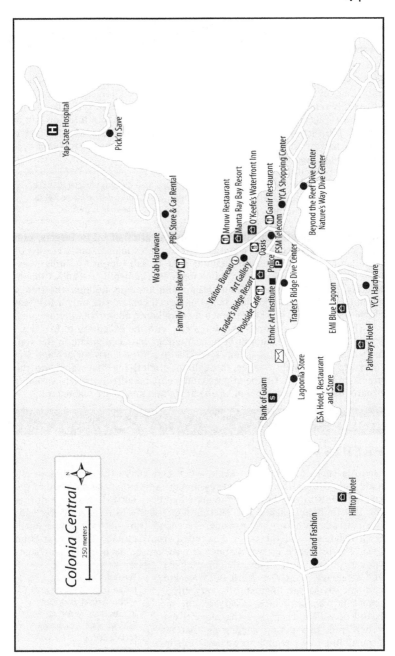

Colonia Central

250 meters

Yap State Hospital

Pick 'n Save

PBC Store & Car Rental

Wa'ab Hardware

Family Chain Bakery

Mnuw Restaurant

Manta Ray Bay Resort

O'Keefe's Waterfront Inn

Ganir Restaurant

YCA Shopping Center

FSM Telecom

Beyond the Reef Dive Center

Nature's Way Dive Center

Oasis

Visitors Bureau

Art Gallery

Police

Trader's Ridge Resort

Trader's Ridge Dive Center

Poolside Cafe

Ethnic Art Institute

EMI Blue Lagoon

YCA Hardware

Pathways Hotel

Bank of Guam

Lagoonia Store

ESA Hotel, Restaurant and Store

Hilltop Hotel

Island Fashion

Geography

The state of Yap consists of the island of Wa'ab, the capital island, and 14 atolls spread over a 500 mile (800 kilometer) range. In total, the land of Yap state covers only 38.7 square miles (101 square kilometers). Wa'ab lies at roughly nine degrees north latitude, and the temperature is a comfortable 75-90° Fahrenheit (24-32° Celsius) year-round. Annual rainfall on Yap is around 100 inches (250 centimeters), and the neighboring islands receive roughly half of that average, depending on the severity of typhoon systems passing near the state.

The island of Wa'ab, which is sometimes referred to as Yap or Yap proper, actually consists of four separate islands that share the same reef structure. All are connected by man-made bridges. Wa'ab's soil supports a

> Yap can both refer to Wa'ab, the capital island, as well as the state as a whole.

wide range of food crops as well as a diverse array of birds, insects, reptiles, and a few introduced mammal species. Yap's main exports consist of fruits and vegetables sent to Guam as well as fish caught by foreign vessels. Wa'ab is divided into ten municipalities: Dalipebinaw, Fanif, Gilman, Kanifay, Rull, Weloy, Gagil, Tomil, Ma'ap, and Rumung. Colonia, the state's capital and largest population and commercial center, sits only a few feet above sea level and can be traversed by a walker in about 20 minutes.

The neighboring islands and atolls are, with the exception of Fais, low-lying. This limits the amount of nutrients that can accumulate in the soil, as usually the water table is only a few feet from the soil's surface and any nutrients are quickly washed through the underlying limestone into the brackish water table. On the other islands, only breadfruit, certain varieties of taro, bananas, papayas, and small shrubs and spices are viable crops.

History

PREHISTORY

There is some disagreement about when and where the Micronesian islands were first settled, but most researchers agree that the majority of the currently inhabited islands in Yap state had been settled sometime during the first millennium BC. The Micronesian islands can generally be split linguistically into two groups: one descended from settlers sailing north from Polynesia and the other descended from settlers sailing east from Asia. The influence of two distinct groups can be seen in the languages spoken in Yap state today. Neighboring island languages, such as Ulithian, Woleaian, and Satawalese, are linguistically very different from Yapese, which is spoken on the island of Wa'ab. There is archaeological evidence from this period suggesting that the Yapese and their neighboring island inhabitants used large voyaging canoes very similar to canoes used today.

The visitor to Yap has a unique opportunity to see an ancient form of navigation used by these settlers at Yap's Traditional Navigation Society. See pg 159 for more information.

COLONIAL PERIOD

Yap was most likely first discovered by the Western world on October 1, 1525 by the Portuguese explorer Dioga da Rocha, who landed on what was most likely Ulithi and stayed for four months. For the next three hundred years, Yap and its associated islands were visited by Spanish, British, Dutch, and American explorers and traders, including Father Jan Cantova, who brought Roman Catholicism to the island of Mogmog, Ulithi in 1731. The 1800s marked a time of trade and minor development of Yap by Western people, including the establishment of the first permanent trading station by the German Alfred Teten in 1869. It was also during this time that the now-famous trader David Dean O'Keefe became shipwrecked on Yap and was rescued by the Yapese.

In 1874, Spain claimed sovereignty over Yap, leading to a feud between Germany and Spain over control of Yap, which had become the center of trade for all of the Caroline Islands. Pope Leo XII settled the feud by awarding Yap and the other Caroline Islands to Spain and granting commercial rights to Germany and other nations. A few decades later, Spain sold its interests in Micronesia, including Yap, to Germany.

WORLD WAR I AND II

World War I began for Yap with the British shelling of the island in a successful attempt to destroy German communications equipment. Eventually, the Japanese seized Wa'ab on October 7, 1914. After WWI, the Japanese took control of all Pacific islands north of the equator in accordance with an agreement in the Treaty of Versailles. This led to rapid settlement by the Japanese, and the ruins of many Japanese buildings from this time can still be found on Yap and some of the outer islands. During this time the Japanese set up schools and hospitals, and outlawed many local traditions, such as tattooing. The Japanese also mandated that all Yapese children learn Japanese, and many of the older islanders can still speak the language.

Yap and its neighboring islands played an important role in World War II. Woleai was used as a seaplane anchorage and airstrip, and Ulithi served as a staging point for 617 American ships prior to the operation in Leyte

David Dean O'Keefe

O'Keefe was an Irishman who immigrated to Georgia in 1848, where he worked as a skipper of several different ships. He then set sail for Asia after spending nearly a year in jail for murdering a fellow ship-mate in self-defense. He arrived in Yap as a copra trader and soon began to expand his copra trade throughout the Caroline Islands. He used his forays throughout the Caroline Islands as opportunities to ferry Yapese stonemasons, who quarried stone in Palau to make *rai*, the famous Yapese stone money. Before O'Keefe's vessels took the Yapese stonemasons, the process was very labor intensive, and a single large *rai* or several smaller ones could take nearly a year to quarry and transport to Wa'ab. O'Keefe's success as both a copra trader and a source of transportation for the stonemasons made him very powerful, so that some historians called him a near-king of Yap. Today visitors can take a kayak to O'Keefe's Island (Tarang Island) in the channel not far from Colonia.

Gulf, Okinawa. On November 20, 1944, a Japanese *kaiten* kamikaze torpedo sank the *USS Missisinewa* spilling nearly three million gallons of oil and aviation fuel and killing 63 American sailors in the Ulithi lagoon.

Following the war, the U.S. Navy continued to oversee Micronesia for a few years. The Navy set up long-range plans for Micronesian self-governance and repaired some of the damage done to the islands. The managing responsibility was later shifted to the Interior Department of the United States. There were challenges from the start of the American administration. The Trust Territory management was at first primarily Navy personnel on 18-month foreign rotations, which left little continuity in management or ideology. Also, post-war staffing reductions left a large gap in needed administration experience, and the Navy approached management of the islands in a laid-back, "island style" fashion. The Navy argued that it did not want to push change faster than the island would assimilate it.

> Later, a memorial on Mangejang Island in Ulithi was erected, following the rediscovery of the wreck, to commemorate the loss of life in this attack. The memorial is periodically maintained by visitors and Ulithians.

SELF-MANAGEMENT

Finally in 1971, the Federated States of Micronesia adopted a constitution. It later became an independent state by signing a Compact of Free Association with the United States, which permitted FSM citizens visa-free work opportunities in the U.S. as well as the opportunity to join the U.S. mili-

Current Events and Political Life

Yap State's political life is quite different from most of the other FSM states and most countries world-wide in that it is rather sedate. Nevertheless, Yap is known as a relatively well-managed government with regular budget surpluses and an increasingly efficient, well-connected, and technologically savvy government, of which Yap State's website (www.yapstategov.org) is evidence. The interested visitor can sign up for nearly daily news updates from the state government about news on the island and in the region.

The state has an interesting government structure, including an executive (governor/lieutenant governor), a legislature, a judiciary, and two councils of chiefs, the Council of Tamol, which oversees neighboring islands, and the Council of Pilung, which is responsible for Wa'ab island. The traditional councils serve in adjudicating issues of traditional nature, such as family matters, preservation of culture or relics, and land issues. The interplay of the three branches of government and the Councils can be convoluted, but quite interesting, and the Councils are strong evidence of the State's commitment to the preservation of their traditions.

Over the past several years, there have been rumblings amongst the members of the Legislature and those who are interested in such matters of a move to secede from the national government in Pohnpei. This is a response to many Yap residents' anger and frustration at having to loan and grant their carefully budgeted surpluses away to other states in fiscal trouble, and as a reaction to the perception that Pohnpei isn't receptive enough to the issues particular to Yap State. The Legislature has made several efforts toward consensus-building on the issue, the most recent being in July 2010, but these attempts have fallen far short.

tary. Also, the Compact allowed for nearly two billion dollars of aid between 1986 and 2001 and federal disaster relief. In return, the United States has exclusive military access to the FSM's territorial waters and can demand land for military use. Compact funds and U.S. grants now account for the majority of the FSM's economy, and the public sector is the largest source of employment in the country. Yap state is known in the FSM as being quite responsible with its funds and frequently loans money to other states to balance their budgets.

Culture and People

The people of Yap are reserved, but warm. These islands are the least influenced by Western culture of all islands of the FSM and Palau. The majority of Yapese people continue to live in the same family compounds as their ancestors. Each immediate family unit typically has its own sleeping quarters, in the form of small local houses either made from concrete and modern building materials or from local lumber and thatched roofs woven from various plants. All family members share an outdoor cookhouse and showering facilities, although some of the more modern homes have indoor kitchens. Families here also maintain taro patches, vegetable gardens, and fruit trees as their main source of food. Indeed, gardens are a very important part of everyday life for most residents of Yap. Most property on Yap has been passed down in the same families for generations.

Yap is world-renowned for its use of stone money, or *rai*. *Rai* are large limestone disks with central holes, some 10 feet (3 meters) in diameter and weighing nearly 3 tons (2700 kilograms). No longer used in day-to-day transactions, *rai* were quarried in Palau and returned to Yap on rafts and sailboats, a very labor-intensive process. Part of O'Keefe's success was his ability to ferry *rai* to Yap very quickly, and the sudden influx of *rai* led to a form of inflation, with newly-quarried *rai* worth less than the older stones. *Rai* are still used today by the Yapese in land exchanges. Though the stone money is rarely moved, most Yapese know to whom a given *rai* stone belongs.

> Visitors can see several stone money banks throughout the Yap. The banks are usually paths with an embankment along one side upon which the *rai* stones are placed.

Yap is also known as being home to some of the last traditional navigators in the world, men who are able to navigate the seas using stars and constellations. Yapese navigation is still a living art, and their method of navigation is particular to these islands. Visitors may be able to see a voyaging canoe being hewn from huge trees, watch students learning to navigate from master navigators, or even take a trip on a voyaging canoe. For more information on the Yap Traditional Navigation Society, see pg 159.

The women of the neighboring islands are known for weaving traditional *lavalavas*, wrap-around skirts woven by hand using hibiscus, banana fibers, or commercially produced thread. Wearing a *lavalava* is what differentiates an outer island woman from a Yapese woman. While outer island women can occasionally be seen wearing Western dress, women of Yap never wear *lavalavas*, as doing so is taboo. Outer island girls wear grass skirts made from palm leaves. Upon reaching puberty *lavalavas* are gifted to girls, and their role in the family shifts from that of a child to that of a caregiver, cook, and gardener.

The tradition of weaving patterns into *lavalavas* has evolved over centuries. Today, each neighboring island, and sometimes each family, has a particular style of weaving, and one can learn to tell from which island a woman hails by the patterns and style of her *lavalava*.

The process of making a *lavalava* can begin by simply purchasing a spool of thread, but traditionally, banana fibers are procured and refined to create a spool of fiber. Spools of thread or fiber are then used to create a specific pattern of colors. The result of this step is called a *choh*. The

Local Languages

Yapese is most commonly heard on Wa'ab, but Ulithian is often heard on Wa'ab as well. Almost everyone on the islands speaks English very well, so the visitor will have very little need for language skills. However, Yapese and neighboring island people generally appreciate visitors who make an effort to learn a bit of the local languages. Note that while there is an official spelling for both Yapese and Ulithian, neither are commonly used, and travelers will be hard pressed to find signs, menus, or other printed materials written in either Yapese or any outer island language.

For phrases in Yapese, see pg 223. Here are a few phrases in Ulithian:

English	Ulithian
Hello/goodbye	Adios
See you later	Ilanga ("ee-la-ngaah")
Good morning	Mwommwaay lemaeliyel ("mwo-mwahee le-mal-ee-el")
Good night	Sa bong
Please	Falpachim
Thank you	Sa chig chig
You're welcome	Toar
Excuse me/I'm sorry	Sorrow
Come and eat	Buddoh mongoay ("bu-tho mo-ngoy")
I'm full	Isa meth ("ee-saw meth")
How are you?	Hosa hatefah? ("ho-saw hat-eh-fah")
I'm fine	Faroey chog ("feh-royee chog")
What is your name?	Ifae idem?
My name is _____.	Iday _____.

choh is painstakingly placed onto a local loom. Creating a *choh* takes around 18 hours of work, and placing the *choh* on the loom takes another 6 to 8 hours. Weaving the *lavalava* takes another 36 to 48 hours of back-breaking work, as the loom is entirely manual and functions according to the tension maintained by the weaver's legs. The finished product is truly splendid. *Lavalavas* are not only important as an outer island woman's only dress but also as gifts given during ceremonies, especially funerals, and occasionally as a traded commodity. Traditional weaving can be observed at the Micronesian Ethnic Art Institute at Trader's Ridge Resort (pg 154).

Visitors to Yap who are unfamiliar with betel nut may be taken by surprise upon visiting Yap, as the Yapese are known as avid betel nut-chewers. It is very common to see people carrying small bags solely for the accoutrements for chewing. One of the effects of betel nut is the creation of dark red saliva, and long-term betel nut-chewers have red teeth. However, this should not dissuade the adventurous visitor from trying betel nut, as short-term use has no ill effects and can be a great way to start a conversation with Yapese or neighboring island people.

SOCIAL NORMS

The islanders greatly appreciate visitors who are conscious of locally accepted behavior and dress. It is also appreciated when visitors express interest in the local lifestyle: how local food is prepared, how local goods are made, and Yapese social traditions. It is this traditional lifestyle that draws adventurous travelers to Yap state.

Alcohol

Alcohol is a daily part of life for both Yapese and neighboring island people. The consumption of alcohol is segregated based on sex. Men usually get together nightly or on the weekends in drinking circles, where *achiif* (Yapese) or *faluba* (Ulithian), known elsewhere as palm wine, is consumed, and events of the day and the next are discussed and decided upon. Women, on the other hand, seldom drink in public; female tourists should keep their consumption inconspicuous. For men, the opportunity, should it arise, to join a drinking circle should not be missed. It is always completely acceptable for a visitor to refrain from drinking.

Dance

The people of Yap have a large repertoire of traditional dances, which are usually performed during ceremonies or holidays. There are many different kinds of dances, but most tell a story from Yapese or neighboring island mythology; some tell about the formation of the islands, others about different facets of life in the sea, and others stories of wars or loss. The neighboring islands have a different set of dances from those of the Yapese, but both make use of sticks and chanting while dancing. To see these traditional dances, pay a visit to one of the culture classes at any elementary school. Any hotel staff member can provide information about possible school visits.

Dress

It is very common to see topless women, mostly from the neighboring islands, in public areas, but this is a long-standing tradition, and visiting women are expected to dress very modestly. Female tourists should always wear knee-length shorts, dresses, and skirts while outside of their resorts. Spaghetti straps are also inadvisable. There are no restrictions on dress for male travelers. It is viewed especially favorably for women to wear local attire. Search any stores for cloth skirts or *lavalavas*.

Passing Others

Try to avoid walking between two people who are talking, even if they are standing some distance apart. Walking between two people mid-conversation is considered very rude, even if they are standing in a door-way. If it cannot be avoided, always bow and say "*siro*" ("see-row") apologetically as you pass.

Photographs

Always ask permission before taking a photograph of a Yapese person. They are shy people, but are likely to oblige if asked for a picture.

Reserved Behavior

Walking around town, it is easy to see how quiet and reserved the citizens of Yap are, and the visitor would do well to follow their example by not running or yelling in public, which can be construed as either rude or a sign of an emergency.

Travel Information

GETTING THERE AND AWAY

Air

Continental Airlines is the only carrier that services islands in the FSM. There are flights from Guam into Yap on Tuesdays, Thursdays, and Saturdays. Flights to and from Palau are also available through Continental. See pg 27 for more information about flying with Continental Airlines.

Sea

There are no sea routes to Yap from outside the FSM, although it is potentially possible to take one of the FSM's field trip ships from Pohnpei to Yap. See pg 29 more information.

HEALTH AND SAFETY

There is very little personal crime in Yap state, although, as outside cultures encroach upon Yap, this is slowly changing. Petty theft can sometimes be an issue. If you are careful about what you leave lying around, your trip to Yap will be uneventful. For those rare instances where **police** intervention may be required, the police station is located to the left of the road leading up the hill toward Trader's Ridge Resort along with the fire station. The police can be reached by dialing 911. The police force in Yap is very helpful and is always willing to lend a hand or answer a question.

There is no malaria in Yap, but there are very limited outbreaks of dengue fever. This illness is spread by infected mosquitoes, so wear long-sleeve shirts and pants or insect repellent to avoid bites.

The tap water is generally unsafe to drink; for clean, filtered water contact Drops of Life (350-7800) or purchase bottled water at a store in Colonia. Ice and water served by food vendors or hotels is safe to consume.

Yap's **state hospital** (350-3446) is Spartan but efficient and is able to deal with simple to moderately complex cases. The doctors are all trained in the United States or the Philippines.

There are **dispensaries** on the neighboring islands, but licensed medical staff is nonexistent. Medical treatment is extremely limited in these locations. Traveling to neighboring islands is not recommended for visitors with any medical conditions. That being said, Pacific Missionary Aviation (see pg 151) has standby reserves of fuel for emergency medical evacuations.

MR&T's Drugstore (350-3322 or 350-5355) is located in the Yap Cooperative Association complex. This drugstore is a good place to find sinus, allergy, and cold medicines.

Pharmacies and Medications

Over-the-counter medicines can be found in most grocery stores on Yap's capital island. No medicine, even over-the-counter drugs, can be found on neighboring islands. Be sure to bring all needed supplies when traveling to the outer islands.

SERVICES

For access to cash, visit the Yap branch of the **Bank of the FSM** (Mon-Fri, 10 AM-5 PM; 350-2329 or 350-2417) or go by the **Bank of Guam ATM** recently installed near the post office.

Getting Around

AIR

Pacific Missionary Aviation (info@pmapacific.org, www.pmapacific.org) flies from the capital island of Wa'ab to the three outer islands that have airstrips: Falalop Island of Ulithi Atoll, Fais Island, and Woleai Atoll. The independent airline offers inexpensive flights to and from Wa'ab for neighboring islanders, and with any proceeds, PMA is able to provide free medical evacuations and search-and-rescue services to the neighboring island communities. PMA generally flies to Falalop, Ulithi twice weekly, but each plane can only carry 8 passengers, so book tickets well ahead of time. Arrangements to fly to Fais Island or to Woleai must be arranged on a case-by-case basis. Adult tickets are $192 round-trip from Wa'ab to Falalop, Ulithi, $100 round-trip from Falalop, Ulithi to Fais, and $240 round-trip from Wa'ab to Fais. Tickets for children ages 3-12 are half the price of adult tickets, and children under 3 may fly for free on a parent's lap. Pack lightly

> Pacific Missionary Aviation was founded by missionaries in 1974.

because only 30 pounds (14 kilograms) of luggage per passenger is free with the purchase of a ticket. Any additional luggage costs 95 cents per pound. Chartered PMA flights are also available beginning at $1500.

LAND

Taxis

Taxis are readily available and very inexpensive. Rides after 10 PM will most likely require a call-ahead reservation. Ask management at hotels and restaurants to help you arrange taxi rides.

Hitchhiking

Hitchhiking is not recommended in Yap; while the locals are friendly and always willing to help, taxis around the island are so inexpensive that the risk is generally unwarranted.

Car Rentals

Car rentals are not necessary while visiting Yap, as the taxi services are very efficient and much cheaper than renting a car. Also, rental prices can be four to five times what visitors would pay elsewhere, but if a rental car is what is desired, arrangements can be made through the following businesses:

7-D *350-2566, 7d@mail.fm*

ESA Car Rental *350-2139, esayap@mail.fm*

Hilltop Hotel *350-3185, hilltop_yap@mail.fm*

PBC Car Rentals *350-2266, 350-2288, pacificBusCo@mail.fm*

SEA

Most of Yap's 14 outer islands are reached via the **HMS Hapilmohol**, Yap state's field trip ship. The ship is generally scheduled to depart once a month, but due to the vagaries of government funding, availability of fuel for the ship, and the captain's whims, it travels on average every other month. If you are planning to join the *Hapilmohol*, begin planning three to six months in advance. All travelers to any of the neighboring islands need to contact the Council of Tamol (see pg 162).

Accommodations on the *Hapilmohol* are either private or semi-private cabins or deck space. Traveling on the deck can be quite cramped, but it is also the best way to interact with the others on the ship. The field trip ship's itinerary usually takes 14 to 25 days round-trip, depending on weather and any stops that are added to the trip. Do not expect a rigid schedule for arrivals and departures, as departures from Yap are routinely canceled or rescheduled and arrivals on individual islands are dictated by a given trip's requirements. Also, the deck can get very crowded; the ship is rated for about 250 passengers but will often carry nearly twice that number. Nevertheless, we can personally attest that any efforts and discomforts paid to get to the neighboring islands is more than made up for upon arriving on the islands.

It is also possible to charter a fishing vessel through the **Yap Fishing Authority** (350-2394).

Where to Stay

Most hotels are situated in or near central Colonia and are within walking distance of restaurants, dive shops, and stores in the area.

Inexpensive

EMI Blue Lagoon Apartments These accommodations are bare bones and are best for long-term, budget travelers. Rooms include TVs, VCRs, kitchens, hot water, and air-conditioning. EMI Blue Lagoon Apartments are located within walking distance of downtown Colonia, and chances are that visitors here will have many opportunities to interact with Yapese people, as this building is located very close to island residences. Contact hotel management for more information about arranging airport shuttles and island tours. *In Colonia; Amenities: A/C, TV, kitchenette; Cost: room $35-45 daily or $350-450 monthly; 350-2136, emiyap@mail.fm*

Hilltop Hotel Hilltop Hotel is an affordable, family-run business. Located just outside downtown Colonia, Hilltop is within walking distance of stores, restaurants, and dive shops in town. Rooms here are cozy and clean with brightly colored walls and window dressings. There are also fully furnished apartments for guests planning a longer stay. Free airport shuttle is included, and rental cars can be arranged through hotel management. All rooms include air-conditioning and hot water, while some rooms include refrigerators and coffee makers. *In Colonia; Amenities: A/C, refrigerator, coffee maker; Cost: room $45-55; 350-3185, hilltop_yap@mail.fm*

Moderate

The Pathways Hotel The Pathways Hotel has a very unique look, as the units are separate, locally styled cottages on a hillside overlooking Chamorro Bay in Colonia. Each cottage has its own balcony so that guests can enjoy a breathtaking lagoon sunrise or sunset. Guests can enjoy local craftsmanship in their cottage, arrange daily island tours through the hotel, and dine in the hotel's restaurant, complete with cocktail bar. Local crafts are also available for purchase at the front desk. Free airport shuttle is included with each room. *In Colonia; Amenities: A/C, balcony, refrigerator, restaurant, bar, airport shuttle; Cost: cottage $50-125 depending on size; 350-3310, pathwaysres@gmail.com*

Village View Like the Pathways Hotel, Village View Hotel is actually a collection of separate, locally styled cabins situated on a sprawling white sand beach. Located the farthest from local residences, hotel guests have access to a private beach and can dress in comfortable swimwear. A stone path, a local village, and a men's house are all within walking distance of this hotel. Please arrange tours and obtain permission to view any private properties through hotel management. Village View hotel is a 20 minute taxi ride from Yap International Airport in Ma'ap Municipality. Rize Dive Shop is conveniently located on the premises for guests who want to arrange snorkeling or scuba diving trips. Moonrise Restaurant is also situated on the property. *In Ma'ap; Amenities: restaurant, beach access, tours; Cost: cabin $65-75; 350-4679, 950-6646, villageview@mail.fm*

ESA Bay View Hotel ESA Bay View Hotel is situated right on the lagoon, making for a beautiful view, and the rooms are comfortable, roomy, and reasonably priced. Many rooms have balconies, and all include hot water, refrigerators, air-conditioning, and TVs with DVD players. DVDs are available for rental at the front desk. The staff here is very friendly and accommodating.

There is a restaurant on the premises, which serves breakfast, lunch, and dinner. Rental cars and free airport shuttle services can also be arranged. *In Colonia; Amenities: A/C, TV, refrigerator, balcony, restaurant, airport shuttle, car rental; Cost: room $94-132 depending on season; 350-2138, esayap@mail.fm, www.esayap.com*

O'Keefe's Waterfront Inn Walking into O'Keefe's Waterfront Inn feels like walking into an island resort of the 1920s. The older, Western-style decor is charming and well-kept. On the premises is a fully stocked bar, which includes tables on a waterfront veranda and is ideal after a full day of water sports and cultural tours. *In Colonia; Amenities: TV, A/C, bar; Cost: room $155; 350-6500, okeefes@mail.fm*

Expensive

Manta Ray Bay Resort This family-run resort is situated on a picturesque bay and is known for its accommodating staff and adventurous tours. This is an upscale resort, complete with an outdoor waterfall pool, the luxury Taro Spa, which specializes in local massage, a PADI Dive Center offering dive and boat tours, full dive course instruction programs, and kayaking, snorkeling, and fishing charters. Standard rooms are spacious and completely equipped with refrigerators, air-conditioning, hot water, TVs and DVD players, pay-by-use wireless internet access, and blow dryers. Two Deluxe Ocean View rooms are available; each includes a canopy bed, private plunge pool, and gazebo. There is also a Deluxe Ocean View Suite, which has access via a spiraling staircase to a private, rooftop hot tub. Cultural and hiking tours can also be arranged through this resort. Free airport shuttle is included with a room reservation. A free email kiosk is located in the lobby, as are DVD rentals, a gift shop selling Yapese handmade goods, and a desert center.

The M'nuw Restaurant is also located on the premises, as is Yap's only microbrewery, Stone Money Brewing Company. *In Colonia; Amenities: A/C, TV, refrigerator, restaurant, bar, internet access, pool, spa, tours; Cost: standard room $175, room with private pool $258; 350-2300, (800) DIVE-YAP, global@mantaray.com, www.mantaray.com*

Trader's Ridge Resort Trader's Ridge Resort offers upscale accommodations, an outdoor pool, a bar, two restaurants, and a local crafts gift shop. This resort is unique in that it houses the Ethnic Art Institute of Micronesia where guests can view Yapese men and women carving model canoes, weaving local sails, and working on their looms to create local wrap skirts, or *lavalavas*. Trader's Ridge Resort also includes a PADI Dive Center that offers snorkeling tours, scuba diving expeditions, and kayak rentals. *In Colonia; Amenities: A/C, TV, pool, restaurant, gift shop; Cost: room $215-375 depending on size; 350-6000, resv@tradersridge.com, www.tradersridge.com*

OUTER ISLAND ACCOMMODATIONS

A neighboring island trip is great for travelers looking for a local experience. The Ulithi Adventure Resort is located on the island of Falalop, Ulithi and is the only hotel on the neighboring islands.

Ulithi Adventure Resort If a genuine experience of a traditional island culture is what you seek, this is the hotel for you. Very few travelers, less than two dozen annually, visit here. Chances are that your group would be the resort's only guests and that you would have the staff and island to yourselves. Daily sights on the island include men building local huts and cookhouses, cutting palm wine from young coconut trees, and participating in nightly drinking circles. Visitors would also see women wearing colorful *lavalavas*, working in their gardens, and cooking reef fish over coconut husk fires. Additionally, the hotel is situated on a beautiful beach that is ideal for snorkeling. There are no ATMs or banks on this island, so come prepared. Cash is accepted at the two or three tiny island stores, located on family compounds.

There are 14 rooms, each with a twin-sized bed, hot water, and air-conditioning. Room rates also include island tours. There is a dive shop on the grounds, but the air pump has been out of service for some time, so check with management before planning a dive from here. Visitors can also arrange fishing charters and tours to other islands in the Ulithi Atoll through hotel management. Meals are provided by the hotel in generous portions for a reasonable rate along with safe drinking water. The resort employs several local ladies as well as a few men and is a great source of local income.

At the time of this writing, the resort is in operational flux due to the death of the previous owner, John Rulmal. *Ulithi Atoll; Amenities: A/C, hot water, beach access, tours; Cost: room $100-125 depending of cost of supplies on island; Ulithi Post Office, Falalop, Ulithi, Yap, FM 96943, 350-2360, pmayap@mail.fm, info@diveulithi.com*

Homestays

There are also homestays available on the outer islands, including on Falalop, Ulithi, which give guests a personal cultural experience. Guests choosing a homestay will eat meals with the family, sleep in the same quarters, and experience island life as a local.

> If you arrange a homestay, bringing gifts, such as food or cigarettes, is a great way to show your appreciation for the hospitality of your hosts.

Before planning a neighboring island visit, contact the Council of Tamol, (pg 162) to arrange permission and transportation. Keep in mind that a small fee will be due to each neighboring island that you choose to visit.

Where to Eat

Inexpensive

Oasis Oasis, located in Central Colonia, serves a mix of Asian and Yapese cuisine for breakfast, lunch, and dinner at reasonable prices. The lunch special every weekday includes generous portions of local food for only five dollars. The staff is notably friendly and accommodating, and indoor and outdoor tables are available. *In Colonia; Cost: meal $5-12; Hours: Mon-Sat 10 AM-1 PM, 5-9 PM*

Ganir Ganir is located in Yap Cooperative Association Complex above IES convenience store. Meals are a mix of American and Asian cuisine. The restaurant is open for breakfast, lunch, and dinner. Prices are very reasonable, and there is a happy hour on weekdays from 2 to 4 PM. *In Yap Cooperative Association Complex; Cost: meal $5-14; Hours: Mon-Fri 7 AM-8:30 PM, Sat 7-9 AM, Sun 7 AM-2 PM, 4:30-9 PM; 350-5222*

Bay View Restaurant Located on the premises of ESA Bay View Hotel on the southwest side of Chamorro Bay, Bay View Restaurant is right on the lagoon. It features beautiful views of Yap's mountains. This restaurant serves generous portions of American and Asian meals at low prices. *At ESA Bay View Hotel; Cost: meal $5-14; Hours: Mon-Sat 9 AM-8 PM; 350-2139*

Moonrize Restaurant Specializing in Japanese cuisine, these dishes are delicious and affordable. The restaurant is also beautifully situated on a white sand beach. *At Village View Resort in Ma'ap; Cost: meal $5-19; Hours: Mon-Sat 8:30 AM-9:30 PM, Sun 11 AM-3 PM; 350-2031*

Moderate

Poolside Café Located at Trader's Ridge Resort, this restaurant serves breakfast, lunch, and dinner at mid-range prices. Meals follow a Western theme but include some local ingredients. Guests are encouraged to sample a Betel Nut Martini, complete with a local betel nut preparation that is dropped into top-shelf gin. *At Trader's Ridge Resort; Cost: $7-30; Hours: 10 AM-8 PM daily; 350-6000*

M'nuw Ship's Bar & Grill Dining at M'nuw, which is located at Manta Ray Bay Hotel, is a unique experience; the ship is a 170-foot Phinisi Schooner from Indonesia with three dining decks, two bars, and a kitchen all onboard. The American dishes are moderately priced. Each evening, there is a multi-media presentation of dive photography and video from the waters surrounding Wa'ab Island. No meal here is complete without a pint of beer from the local Stone Money Brewing Company. *At Manta Ray Bay Resort; Cost: meal $8-30; Hours: 6 AM-9 PM daily; 350-2300, 350-2319*

Expensive

The Veranda View Restaurant This dining room is located upstairs from the Pool Side Café at Trader's Ridge Resort and is a formal setting, open only for dinner. Prices are more expensive than guests will find in other establishments, but there is an accompanying increase in quality and creativity. *At Trader's Ridge Resort; Cost: $12-40; Hours: open for dinner daily; 350-6000*

What to Do

SIGHTS

While traveling through Yap, visitors can expect to see breathtaking greens, blues, and fluorescent colors in the lush vegetation covering the land. Local people incorporate these bountiful natural resources into the activities of their daily life, such as building, cooking, and creating local medicines. In every village, local people will be seen living as their families have done for centuries.

Simply walking through **Colonia**, travelers can expect unique views, including topless men, women, and children wearing grass skirts, *thus*, or *lavalavas* and carrying elaborate baskets woven from dried palm leaves or hibiscus. You might hear four very distinct local languages in a single store, as traditionally dressed islanders purchase rice, sugar, coffee, and other imported, Western goods. Juxtapositions of the traditional with the modern are common in Yap.

It is fascinating to see Yapese people practice ancient skills, but it is extremely important that visitors travel with caution by seeking permission and going through the proper channels, such as hotel tour guides. Before visiting a village, a stone money bank, or trail, always ask permission. Yapese people are happy to share their lives with travelers, but visitors are expected to be respectful of local practices.

It is highly recommended for all travelers to Yap to participate in a **cultural tour**. All hotels in Yap will arrange cultural tours. On one of these tours, you might drive around the island, walk along a stone path, see a stone money bank, visit a village, eat locally prepared foods, or even observe a traditional dance. A popular stop on these tours is **Kaday Village**, which features traditional dances on Tuesdays and Saturdays when weather permits. Visitors may also have the opportunity to don local attire during their tour.

The Micronesian Ethnic Art Institute, located on the grounds of Trader's Ridge, is a great place for visitors who may not have the time for a full island tour. Here, guests can observe local weaving, carving, and building skills that have been passed down through Yapese families for centuries. There are several thatch roof huts where these crafts are demonstrated. Contact Trader's Ridge Resort (pg 154) for details.

Stone money banks are sites where Yapese families leave stone money that has been passed down through generations. Here, travelers have the opportunity to pose next to the largest money in the world. Stone money ranges from 3 inches (8 centimeters) in diameter to greater than 6 feet (2 meters). These disks are centuries old and worn down by weather and time, making for beautiful sights and pictures. Stone money banks are found throughout the capital island of Yap, and visits can be arranged through any taxi company or hotel.

WATER AND OUTDOOR ACTIVITIES

Diving

Yap is world renowned for its reliable giant manta sightings, and it is not uncommon to see a dozen mantas in the space of a single dive. The island's structure lends itself to incredibly diverse dive environments, from shallow sandy bottoms to outer reefs 200 feet (60 meters) or more deep, swift channel drifts, and leisurely soft coral-laden walls.

> The manta mating season runs from November to April, but it is probable that, during a typical week of diving, divers will spot at least a few mantas any time of the year.

Yap Caverns, the southernmost dive site, numbers among the most popular. A good first or second dive, these caverns are cut into the reef wall and are interspersed with large coral heads, chasms, and chimneys. The photographic opportunities here are endless, as the visibility is generally around 40-100 feet (10-30 meters), and the light filtering through the chimneys leads to some dramatically lit scenes. A large school of bumphead parrotfish call this area home as well as grey reef sharks and an abundance of lionfish.

Mandarinfish Ledge is an excellent twilight or night dive featuring mating mandarinfish in surprisingly large numbers. Average depths are 20-30 feet (6-9 meters), so long bottom times allow divers the chance to watch the mating ritual. The male swims excitedly around a prospective female. If she deems him fitting, they rise belly to belly slowly into the water column a few feet from the reef and at the apex release an explosion of gametes.

Mi'il Channel is another amazing drift dive. This channel can see currents near four knots. While ripping through the channel, be sure to keep an eye out for the copious fish and invertebrate life, including various skates and rays, bumphead parrotfish, large moray eels, and large schools of jacks and snappers. Hawksbill turtles and various species of reef shark are common here, and if you catch a low-current break around slack tides, be sure to take a look around the nooks and crannies for members of the thriving lobster and octopus communities.

Goofnuw Mini-wall, often coupled as a drift dive with Mi'il Channel and the mantas, is not to be missed. This site has steep walls broken by sand or coral slopes, and opens out into the Valley of the Rays. Sleeping leopard sharks, whitetip sharks, lobsters, pelagic fish, and mantas transiting to the Valley of the Rays can all be spotted here.

Slow n' Easy 1 and 2 are good sites for macro-photographers and those looking for an easy, shallow dive or a third dive at the end of the day. An abundance of gobies, alpheid shrimp commensal pairs, soft and hard coral and lots of interesting, tiny invertebrates may be found here. Ask the dive guide to point out the large burrowing mantis shrimps at Slow n' Easy, and keep an eye out for the numerous nudibranchs that abound here.

Manta Ray The largest dive center, Manta Ray Bay Resort and its dive center are well oiled machines. This dive shop offers multiple scheduled dives every day, incredibly helpful staff, and accommodating and experienced dive guides. Signing up for a dive is easy; walk up to the dry erase board outside the dive center and put your name under any dives that you would like to join. Manta Ray will also set up custom dives, and dive groups are generally fairly small. *At Manta Ray Bay Resort; Cost: two-tank dive $120; 350-2300, (800) DIVE-YAP, www.mantaray.com*

Trader's Ridge Trader's Ridge dive shop is just like the resort: professional and classy. They are the only nitrox-capable fill station on island, although all dive shops offer nitrox to those certified to use it. *At Trader's Ridge Resort; Cost: two-tank dive $108; 350-6000, www.tradersridge.com*

Beyond the Reef This dive shop has recently changed ownership due to the passing of the previous owner, Dave Vecella, in a dive accident in 2008 and is now run by co-founder Jesse Faimaw. The dive staff has undergone staffing changes, but Tony Piosca, one of the new guides, is relaxed and very accommodating. Beyond the Reef takes a maximum of four divers per boat for the most personal experience possible. *In Colonia; Cost: two-tank dive with snack $99; 350-3483, beyondthereef@mail.fm, www.diveyap.com*

Nature's Way A small shop with a very small staff, Nature's Way specializes in catering to Japanese-speaking visitors and is perfect for those staying for awhile and wanting to focus on custom, small group dive trips. *In Colonia; www.naturesway.fm*

Rize Divers Rize generally caters to Japanese-speaking customers, although they serve English-speakers as well. Located in Ma'ap, Rize is a great place to visit the manta sites quickly while staying out at Village View Hotel. *In Ma'ap municipality; Cost: two-tank dive $100; rizedivingcenter@mail.fm, www.rizedivingcenter.com*

Fishing

Fishing charters can be arranged through any dive shop (see above). Wahoo, yellowfin tuna, and a few billfish species are regularly caught in the waters surrounding Wa'ab, and trolling is a wonderful way to spend an afternoon. It is also possible to hook-and-line fish, and various grouper, snapper, and trevally species are regularly caught around the island.

Hiking

Any hotel or resort can arrange a guided hiking tour so visitors can admire the local flora and fauna. Simply inquire at the front desk about prices and scheduling. The **Tmilyog Trail** is the most popular. It is about 3 miles (5 kilometers) in length and bisects the island, cutting down through forest and up through grassy highlands. Hikes take an average of two hours to complete, and beginning early in the morning will allow you to avoid the hottest hours of the day. Pictures taken from the peak will capture a beautiful, panoramic view of Colonia and the azure waters of the surrounding sea. Sturdy, gripping shoes are recommended as some of the paving stones can be extremely slippery. Also, visit the **Visitors Bureau** (350-5005 or 350-5567) for information on some of the stone money hikes that can be found just a few minutes from Colonia.

> You could also arrange a visit to the old, retired Japanese airfield to check out the downed aircraft strewn about the airfield in various states of disrepair.

Sailing

Traditional canoe sailing is a very unique experience and highly recommended to anyone passing through Yap. These can be scheduled through Manta Ray Bay Resort, Trader's Ridge Resort, ESA Bay View Hotel (see *Accommodations* on pg 153), and **Yap Traditional Navigation Society** (www.ytns.org). It is highly advised to give the Traditional Navigation Society a call as they may be able to accommodate a tour of their classes where traditional canoe-building and navigation skills are handed down from the older navigators to the younger generation. Seeing a large canoe being hewn from a newly felled tree is a once-in-a-lifetime experience. Ask your hotel for help in contacting the Yap Traditional Navigation Society as their contact information changes frequently.

Snorkeling

Many of the dive sites in Yap are excellent locations for snorkelers or free-divers. Ask a dive shop about good sites for your experience and comfort level. There are some good spots within the channel near Slow n' Easy that are excellent for snorkelers; these spots usually average 15-20 feet (5-6 meters) in depth with decent visibility depending on the tides.

Private property

All property is privately owned in Yap, including beaches, so ask permission before settling in for a picnic or snorkeling at any beach outside of a resort. Travelers can ask at the Visitors Bureau (350-5005 or 350-5567) for suggestions about what beaches would be appropriate for recreation. Hotels, resorts, and restaurants can also provide this information.

Thatch roof houses and outdoor cookhouses are still standard in family compounds on Yap. These are beautiful and interesting sights, but take care before approaching or exploring a village or residence. Yapese people are very private, so always ask permission before entering a village or approaching a residence. If you are traveling with a guide from your resort or hotel, he or she can bring you to places where exploring and picture-taking are accepted. The best tours are often arranged through a new Yapese friend who may offer to take you to his home or village.

Surfing

There is no surfing on Yap. Most of the breaks in Yap either break directly on shallow, jagged reefs or are so small as to be useless. Spend the time kayaking and, if you really want to surf in Micronesia, visit Pohnpei.

Other Water Activities

General beach lounging should be arranged through hotels, as all land is privately owned. If guests are interested in a relaxing kayak ride through mangrove-lined channels, activities can be arranged through the dive shops at Manta Ray Bay Resort or Trader's Ridge Resort. You can stop at O'Keefe's Island where you will find a picnic table and lots of opportunities for exploring the mangroves.

SHOPPING

Souvenirs

A visit to Yap is a once in a lifetime opportunity to bring home some truly unique and beautiful, locally made goods, such as *lavalavas*, grass skirts, woven baskets, and local coconut oil. These items are made through hours of painstaking, intricate work, and by purchasing them, tourists are supporting the local economy and providing income to otherwise unemployed island women. Be sure to check laws regarding importation of various types of shell, especially turtle shell, before planning to purchase jewelry or other items made from shell. If you are looking for particularly rare or expensive goods, such as banana fiber, hibiscus fiber *lavalavas*, or handmade model canoes, ask for help at your hotel. Asking a local for information about purchasing locally made goods can ensure that those who produced the goods will receive the majority of the profits from the sale. It can also be helpful to check with the **Visitors Bureau** (350-5005 or 350-5567), as they may be able to set up a tour or a visit to where these items are made.

For local handmade crafts, a good place to look is **Island Fashion clothing store** (Mon-Fri 8 AM-5 PM). This business has more competitive rates for these goods, and the creators of the goods receive the money paid for the items.

The **gift shops** in both Trader's Ridge Resort and Manta Ray Bay Resort carry Yapese goods, Yap T-shirts, and other souvenirs. The gift shop at Trader's Ridge also carries higher end sunglasses and T-shirts featuring the logo of their dive shop and their microbrewery, Stone Money Brewing Company.

At **Lagoonia Store** (Mon-Fri 9 AM-5 PM), shoppers can find locally made goods, such as jewelry, clothing, bags, models, and fishing supplies. **Yap Art Studio and Gallery** (Mon-Sat 9 AM-5:30 PM; www.yapinstitute.com), which employs local artists, is a great place to shop for original artwork or small carvings. Original paintings, as well as printed copies in the form of post cards and greeting cards are available for purchase here. There are also numerous locally made goods, such as *lavalavas*, grass skirts, baskets, wallets, and change purses made from hibiscus leaves. Goods here are of very high quality, but the prices are also high.

Groceries

With a central location, most shoppers stop at **YCA** (Mon-Fri 8:30 AM-5:30 PM, Sat 8:30 AM-1:30 PM, Sun 9 AM-12 PM; 350-7027 or 350-7028) first. This is the best place to shop for general groceries, such as meats, vegetables, and bread. However, their prices are slightly higher than EMI Blue Lagoon and Pick n' Save. Yap T-shirts, other clothing, sunglasses, and locally made goods, such as baskets and model canoes can also be purchased here. YCA is located in the Yap Cooperative Association complex in Colonia's town center. **EMI Blue Lagoon** (Mon-Sat 8 AM-8 PM, Sun 8 AM-3 PM; 350-4961) is located on the other side of Chamorro Bay next to Pathways Hotel.

Take the first right just before reaching Yap State Hospital to find **Pick n' Save** (Mon-Fri 8:30 AM-5:30 PM, Sat 8:30 AM-1:30 PM, Sun 9 AM-noon; 350-2149) at the end of the road. This small mart is the perfect place to look for imported toiletries and packaged foods that are rarely found in other stores in Yap. The liquor and beer selection is also impressive for this island state. Prices are reasonable.

The perfect stop for a quick breakfast, **ESA Bakery** (Mon-Fri 7 AM-4 PM) offers takeout pancake breakfasts, donuts, bread, and other baked goods along with freshly brewed coffee and other beverages. This bakery is located in the same complex as the ESA Bay View Hotel.

The family-owned **Family Chain Bakery** (Mon-Sat 8 AM-10 PM, Sun 8 AM-4 PM; 350-2377) carries breads, cakes, soft-serve ice cream, and other sweets but also serves lunch items, such as sandwiches, pizza, and fried chicken. Most items are made the morning of the sale, and prices are very reasonable.

Imported vs. Local Goods

When searching for imported goods, such as toiletries, over-the-counter medicines, and packaged foods, expect prices to be high. Shipping overseas adds significantly to the cost of goods in Yap state. Local fruits, vegetables, and baked goods are the most budget friendly and eco-conscious choice.

Other

Wa'ab Hardware has general and specific hardware along with fishing and snorkeling gear. The store is located past Family Chain Bakery before reaching PBC. **YCA Hardware** (Mon-Fri 8 AM-5:30 PM; 350-2207) does not carry fishing gear but does have some specific hardware that is not found at Wa'ab Hardware Store.

For fishing gear, toiletries, and small traveling bags, **PBC Home Appliance** (Mon-Sat 8 AM-5:30 PM; 350-2270) is the place to shop. Their rates are more competitive than YCA, and they are within walking distance of central Colonia. Head towards the hospital, and PBC will be about a five-minute walk from Manta Ray Bay Resort.

Nightlife

Nightlife is calm and sleepy on these tropical islands. The best way to spend an evening is to secure an invitation from a local man to a drinking circle where you will get a true cultural experience and share stories of your home, which are always popular in these crowds.

For a different dive experience, all dive centers on island offer night dives, which is the best time to observe mating mandarinfish.

Visiting Local Bars

Restaurants typically close around 8 PM, and while there are local bars that are open until the early morning hours, it is not recommended for the safety of travelers to visit remote, village bars. Ask taxi drivers and hotel staff about the hours of bars near you.

O'Keefe's Kanteen Bar Located across the street from Waterfront Inn, this comfortable bar has indoor and outdoor seating and serves appetizers, mixed drinks, and beer at reasonable prices. This is the original site where O'Keefe opened his bar. *Across from O'Keefe Waterfront Inn; Cost: drinks $3-6; Hours vary, but usually 4pm-11pm; 350-4539 or 350-4577, donevans@mail.fm*

Waterfront Inn Pub With antique, 1920s Western décor, this is a charming and relaxing place to sip top shelf liquor and gaze at the ocean view. Seating is available inside and outside on a waterfront veranda. The pub is located in the town center of Colonia between YCA complex and Manta Ray Bay Resort. *In Colonia, between YCA complex and Manta Ray Bay Resort; Cost: drinks $4-12; Hours vary; 350-6500, okeefes@mail.fm*

Outer Islands

For visitors wishing to experience island life of the most basic, traditional style, a voyage to the neighboring outer islands is highly recommended. On the outer islands, a traveler might find himself or herself, with a small amount of coaxing, assisting with a chore, like shaving copra or weaving a basket to carry taro. These types of experiences are common in the neighboring islands, and it is this traditional lifestyle that draws adventurous travelers to Yap's outer islands.

The **Council of Tamol** (PO Box 402, Colonia, Yap, FM 96943, 350-2343) must grant permission for any travel to the neighboring islands. Visitors will pay a fee of 20 dollars per island plus another 20 dollars paid upon arrival to the chief of each island. Travelers visiting islands for only a few hours can forgo the 20 dollar fee paid to the chief of the island, although the money is much appreciated by the local communities. Generally, this money goes toward island-wide projects, so the money is well spent.

> The bank and fuel station that were once open on Falalop are no longer in operation, so bring any cash that you will need with you before you leave Wa'ab. Also, be sure to arrange for fuel for any off-island forays that you may wish to take before arriving in Ulithi.

See pg 151 for information on travelling to the outer islands and pg 154 for information on accommodations.

ULITHI

Ulithi atoll consists of about 40 islands and islets and is home to around 700 people as of the last census. Ulithi is also the fourth largest atoll in the world, with 210 square miles (540 square kilometers) of lagoon. There are four inhabited islands: Falalop, Mogmog, Asor, and Federai. Ulithi is the easiest of the neighboring islands to visit due to the well-maintained airstrip located on Falalop. Permission to visit Ulithi is automatic, but visitors must still register with the Council of Tamol in Wa'ab before arrival. There are many attractions in Ulithi, including fishing (trolling, shore fishing, and spear fishing), snorkeling, and diving, although you will have to bring your own air and equipment.

Mogmog is the chiefly island and the most traditional island in the atoll. No Western-style clothing is allowed; all women are topless, and men wear *thus* exclusively. The culture is very family oriented here, and alcohol is periodically banned by the chief when it becomes a social problem for the people of the island. Male and female visitors are encouraged to remove all headwear, and male visitors are encouraged to remove their shirts as a sign of respect to the local culture. Federai and Asor just had large solar arrays installed in 2009, thanks to an EU development grant, al-

---

Dive and Fishing Sites in Ulithi

The phrase *an undiscovered paradise* is overused and generally untrue, but this is a very apt description of the diving and fishing possibilities available to intrepid sportsmen visiting Ulithi. Diving or snorkeling in Ulithi is a singular experience. The amount and diversity of fish, crustaceans, and other invertebrates will leave even the most seasoned diver speechless. Visibility is regularly well above 100 feet (30 meters) in channels and outside the lagoon. Here, you are apt to encounter mantas, dolphins, yellowfin tuna, wahoo, mahi mahi, and innumerable reef and pelagic fish species. Some good spots to try snorkeling are the lagoon side of Asor for large aggregations of various parrotfish, Napoleon wrasse, visiting pelagic species, and a large nesting area of triggers. Ask your boat driver to take you to visit the large group of scuttled World War II vehicles and ships near Asor as well for sightings of various trevally and jack species, including a standing school of giant trevally.

As you follow the reef out toward the large channel between Falalop and Asor, you can sight many giant sweetlips, rainbow runner, and other pelagic fish. Be aware that the current here can become quite strong. Pay a visit to the Asor side of the channel between Falalop and Asor for a few drift dives and the chance to sight large standing schools of gray and whitemargin unicornfish, oriental and giant sweetlips, a large and very curious school of big-eye jacks, the occasional yellowfin tuna, and a very healthy population of reef and oceanic sharks. The lagoon is peppered with many small seamounts, which are excellent places to catch a fleeting glimpse of mantas and other rays. If you can get permission, make it a point to dive or fish the outlying "turtle islands" for a chance at some amazing fishing as well as a view of an incredibly vibrant and healthy population of reef and pelagic shark species. Beware, while fishing these islands, the sharks can be aggressive, and it is better to lose your catch than anything else.

though they are still working out the kinks in the system.

There are several islands outside of the atoll that are home to a large population of nesting green and loggerhead turtles, which usually nest during the summer months. There has been an active scientific program to study the range and distribution of these turtles using both traditional and satellite tags.

FAIS

Fais is a very traditional island and is also very physically different from the other neighboring islands, since it is a high island. This provides the people of Fais with many more food resources than atoll islands as well as mineral deposits that were exploited by the Japanese following WWI. Traveling to Fais is possible both using the *Hapilmohol*, as well as the infrequent charter flights flown by PMA. The reefs surrounding the island are very small, and fishing is comparatively limited. The people of Fais are known for their skill in weaving the more intricate patterns on *lavalavas*, and the vast majority of the fishing done on the island is done by traditional outrigger canoe.

WOLEAI

Woleai consists of 22 islands, including Falalop, Falalus, Tagaulap, and Sailap. Woleai is home to the second of the neighboring islands' high schools and is also one of the more developed of the neighboring islands, as it has a power generation station on the island of Falalop. Still, it is a very traditional and tightly knit group of islands. Woleai was used as a Japanese seaplane anchorage during most of WWII, and to this day, many remnants from this era can be seen around the island, including several anti-aircraft guns, building and railway remnants, and a Japanese monument to the thousands of Japanese soldiers who were bypassed in 1945 and starved on the island. While there is an airstrip on Falalop, it is usually flooded or unserviceable, and flights via PMA, when the airline is able to service the atoll, only happen a few times a year. If you can plan your trip to coincide with the high school's graduation you are in for a supreme treat; the graduation is a huge event, and the *Hapilmohol* usually brings visitors from across Yap to join in the celebrations. The students and teachers, along with the entire atoll community, prepare for the celebration weeks in advance, and the students show off their best local dances.

ELATO

Elato, along with the island of Olimarao, is part of a double lagoon formed by a shared seamount. Recently the atoll has become the center of quite a bit of foreign press as an example of things to come for small, low-lying atoll islands, as Elato is losing portions of its beaches to erosion and its crops to unusually high "king tides." This is becoming a more and more common occurrence for not only the residents of Elato but also those inhabiting other small atolls throughout the Pacific.

SATAWAL

Satawal is known for its traditional celestial navigators, including Mau Pilailug, otherwise known as Papa Mau. Papa Mau sailed a local canoe, the *Hokule'a*, from Hawaii to Satawal, using only ancient stories and the stars as reference points. The island's collection of large voyaging canoes includes some of the best examples of the art of canoe-building in Micronesia. These canoes are still used on a regular basis for fishing and travel. The island, as well as the rest of Yap state, has been hit hard by several typhoons over the last 20 to 30 years and now has several concrete buildings thanks to grants from the FSM and abroad.

Annual Festivals on Yap

Annual Yap Day Festival

Yap Day is dedicated to commemorating the cultural traditions specific to the people of the capital and neighboring islands. This state holiday is always March 1st, and the festivities are held during the weekend closest to that date. This occasion is of paramount importance to the Yapese people, and it is always celebrated grandly, with numerous traditional dances, handicraft demonstrations, food sales, and locally made goods available for purchase. Men and women are topless for the events, wearing conventional dress of brightly colored *thus*, loincloths for men, and *lavalavas*, wrap skirts woven from hibiscus or banana leafs for women.

The various types of dances that take place on this occasion include stick dances, kneeling dances, standing dances, and sitting dances. These movements have been passed down, generation to generation, over centuries. Preformed to the beat of claps, stomps, strikes of sticks, and the chants of the performers, these displays are captivating and transport the audience to ancient times. More information about Yap Day festivities can be found at www.visityap.com and by contacting the site's webmaster.

Annual Yap Canoe Festival

The Yap Canoe Festival is usually held in October or November each year. For exact times and locations, visit www.visityap.com.

Yap state honors its seafaring tradition by showcasing all aspects of traditional navigation and canoe-building. Visitors can observe canoe races and rides and demonstrations of local coconut rope making, carving, traditional sail weaving, local skirt weaving, dances, and food preparation. The first annual festival in 2009 proved to be very successful, and it is sure to improve in the future.

Annual Manta Fest Photography Festival

Come meet and learn from top underwater shooters from around the world. There are always great dives with once-in-a-lifetime views of mating mandarinfish, sharks, and mantas. Professional digital still photographers and videographers are present to help guests with any questions or needs. There are also nightly presentations on a large outdoor screen at M'nuw Restaurant as well as individual classroom seminars in the afternoons. The professionals also compile a presentation from the guests to show on the last day and give awards to participants. Various prizes are up for grabs, and competition is quite fierce. For more details and to confirm the dates for the next Manta Fest Photography Festival, visit www.mantafest.com.

Previous pages: Yap Day dancers and festivities
Above: Prestine beach, Yap
Below: Mortlockese children playing outside church, Chuuk

Above: Stone money bank, Yap
Below: Woman using traditional loom, Yap
Following pages: Sunset on Pisar, Chuuk; Smiling child on Ta Island, Chuuk

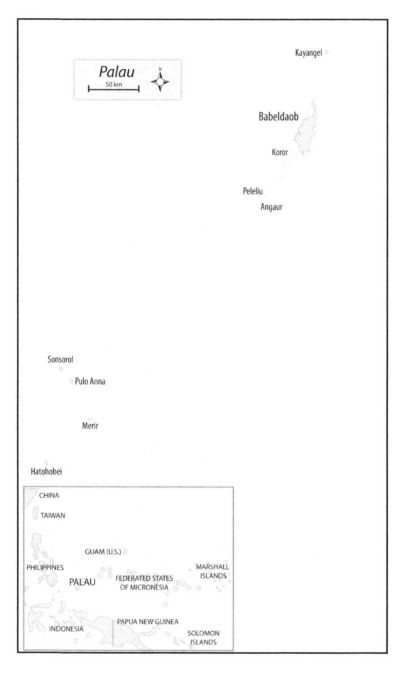

Palau
50 km
N

Kayangel

Babeldaob

Koror

Peleliu
Angaur

Sonsorol

Pulo Anna

Merir

Hatohobei

CHINA
TAIWAN

GUAM (U.S.)
PHILIPPINES
PALAU   FEDERATED STATES
OF MICRONESIA
MARSHALL
ISLANDS

PAPUA NEW GUINEA
INDONESIA
SOLOMON
ISLANDS

Palau

Babeldoab
5 km

Ngarchelong Dock
Badrulauch

Ngarchelong

Choll
North Beach Cottages

Ngarrad

Ngardmau
Ngardmau Waterfall

Sunken Village
of Ngibtal
Public Beach

Ngiwal

Japanese Cannons
Imeong Village
Lake Ngardok

Ngaremlengui
Melkeok
Public Beach

Public Beach
Karamadoo Bay
Palau Beach Bungalows

Ngatpang Waterfall

Ngatpang

WWII Monument

Aimeliik Bai
Jungle River Cruise

Malsol's Tomb
Aimeliik
Ngchesar

Airai
Ngerekesbesang Island
Koror
Airai View Hotel
Arai Bai

Malakal Island
See Detailed Map

Dolphins Pacific

Palau

Welcome to the Rainbow's End, a land of enchantment and underwater wonders. Natural bridges spanning crystal clear waters, enormous waterfalls plunging into mist shrouded pools, and brilliant flora and fauna hidden in dense jungles are just a few of the marvels that you can find on the Palauan islands. The beauty above the water is matched by the incredible fish, sharks, rays, dolphins, turtles, crustaceans, and 100-mile long barrier reef that have made Palau one of the Seven Underwater Wonders of the World, according to CEDAM International.

At first Palau appears to be just a speck on the map, but after spending a few days here, you will discover the rich culture and heritage of a people that has survived centuries of occupation and modern warfare. More than 250 islands spread across 400 miles of ocean comprise the Republic of Palau. Pictures and words, however, cannot do justice to the incredible beauty of this young republic. You will just have to see for yourself!

HIGHLIGHTS OF PALAU

Scuba diving: Explore some of the top dive sites in the world, including amazing naturalist, wall, and drift dives. pg 208

Snorkeling in Jellyfish Lake: Discover an amazing scientific wonder found only in Palau. pg 205

Hiking to Ngardmau Waterfall: Walk through the Taki Nature Reserve along the historical remains of the Japanese railway system to reach the 100-foot (30-meter) waterfall. pg 208

Kayaking among the Rock Islands: Paddle into the heart of the limestone rock islands that surround the city of Koror. pg 204

Helicopter tour of Palau: Fly above Palau and view the mushroom-shaped Rock Islands, the natural bridge, Jellyfish Lake, and Milky Way and possibly catch a glimpse of the endangered dugong. pg 205

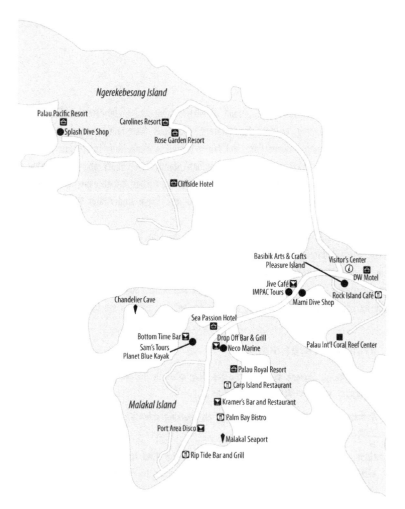

Ngerekebesang Island

Palau Pacific Resort
Splash Dive Shop

Carolines Resort
Rose Garden Resort

Cliffside Hotel

Basibik Arts & Crafts
Pleasure Island

Visitor's Center
DW Motel

Jive Café
IMPAC Tours
Mami Dive Shop

Rock Island Café

Chandelier Cave

Sea Passion Hotel

Bottom Time Bar
Sam's Tours
Planet Blue Kayak

Drop Off Bar & Grill
Neco Marine

Palau Int'l Coral Reef Center

Palau Royal Resort

Carp Island Restaurant

Malakal Island

Kramer's Bar and Restaurant

Palm Bay Bistro

Port Area Disco

Malakal Seaport

Rip Tide Bar and Grill

Koror

500 meters

N

T-Dock

Red Rooster Café

Etpitson Museum   Tree D Hotel

Dragon Tei

Budget Car Rental

Communications Corp.

Emaimelei

Joe's Bar

Rur Gift Shop

Palau Shop

Palasia Hotel

Sakura

The Taj

Greenbay Hotel

Bem Ermii

Police

Prison
(Subilik Shop)

Yolt Gift/Bike Shop

WCTC Shopping Plaza
Surangel's Shopping Center

Suriyothai

Penthouse Hotel

Fresh Noodle

Lehn's Motel

Keam

Belau Museum

Geography

The Republic of Palau, located in the northern Pacific Ocean southeast of the Philippines, is an island chain composed of eight principal inhabited islands and more than 250 smaller rock islands. The largest of the islands, Babeldaob, contains eleven of the sixteen states which comprise the Republic of Palau, including the capital of Palau in the state of Melekeok. Just south of Babeldaob but connected by a bridge, is the island of Koror. Koror is the metropolitan center of Palau and host to the majority of the businesses and shopping centers of the country.

The coral atoll of Kayangel is located 22 miles (35 kilometers) north of the island of Babeldaob. Less than one mile (2 kilometers) long, the largest and only inhabited island of Kayangel is home to fewer than 150 people. The first inhabited island southwest of Koror is Peleliu, the most populated and developed of the outer islands. Peleliu is famous as a battleground during the Second World War. Further south and outside of Palau's barrier reef is the island of Angaur. Angaur is the only island of Palau to host the invasive species of macaque monkeys. Located about 370 miles (600 kilometers) away from the main island chain of Palau are the seven Southwest Islands, which are grouped into 2 states, Sonsorol and Hatohobei. In addition to the inhabited islands are the limestone or coral rock islands of Palau. Hundreds of scattered islands, many rising out of the water like giant mushrooms, are home to beautiful beaches, blue lagoons, and ancient remnants of previous inhabitants.

Surrounded by the Great Barrier Reef, the many islands of Palau vary greatly in terrain. The islands of Palau are composed of four different land formations: high limestone, volcanic, low platform, and coral atoll. These different formations sustain diverse varieties of vegetation. The elevations of the islands also vary from the highest point, Mount Ngerchelchauu (794 feet, 242 meters) on the island Babeldaob, to the many sea level atolls. Most of the Palauan islands are covered by rock or tropical forests. Mangrove swamps or white sand beaches are often found on the coasts of the islands.

There are roughly 80 saltwater and freshwater lakes throughout the islands of Palau. Ngardok Lake on Babeldaob is the largest freshwater lake and serves as the largest rain catchment for the islands. There are also many small streams and waterfalls throughout the islands. The largest and most renowned waterfall is Ngardmau Falls, located in the state of Ngardmau on Babeldaob. A large number of underwater caves and caverns are scattered throughout the reefs of Palau, including Chandelier Cave, a popular site for scuba divers.

Although most famous for its abundant ocean life, the islands of Palau harbor a wide variety of flora and fauna. The rock islands are covered with rainforests and harbor a great diversity of plant life. Trees commonly found in Palau include ironwood, pandanus, and banyan. Coconut, breadfruit, mango, banana, and betel nut grow naturally throughout the islands. Taro, cassava, pineapple, and tobacco are also farmed in the country. The islands of Palau also host a variety of animals. There is a particularly wide variety of reptiles found on or near land, including crocodiles and monitor lizards. Non venomous snakes, two species of bat, the rare flying fox, the aforementioned monkeys, and a huge diversity of birds are also found on the islands.

Palau is located at 7° 30' north latitude and 134° 30' east longitude. The climate is hot and humid year round, averaging 82% humidity and 82° Fahrenheit (28° Celsius). The wet season runs from May to November, although brief torrential storms occur throughout the year, producing 150 inches (380 centimeters) of rainfall yearly. Typhoons generally occur between June and December. The islands of Palau, however, are fairly well protected by the reef from all natural hazards, and typhoons are rare.

History

PREHISTORY

The prehistory of Palau and the origins of its people are still vague due to centuries of relative isolation and a lack of written historical records. Early history was primarily recorded through Palauan mythology.

Many archeologists believe the original settlers arrived from Indonesia as early as 1000 BC. The language and culture of Palau display similarities to the people the Philippines, Indonesia, and Melanesia. Between 1200 and 1600 AD, over 60,000 Palauans occupied villages on the majority of the Rock Islands. During this period there is evidence of contact between the people of Palau and many surrounding islands including Yap, New Guinea, and Indonesia. The extensive interaction with the people of Yap is well recorded in the mythology of both cultures, and Palau is the source of the well-known Yapese stone money.

> Lost Palauan sailors sometimes drifted as far as Guam and the Philippines in these prehistoric times.

FOREIGN GOVERNANCE

The Spanish recorded the first European sighting of the islands of Palau in the early 1500s, naming the islands "Los Palaos." The first recorded European contact occurred in 1783, when a British vessel, the *Antelope*, under the command of Captain Henry Wilson, shipwrecked on Palau's reef. By this time, many of the Rock Island villages had been abandoned, and the majority of the population lived on the islands of Babeldaob, Koror, Peleliu, and Angaur. Shortly after the shipwreck of the *Antelope*, trade between Palau and Europe began in earnest. The introduction of firearms and an outbreak of smallpox during the late 1800s decreased the population of Palau by more than nine tenths.

Foreign governance of Palau began in 1885, when Pope Leo XIII recognized Spain's rule of Palau. Catholic missions and school systems were established, local warfare was reduced, and trade was established with the Japanese.

Palau was sold to Germany in 1899. The German legal system was thus recognized, and a jail was opened. Additionally, the German administration began mining phosphate in Palau, and the use of foreign currency commenced.

When Japan declared war on Germany in 1914, Palau became a naval district under Japanese command. Following World War I, a League of Nations mandate officially awarded the islands of Palau to Japan. The Japanese continued to mine phosphate and bauxite and to enhance the infrastructure of Palau. Under Japanese rule the tourism industry of Palau began gaining value.

WORLD WAR II

Palau is known internationally as the location of several battles during World War II. Through the war, the Japanese and American militaries battled over Palau as a military stronghold. Particularly notable battles occurred on the islands of Angaur and Peleliu. The Battle of Peleliu, which raged from September to November of 1944, had the highest casualty rate of any battle in the Pacific.

The horrors of World War II have had a lasting impact upon the islands of Palau, and remnants of the war are still found throughout the islands. Bombings and Japanese executions resulted in the deaths of many Palauans. The people of Palau were forced to flee their homes and hide in the jungles and caves throughout Babeldaob only to return later and find their villages had been destroyed.

U.S. GOVERNANCE AND INDEPENDENCE

Following World War II, Palau became a United Nations Trust Territory under U.S. administration. The United States was tasked with improving the infrastructure of Palau in order to build a self-sufficient nation. However, agriculture and industry were never developed, and Palau became economically dependent on foreign aid. Half of the population became govern-

---

The Battle of Peleliu

From September to November of 1944, the beautiful Pacific island of Peleliu was the stage of death and carnage as the United States and the Empire of Japan engaged in one of World War II's bloodiest battles. U. S. Major General William Rupertus predicted that Operation Stalemate II, which was over control of a tiny airstrip on the small island, would only take four days. It lasted instead for 73 days and claimed the lives of 18,800 American and Japanese soldiers.

The Battle of Peleliu remains one of the most controversial battles of the war due to the incredible death toll and the questionable value of the airstrip. On September 14, 1944 the 1st Marine Division attacked the "White Beach" and "Orange Beach" to find the Japanese forces dug into a honeycomb defense system that utilized fortified bunkers, underground tunnels, and the caves of the island. The Battle of Peleliu culminated with the infamous attack on Bloody Nose Ridge, an attack during which 60% of the Marines involved became casualties. Following the capture of Bloody Nose Ridge and the island of Peleliu, 35 Japanese soldiers held out in the cave systems of Peleliu until April 22, 1947, becoming the final surrenders of World War II.

Despite the brutal battle needed to capture Peleliu from the Japanese, the airfield was of little military use for future American battles in the Pacific. However, the battles fought on the islands of Peleliu and Angaur prepared the American forces for the defensive tactics used by the Japanese on Okinawa and Iwo Jima. There are monuments and memorials throughout the islands of Angaur and Peleliu, which mark and honor the battles that occurred there.

ment employees funded by the United States.

In 1980, Haruo Remeliik was elected the first president of the Republic of Palau. The next year, Palau's constitution was finalized and signed. The constitution of Palau is particularly noteworthy as it declared Palau the first nuclear-free nation in the world.

Negotiations for a Compact of Free Association between Palau and the United States began in 1982. As part of the contract, the United States demanded the right to dock military vessels, which may contain nuclear arms, in Palau's waters. It took over a decade and a constitutional amendment for the Compact to be finalized. On October 1, 1994 Palau gained its independence by signing the Compact of Free Association with the United States and thus becoming a sovereign nation. The Compact provided Palau with $450 million in aid over a fifteen year period. Later that year, Palau became the newest member of the United Nations.

The Republic of Palau is a presidential representative democratic republic. In Palau, the president serves as both the head of state and the head of government. Like the United States government, the government of Palau is divided into an executive branch, a legislative branch called the Palau National Congress, and an independent judiciary. Palau does not possess an independent military and relies upon U.S. protection, but many Palauans serve in the U.S. Armed Forces. The Compact also guarantees financial assistance from the United States.

Culture and People

Traditional Palauan culture is based on complicated political and social structures and features a variety of unique and interesting customs. Modern Palauan culture is a codependent balance between local tradition and Western influence. Palau has managed to remain more traditional than other Westernized islands, such as Guam, while offering more of the comforts of Western society than traditional Pacific islands, such as the islands of the Federated States of Micronesia.

Traditional Palau was divided into villages, each with its own chief. These chiefs were men from the most powerful families, or clans, in the village and were selected by the powerful women of the village. The whole of Palau was governed by a council of chiefs representing the different villages of Palau. This council held its political meetings in traditional men's houses, known as *bais*, and was led by two High Chiefs known as the *Reklai* of Melekeok and the *Ibedul* of Koror.

> The general state of traditional Palau was one of conflict, as wars between villages were very common.

Gender roles and the Palauan family structure are specified by an intricate and complicated system. The matrilineal lineages of the Palauan family were the most important familial relationships, and although families lived with the father's family, they were members of their mother's clan and would return to their mother's village following the death of the father. A Palauan marriage occurred when a man or his family offered money beads, the traditional currency, to a woman's family in exchange for a woman. This union required the husband and his family to present money and gifts periodically to the family of the wife at major customary events.

For this reason daughters are viewed as more valuable children and sons as more expensive for a family.

In Palau there was a fairly rigid separation of genders. Traditionally, the men of Palau spent their days fishing, engaged in local warfare, or headhunting for men of other tribes. The local crafts for men include woodcarving, jewelry-making, canoe-building, and practicing magic. The women of the village were responsible for farming, preparing food, and caring for children. They also spent their time weaving, making pottery and herb medicines, and tattooing. Although there are still gender roles in Palau today, the taboos are much less rigid.

> The wealth of a Palauan man is often measured by the number of sisters he has.

The first Spanish sailors to explore Palau reported the traditional attire for the Palauan man to be complete nudity. When the influence of Western society pressured more modest dress, it became common for the local men to don long, red loin cloths, known as *osakas*. Traditionally, Palauan women wore grass skirts and remained topless. You will also see many Palauan women wearing one or more small clay beads on strings around their necks. These beads are money beads, the traditional currency of Palau. An unmarried girl wears the beads of her parents, while a married woman is presented money beads by her husband's family. These beads, which are a variety of shapes, sizes, and colors representing different values, are signs of wealth and social status in Palau. The historical origin of these beads remains a great mystery. Women in Palau continue to wear the traditional money beads. These beads, however, are becoming rarer, as over the years many have been lost or taken away from Palau. Today, Palauans wear modest, Western clothing. It is considered disrespectful, particularly among older and more traditional Palauans for women to expose their thighs, so long shorts or skirts are worn.

Many traditional Palauan customs and ceremonies that have existed for centuries are still practiced today. Each ceremony has its own rituals and practices. There is, however, a common thread throughout all ceremonies held in Palau: feasts. Palau has a culture which places great emphasis on food, and all of the customs of Palau include an elaborate and abundant feast.

The First Birth Ceremony is a very unique Palauan tradition. After delivering her first child, a Palauan woman undergoes a traditional bathing ritual which concludes with a ceremony presenting the new mother and

Gun Violence and the Presidents of Palau

According to Article 13 of the Constitution of Palau, it is illegal for anyone but military personnel and law enforcement officers to bear firearms or ammunition. However, firearms have had a major impact on the government of Palau in spite of the constitutional ban.

On the night of June 30, 1985, President Haruo Remeliik, the first president of Palau was assassinated in front of his home. Former Minister of State, John O. Ngiraked, and his wife were later convicted, but the murder weapon was never recovered. On August 20, 1988, the second president of Palau, Lazarus Salii, was also found shot to death in what was later ruled a suicide.

child to the community. This custom begins with the *Omesur*, or bathing. The new mother returns home to her parents, and a hut is erected for her. Inside the hut the mother is covered with a combination of ginger and oil (to prevent her skin from being burned) and is bathed with a mixture of hot water and medicinal leaves and herbs. Traditionally, this ceremony might take up to ten months, but modern bathing ceremonies usually last from five to ten days. At the end of the bathing ritual, on the day of her presentation ceremony, the new mother takes her *Onemgat*, or final steam bath. During this bath the woman sits above a pot of steaming herbs selected for their smell or medicinal qualities and is cleansed.

The final stage of the First Birth Ceremony is the *Ngasech*. The mother is dressed in a decorative skirt featuring the colors of her clan, her hair is pulled back and decorated with flowers, and her body is covered in yellow oil. Tradition mandates that the woman is topless during the ceremony, and although most women continue this practice, some women choose to wear a woven coconut bra. Following the arrival of the husband and his family, the mother will emerge from her hut and walk across woven coconut mats to be presented to the husband's family and the community. The woman will also hold up a bouquet of flowers, specific to her clan, while holding her breasts with her other arm.

This is a ceremony which has remained particularly consistent with its origins. A visitor to Palau is likely to see photos of women during their First Birth Ceremonies and may be lucky enough to witness one of these ceremonies in person.

House Parties

Social custom grants a member of the community the opportunity to throw a party when purchasing a house. Members of the community will gather to celebrate and to present the homebuyer with monetary gifts. The party is either held at the house of a relative or at a local bar. There is usually a live band or DJ, and it is common for the dance parties to cha-cha well into the night.

The funeral service is another ceremony in Palau marked by a large social gathering and carrying social and monetary obligations for Palauans from many different villages. Palauan tradition dictates that the deceased are to be buried in the village of their mother. Custom requires all family members, friends, and acquaintances to attend the feast and offer monetary gifts to the bereaved family. These gifts are used to pay for the funeral and to aid in filling any void the death may have left in the family's income. The size of the gathering for a funeral in Palau is quite impressive, and the monetary gifts presented are often substantial. At the feast the body will be on display, and the feast will generally conclude with a procession to the burial. There are cemeteries in Palau, but it is not uncommon to see the burial sites of ancestors on the property of a family or clan. A second funeral service is held one year later on the first anniversary of the death. The funeral custom in Palau is an integral aspect of Palauan culture as it warrants a large social gathering, and the tradition of giving gifts at a funeral has an impact on the economy of the nation.

Palauan funerals are often held outside the homes of family members, and are easily identified by large tents and crowds of people. Although these events may illicit curiosity among tourists and observation from a distance is appropriate, please be respectful of the privacy of the locals and resist the urge to impose upon a custom.

Bais are traditional meeting houses crucial to Palauan culture. The surviving *bais* serve as links between modern Palau and its traditional culture. Although the role of the *bais* has evolved, their importance to the people of Palau has not diminished. Traditionally there are two types of *bais*: *Bai ra Rubak* and *Bai ra Cheldebechel*. The *Bai ra Rubak* was built for the chiefs. These *bais* were the venues for important meetings and discussions crucial to village governance. Women were not permitted to enter the chiefs' *bais*. The *Bai ra Cheldebechel* served as a clubhouse for the village. These *bais* served as traditional schools and hosted many other village functions.

The *bai* is a wooden, single-room structure with a peaked roof built on stone platforms. They have been built as long as 80 feet (24 meters), as wide as 20 feet (6 meters), and as tall as 40 feet (12 meters). The rectangular rooms have hardwood floors and often feature multiple fireplaces. Both the inside and outside of the *bai* is decorated with hand carved pictures often depicting the local legends of Palau and noteworthy historic events. The structures are amazing tributes to the traditional architecture of the Pacific islands. The *bais* of Palau are unique among similar traditional buildings in Malaysia and Indonesia in that the *bais* were constructed by hand without the use of nails, screws, or pegs.

Nature and wars, including tribal battles and World War II, have destroyed the majority of authentic *bais*, and many of the *bais* in Palau today

Betel Nut

Chewing betel nut is a traditional pastime that remains very popular for the Palauan people. The betel or areca nut is the seed of the areca palm tree, which grows throughout the islands of the Pacific, Asia, and parts of Africa. The Palauan tradition of chewing usually involves slicing open the nut, filling it with slaked lime, and wrapping it in a pepper leaf prior to chewing. Chewing the betel nut produces red-stained saliva, which chewers spit in voluminous quantities. The practice is similar to its Western equivalent of chewing tobacco. Chewing betel nut produces a feeling of warmth and acts as a mild stimulant. Frequent and prolonged chewing will result in red-stained teeth and can lead to cancer and a variety of other health concerns.

Visitors will notice both the men and women of Palau carrying small woven baskets or a variety of small bags which contain betel nuts, pepper leaves, and jars or plastic bottles of slaked lime. These betel nut kits are known as *tets*. Many people today also add a piece of cigarette or chewing tobacco to their betel nut, and it is common for people to keep a bottle with their *tet* in which they can spit.

Traditionally, chewing betel nut was an important custom for the adults in a village, and betel nuts were often farmed, traded, and given as gifts. A visitor interested in sampling betel nut can purchase the nuts, leaves, and lime at many of the local stores or village stands. Also, many locals would be willing to share their betel nut if asked politely. First-time chewers may want to ask a local to prepare their chew for them as using too much lime can result in burns.

are recreations of their predecessors. The *bai* located in the village of Air-ai, however, is an original *Bai ra Rubak*. Although it has been repaired and renovated, it is the only authentic traditional *bai*, and many of the original materials, such as the foundation and the flooring, remain. This *bai* has served the village Airai for the past 300 years.

SOCIAL NORMS

Palauans are aware of the cultural differences of foreigners and are very forgiving of any cultural faux pas. However, they also greatly appreciate efforts to respect Palauan customs.

Alcohol Consumption

On payday weekends, locals go out drinking, and drunk driving is a major problem on the island. As a visitor, try to set a good example and drink responsibly. For your own safety, call a taxi or arrange transportation back to your hotel before you drink. Some of the states

> Palau and Micronesia are two of the largest per capita consumers of Budweiser products in the world.

of Palau, such as Kayangel and Ngaremlengui, prohibit alcohol consumption. Also, be aware that many older islanders do not approve of drinking or the lifestyle of some younger Palauans in general.

Cultural Conduct

When attending traditional events, it is important to respect traditional customs. Be aware of the general mood of the event. A good guideline is to do as the elders do rather than as the younger, more Americanized locals do.

It is highly recommended that you dress conservatively at all cultural events. Women should wear knee length skirts and tops that cover their shoulders. Men should wear collared shirts and clean shorts or pants. You may feel overdressed, as some locals will be in dirty and even torn clothing, but locals will still appreciate when you dress nicely. Do not drink alcohol at these events, unless it is a house party, even if locals are drinking. Accept food if you are offered it; you may even be served first because you are a guest, but defer to the elders, as local culture deems they should be served before everyone else. Keep your voice low when talking, and be aware that others may be listening to you anytime you are in a public place.

Dining

At most restaurants, food is served as it is made and not when all the dishes for a table are ready. Many locals eat family style and share things as they come out. Also, some restaurants close between lunch and dinner, giving the staff a chance to rest between

> Many restaurants can substitute tofu for meat if you are searching for a vegetarian or healthy option. Just ask!

shifts. Call ahead to make sure the kitchen is open if you are looking for a late lunch.

Dress

Due to the strong influence of Christianity on Palau, many modern Palauans dress modestly. As a guest in Palau, you should consider dressing modestly when you go out into the community. This does not mean covering everything from your neck to your feet; it is the tropics, after all! Just remember to wear longer shorts or skirts; most locals wear shorts and skirts down to their knees. Stay away from skimpy tops; sleeveless tops are acceptable, but spaghetti straps and strapless tops should be avoided. When spending time at your resort or out on the Rock Islands, it is fine to wear a bathing suit, though most locals swim in shorts and a T-shirt. Make sure to dress appropriately when going into town and especially when on Babeldaob or an outer island.

Time

Everything happens slower in the islands! Many restaurants have only one or two cooks and as many stoves. Be patient and enjoy your evening; complaining will not make your food arrive any faster.

What's in a Name?

In Palauan culture, directly asking a person their name is considered taboo and disrespectful. Palauan courtesy dictates that individuals should inquire as to another's name by introducing themselves or by asking a third party. This is a practice which may seem strange to many foreign visitors.

Also, like many Asian cultures, it is degrading to pat a person on the top of his or her head. It is often natural for Westerners to pat children or shorter people on the head, but this action is an insult in Palau.

Travel Information

GETTING THERE AND AWAY

Currently the only carrier that flies to Palau year-round is Continental Airlines. This state of affairs tends to result in high ticket prices. Occasionally, chartered flights from Japan and China are available. All Continental flights arrive and depart in either the evening or late at night.

See page 27 for more information about flying to Micronesia and Palau.

HEALTH AND SAFETY

As a general rule, Palau is a very safe place to visit or live, but it is always good to take precautions. Travelers should be careful when leaving valuables in their rooms; bring a small lock for your suitcase, and lock valuables inside when you leave the room. Do not leave diving equipment on patios or balconies.

When out and about in town, try not to carry a lot of cash. Walk on well lit streets when possible or take a taxi if it is late. If you are not confident that your taxi driver is sober, do not get in the car; the hotel or restaurant can try another company or arrange alternate transportation.

If you do find yourself in a robbery situation, give up your valuables and report the incident to the police immediately. The island is so small that the police can sometimes figure out who committed the crime and recover stolen goods, though the process is sometimes slow. Even if they cannot, losing a few dollars and your camera is a lot better than being physically attacked.

Be wary of drunken locals, particularly males, who can be confrontational. If you are looking to have a few drinks, it is recommended to patronize the tourist bars.

If you are the victim of a crime, call the **police** (911). There are two police/fire stations: one in downtown Koror, the other in Melekeok on the Compact Road.

Staying hydrated is extremely important. Bottled water is available at all markets in Koror and in the villages. Local brands of bottled water will run about $0.50 per bottle. Imported brands are available at higher prices. Avoid tap water, even in Koror where it is processed. Waterborne illnesses, including amoebas and parasites, are common and can result in serious gastrointestinal distress. Ask at restaurants and hotels about the water they serve.

Many locals leave food out all day, so people can eat as they get hungry. Food left out, especially in the tropics, can foster rapid bacterial growth. It is rude to turn down an offering of food, but do not consume any food that you believe may be unsafe.

Palau has three different types of **healthcare facilities**: the national hospital, private clinics, and rural dispensaries. Generally, the medical facilities are adequate for routine medical care but limited in resources and services. If you can wait until you return home to take care of your medical needs, you should. In comparison to the other islands featured in this book, Palau offers the best range of services. If you do find yourself in need of medical services in Palau, be prepared to pay in cash ahead of time for services.

The **Belau National Hospital** (488-2558) is located on Ngerkerbesang Island in Koror. The hospital employs local and international doctors, nurses, and technicians, many with degrees obtained in the United States. The emergency room is open 24 hours daily, and outpatient services are available Monday through Friday 7:30 AM to 4:30 PM except on national holidays. Services are limited, but they can work to arrange a medical evacuation in severe cases. Prescriptions can be obtained if they are in stock, but brands are limited.

There are also two private clinics located in Koror. **Dr. Robert's clinic** is located next to the hospital and is open during regular business hours and some Saturdays. **Dr. Yano's clinic** is located across from Surangels and is open early in the morning and after normal business hours.

Outside of Koror and on the outer islands, you will find **dispensaries** scattered throughout the different states. These remote offices are usually staffed by a nurse, though some are not staffed daily, and can take care of things like changing dressings, diagnosing rashes, and doling out medicines when they are available. These dispensaries should be visited as a last resort, as many services are not available. Many over-the-counter medications, contact solutions, feminine products, and sunblock can be purchased in Koror at Surangels Grocery Store or at the WCTC shopping plaza (see pg 214).

SERVICES

Internet Access

More and more restaurants and hotels are offering patrons internet access, either for free or for low hourly fees. If you brought a laptop, head to Abai Coffee Shop, Drop Off Bar and Grill, Sam's Tours, Palau Pacific Resort, or Penthouse Hotel. There are also a few internet cafés with computer terminals that guests can use for as long as they want to pay the rates. Check out the Island Mart internet café across from Palau High School, Coconut Cyber Café next to the Rock Island Café, and the internet café at the DW Motel in downtown Koror.

Laundry

There are many small laundries scattered around downtown Koror and in Babeldaob where you can wash and dry your clothes or leave them for wash and fold service for a small fee. Washers use cold water only, so whites will never look as good as they did back home, but your clothes will be cleaned, dried, and neatly folded. If you are particular about your laundry soap, pick up some supplies at WCTC or Surangels and ask the attendant to use it; otherwise, you will get the cheapest soap on the island and pay extra for it. Many of the hotels in Koror also offer wash and fold services; ask at the front desk for more details or for the location of the closest laundry. If you are going to wash your own clothes, it is best to go in the morning or during the hottest part of the day; locals bring their wash in the evenings, and it can get very crowded.

Mail

The post office is located in the center of Koror and is open Monday through Friday from 9 AM to 4:30 PM. Palau issues its own stamps. There is a mailbox at the police station, but it is rumored that mail is never collected and rain leaks in the box. Drop off your mail inside the post office when it is open to ensure that it is sent. Stamp collectors should check out the shop attached to the post office for some awesome island stamps.

> Palau was actually the first country to release an Elvis stamp.

ATMs and Banks

The two major banks on Palau are the Bank of Guam (488-2696), located in downtown Koror next to Palau Community College, and Bank of Hawaii (488-6202), located across from Palau High School. Both are FDIC insured and can help you with most of your banking needs on the island. The banks keep very short hours; typically, they are open from 9:30 AM to 3:00 PM, and they tend to get very busy at lunch and at the end of pay weeks. ATMs can be found outside of either of these banks as well as on the bottom floor of the WCTC Shopping Center. Beware that communication errors, power outages, and cash depletion can render these ATMs inoperable, especially on weekends.

Credit Cards

Although many restaurants are accepting credit cards, some still take only cash and the credit machines go down quite often. If you do not have cash, ask before you order to make sure that credit cards are accepted and that the machines are working.

Getting Around

AIR

Currently there are no planes flying to the outer islands, but there has been talk of opening an airstrip in either Angaur or Peleliu. Until that happens, you can take to the air on a **Palau Helicopter Tour** (488-6669). Enjoy Palau's emerald Rock Islands and turquoise waters from the sky. You might even get to see one of the few remaining dugongs – an animal similar to the manatee – in Malakal Harbor! Prices start at $75 per person for a 10-15 minute ride.

LAND

Rental Cars

Renting a car in Palau has its advantages and disadvantages. It is only recommended if you plan on exploring Babeldaob. Taxis and tour companies can take you on guided tours of the big island, but they are often expensive ($50 or more) and less convenient than a rental car. Having your own car will allow you to go off the beaten path and to take your time. It is also a great idea if you are planning to spend a night or two at one of the little beach resorts up north. Depending on your needs and the company you use, renting a car can be less expensive than hiring a taxi, but one disadvantage is the difficulty of navigating the unpaved, unsigned roads, particularly at night. Friendly locals are always happy to give you directions if you stop to ask, but they may be unclear or just plain wrong. If you plan to remain in and around Koror, a rental car is unnecessary. Stop at the Palau Visitors Authority or Palau National Communications Corporation to obtain a road map.

> **Budget Car Rental of Micronesia** Downtown Koror or at Palau Pacific Resort; 488-6232, budgetpalau@palaunet.com

> **PIDC Car Rental** Topside, Koror at the PIDC Center; Cost: sedan $40, SUV $60; 488-8350, 488-8351, pidc@palaunet.com

Taxis

Taxis are available within Koror and to and from the airport, although a hotel shuttle is usually cheaper. Any hotel, restaurant, or bar can call a taxi for you. Tourists should expect to pay $5-7 a ride, though some drivers will try to charge more. Make sure to negotiate a fair price before you take the ride to avoid any surprises at the end. It becomes more difficult and more expensive to find a taxi after 10 PM. Sometimes you can make plans with a driver earlier in the evening to get a ride late at night. Call 779-7730, and ask for Ray for a reliable and sober driver.

Drunk Drivers

Be wary of drivers who appear to be under the influence. If you are not comfortable taking a ride from your cabbie, call another cab company. Report any problems to the Belau Tourism Association or Palau Visitors Authority (488-2793).

Buses

There is one bus company, **Biib** (488-4211, bbi@palaunet.com), which runs a shopping bus around Koror. Stops include the Rock Island Café, WCTC, and Elilai Restaurant. Email for current bus schedules.

Hitchhiking

Hitchhiking is possible around Palau, and some locals are happy to give you a lift. There are always assumed risks, however. Drinking and driving is a growing problem in Palau, and it is usually safer to take a taxi. If you are trying to go to Babeldaob, ask your hotel if they can arrange a ride for you.

Sea

Palau's outer islands are easily accessed by boat. Kayangel is two hours by speed boat; Peleliu is three hours by slow boat or one hour by speed boat; Angaur is four hours by slow boat or one and a half hours by speed boat. The government provides boat transportation to and from the islands on a set schedule. Contact the **Palau Visitors Authority** (488-2793), or the individual state governments for boat schedules and ticket pricing. Be aware that the boats are old and sometimes break down, which could take some time to repair. Also, unfavorable sea conditions could keep the boats docked. Another option is to schedule private transportation through local tour operators via speed boat.

Where to Stay

Inexpensive

DW Motel Tucked down a driveway just off the main road in downtown Koror, DW Motel offers quiet and comfort at an affordable price. Rooms are clean and comfortable and include a private bathroom. Rooms do not have private phones, but there is a communal phone on each floor. *Downtown Koror; Amenities: A/C, mini-fridge, laundry; Cost: room $45 and up; 488-2641, palau7796768@yahoo.com.tw*

Lehn's Motel & Apartments Though technically this hotel is in downtown Koror, it is actually located down a roughly paved road in the neighborhood of Ngerchebed. If you plan to walk, be aware that the road is very dark at night and is a popular spot among local youths who sometimes cause trouble. That being said, Lehn's offers single rooms, double rooms, and suites complete with cooking facilities. The hotel is also home to a very large crocodile (safely enclosed in a pen), and the staff is happy to throw him some meat for your "entertainment." *Ngerchebed, downtown Koror; Amenities: A/C, kitchenette; Cost: single or double $45 and up, suite $75; 488-1486, lehnsmotel@palaunet.com*

Tree-D Hotel Tree-D is located on the main road in Koror and offers private rooms at a budget-friendly price. The staff is happy to accommodate your needs when possible, including airport pick-up for a fee. *Koror; Amenities: A/C, TV, mini-fridge; Cost: single or double $40; 488-3856, treed@palaunet.com*

Palau Beach Bungalows Located in Melekeok state on the big island of Babeldaob, Palau Beach Bungalows are a great place to stay if you want to experience the "local" side Palau. Bungalows are clean and air-conditioned, and most have en suite bathrooms and kitchens, which is good because the restaurant in Melekeok is not always open. The bungalows are located on a sandy road close to the ocean and are perfect for those looking for a quiet night or a morning of surfing off the pier. *Melekeok; Amenities: A/C, kitchenette; Cost: bungalow $40; 587-2533, palaubeachbunglaows@palaunet.com*

Moderate

Penthouse Hotel The Penthouse Hotel offers large, clean, comfortable rooms and the restaurant on the property offers delicious local dishes and freshly baked pies. Located just off the main road in downtown Koror, this hotel is also within walking distance to many stores and restaurants. Additionally, there is a small fitness center and a beauty salon at the hotel. Free wireless internet is available. *Downtown Koror; Amenities: A/C, TV, mini-fridge, wireless internet, room service, fitness center; Cost: single or double $80 and up; 488-1941, manager@penthousepalau.com, www.penthousepalau.com*

Carp Island Resort Carp Island offers guests a unique experience on an isolated island 45 minutes from Koror by boat. Rooms range from rustic cabins with two or three twin-sized platforms, sleeping mats, and shared bathrooms to more comfortable rooms with real beds and private bathrooms. The resort offers three meals a day on a preset menu; meals must be ordered in advance. Note that the meals are very expensive, so bring your own snacks and drinks if possible. You can arrange snorkeling, diving, and kayaking trips from the resort, take a hike around the island, or see some Yapese stone money that was left behind years ago. *Carp Island; Amenities: fan, beach access; Cost: dive house $65 and up, cottage $90 and up; 488-2978, carp@palaunet.com, www.carpislandpalau.com*

Green Bay Hotel Green Bay Hotel offers large, clean, simple rooms at reasonable prices and features spectacular views of the Rock Islands. Though located in Koror, Green Bay Hotel is a little off the main road on a dark and winding road. You will need to take a taxi to most restaurants and sites of interest. *Koror; Amenities: A/C, TV, mini-fridge; Cost: single or double $90 and up; 488-5584, info@greenbayhotel.com, www.greenbayhotelpalau.com*

North Beach Cottages Looking for something a little different? Head to the northern tip of Babeldaob, and stay at the North Beach Cottages in Choll, Ngaraard. Each cottage is made of local mahogany wood, surrounded by lush foliage, and located on a sandy beach. The resort features only four cottages, offering guests a very private retreat. Cottages include air-conditioning, private balconies, and private bathrooms. The restaurant on the property serves local dishes, including fresh seafood and local fruits and vegetables. *Choll, Ngaraard; Amenities: A/C, balcony; Cost: bungalow $120, campsite $25 (tent not provided); 488-8232, northbeachcottages@palaunet.com, www.northbeachcottages.com*

Cliffside Hotel Palau This hotel is located on Ngerkebesang Island on a quiet cliffside overlooking downtown Koror and the Rock Islands. The Cliffside Hotel has a restaurant and bar as well as a swimming pool and hot tub. Rooms are large and comfortable and feature great views! *Ngerkebesang Island; Amenities: A/C, TV, mini-fridge, wireless internet; Cost: single $120 and up, double $180 and up; 488-4590, cliffside@palaunet.com*

Airai View Hotel & Spa You can tell the Airai View Hotel in Airai state used to be a prime destination, but it is now a little dilapidated. At the time of writing the hotel is undergoing renovations, though it is still open for business; beware of construction hazards, power outages, etc. Airai View is the only hotel on the island with a waterslide, a favorite of local children but also in need of repair. The pool also is in need of a good scrub and a large dose of chlorine! Located near the airport, you will need to rent a car to get to restaurants and most sites of interest. *Airai; Amenities: A/C, TV, mini-fridge, pool; Cost: single or double $130 and up; 587-3530, services@airaiview.com*

Rose Garden Resort The rooms at this mountainside resort are simple but clean. They feature amazing views of the Rock Islands and Koror Lagoon. The resort, located on Ngerkebesang Island, features an onsite restaurant with delicious, reasonably priced local and international dishes. *Ngerkebesang Island; Amenities: A/C, TV, laundry; Cost: bungalow $130 and up; 488-7671, rosegardenresort@fastmail.fm, www.palau-hotel.com*

The Carolines Resort Each private bungalow at the Carolines Resort on Ngerkebesang Island is designed in the style of traditional Palauan architecture and built using local resources such as mahogany, bamboo, and mangrove wood. Though they look rustic from the outside, each bungalow comes with a private bathroom, air-conditioning, and television. Enjoy spectacular views of the Rock Islands and Koror Lagoon from your private balcony. *Ngerkebesang Island; Amenities: A/C, TV, mini-fridge, balcony, laundry; Cost: bungalow $155 and up; 488-3754, carolines@palaunet.com, www.carolineresort.com*

Expensive

Sea Passion Hotel Palau's Sea Passion Hotel, completed in 2008, is one of the newest hotels on the island. The hotel, which is located in Koror near the bridge to Malakal Island, features a swimming pool, private beach, kayak and Jet Ski rentals, as well as an international restaurant and ocean side bar. Rooms have an upscale look and views to match. Wireless internet is available. *Koror; Amenities: A/C, TV, mini-fridge, wireless internet, complimentary breakfast, pool, beach access, kayaks, Jet Skis; Cost: single $170 and up, double $200 and up (includes hotel tax); 488-0066, service@palauseapassion.com, www.palauseapassion.com*

Palau Plantation Resort Tucked away from the hustle and bustle of Koror's main strip, the Palau Plantation Resort offers comfort and privacy. Enjoy evenings in the hot tub and views of the Rock Islands. The onsite restaurant has some good dishes, but they often do not have the ingredients to make what is on the menu. You will need to take taxis or rent a car to get to most restaurants and sites of interest. *Koror; Amenities: A/C, kitchenette, pool, hot tub; Cost: cabin $180 and up, villa $350 and up; 488-3631, plantation@palaunet.com, www.palau-resort.com*

Palau Royal Resort The Palau Royal Resort on Malakal Island offers its guests simple luxury. Their rooms are very clean and comfortable and come with all the amenities you would expect from a world class resort. The resort features a pool, spa, diving center, restaurant, fitness center, and beach bar. *Malakal Island; Amenities: A/C, TV, mini-fridge, wireless internet, pool, hot tub, fitness center, spa, restaurant, bar, beach access; Cost: room $230 and up; 488-2000, reservations@palau-royal-resort.com, www.palau-royal-resort.com*

Palasia Hotel Palau At the Palasia Hotel, located in the heart of downtown Koror, you will find peace among the hustle and bustle. The seven story hotel is one of the tallest buildings in Palau, and it offers great views of the northern Rock Islands. The rooms are clean, and the island decorations are bright and cheery if a little dated. The hotel features a pool, two restaurants, a bar, spa, and fitness center as well as meeting facilities. Free wireless internet is available. *Downtown Koror; Amenities: A/C, TV, mini-fridge, wireless internet, pool, fitness center, restaurant, bar; Cost: single or double $200 and up; 488-8888, res.palasia@palaunet.com, www.palasia-hotel.com*

Landmark Marina Hotel Located directly on the water on M-Dock in Koror, Landmark Marina offers clean, comfortable rooms and amazing views of the Rock Islands. The onsite restaurant is a churrascaria (Brazilian barbeque) serving up delicious dishes, and the bar has a quiet and refined atmosphere. The one downside is the hotel's close proximity to the trash repository; on windy nights, avoid sitting outside. Ask at the desk for private boat charters. *Koror; Amenities: A/C, TV, mini-fridge, wireless internet, complimentary breakfast, restaurant, bar, laundry, boat rentals; Cost: double $200 and up (includes hotel tax); 488-1069, service@landmarkmarina.com, www.landmarkmarina.com*

Palau Pacific Resort The most scenic resort on the island, Palau Pacific Resort features a private beach with some of the best snorkeling found in Palau, a swimming pool, multiple hot tubs, and beautiful gardens. Although pricey, this resort offers a pampered stay in paradise. Guests are also invited to attend organized activities by day and observe local dancing by night. The resort includes a fitness center and tennis court. Splash Dive Shop located at the Palau Pacific Resort can accommodate your diving needs. Wireless internet is available. *Ngerkebesang Island; Amenities: A/C, TV, mini-fridge, wireless internet, fitness center, pool, hot tub, beach access, tours; Cost: single or double $280 and up; 488-2600, info@ppr-palau.com, www.palauppr.com*

OUTER ISLAND ACCOMMODATIONS

For more information on visiting one of Palau's beautiful outer islands, please refer to pg 216 where you will learn more about transportation, amenities, activities, and what to expect.

Peleliu

Reiko's Inn Here you will find clean rooms and a friendly host. The inn is just minutes by bike to the beach or dock. Meals can be arranged with the host in advance. *Amenities: A/C, shared bathroom; Cost: single $25 and up; 345-1106*

Wenty's Sunset Inn This converted family home offers visitors an inexpensive place to stay while exploring the island of Peleliu. Kitchen facilities are available to guests and the friendly housekeeper is happy to help you with anything you need, including bike rentals and island tours. The rooms have two or three beds each, and most use a shared bathroom. The facilities could use a good scrubbing. *Amenities: fan, shared bathroom, beach access, bike rentals, tours; Cost: room $25 and up; 345-1080*

Storyboard Beach Resort The Storyboard Beach Resort consists of six traditional style cottages on a beautiful beach. Each cottage has a private bathroom with a hot shower, a ceiling fan, and a spectacular view from its private balcony. If you are looking for a place to relax without the distractions of everyday life, this is your place; you will not find a television, phone, or internet connection in the cottage, although there is a phone and internet connectivity in the office if you do need to plug in for a bit. There is also a dive shop and restaurant onsite. *Amenities: fan, private bathroom, hot water, balcony, restaurant, beach access; Cost: room $60 and up; 345-1019, storyboard@palaunet.com, www.storyboardresortpalau.com*

Dolphin Bay Resort This beautiful resort boasts small, private bungalows for your enjoyment. The rooms include air-conditioning and private bathrooms.

The beach area is great for taking in the island's colorful sunsets. Bikes are available for rent, and the resort has its own dive shop. The onsite restaurant and bar serves breakfast, lunch, and dinner. *Amenities: A/C, private bathroom, mini-fridge, hot water, restaurant, bar, beach access; Cost: bungalow $160 and up; 345-5555, 345-6666, pdivers@palaunet.com, www.dolphinbay-resort-peleliu.com*

Angaur

Island Villas Beach House This beach house has two bedrooms, two bathrooms, a kitchen, living area, and a large porch. Prepared meals are available upon request for an additional fee; please arrange in advance. The house, which is located on the ocean, may be shared with other visitors. *Amenities: A/C, TV, hot water, beach access; Cost: single $20, double $30; 277-1111, islandvillas@palaunet.com*

OK's Motel OK's Motel offers very simple accommodations and is perfect for people who want to experience the island without spending a lot of money on a place to stay. The motel staff can arrange a variety of tours, and meals are available upon request. *Amenities: fan, private bathroom, tours; Cost: single $35; 277-1006, okasiano@yahoo.com*

LIVEABOARDS

For visitors to Palau who are primarily interested in diving, liveaboards are another option for accommodations.

Big Blue Explorer The *Big Blue Explorer* is a 167-foot (51-meter), air-conditioned motor cruiser. Each spacious cabin features a private bathroom. You will enjoy delicious meals prepared by the ship's chef. Divers have the opportunity to make four dives everyday and, on most nights, a night dive for a total of 27 diving opportunities on the seven-day excursion. *Cost: 7 days/nights from $2249 per person for double occupancy; (800) 346-6116, www.divetrip.com/bigblue.htm*

Palau Aggressor II The *Palau Aggressor II* is a 106-foot (32-meter) vessel with eight rooms, accommodating up to 16 divers. Rooms have double or single berths. The ship features a hot tub on the deck, and the ship's chef cooks up delicious meals every night. Each day divers have the opportunity to make up to five dives, including night dives most nights. *Cost: 7 days/nights from $2935 per person for double occupancy; (800) 348-2628, palau@aggressor.com, www.aggressor.com*

The Ocean Hunter Fleet *Ocean Hunter I* is a 60-foot (18-meter) steel motor-sailer designed for up to six guest divers. *Ocean Hunter II* is a motor cruiser with six cabins to fit up to 12 guests comfortably. *Ocean Hunter III* is a 96-foot (29-meter), former research ship that has been transformed into a luxurious 16-diver ship. The *Ocean Hunter III* travels not just in Palau but throughout the Western Pacific and makes trips to the Southwest Islands of Palau and the outer islands of Yap. All three ships offer unlimited diving, personalized service, and delicious, low-fat meals for breakfast, lunch, and dinner. *Cost: 7 days/nights from $3495 per person for double occupancy; (800) 737-3483, reservation@oceanhunger.com, www.oceanhunger.com, www.palau-scuba.com*

Prevous page: Woman in first birth ceremony
Above: The islands of Palau from above
Below: Beach on Kayangel

Above: Traditional bai
Below: Capitol building of Palau

Above: Kids playing on Palau
Below: Sea turtle

Above: Snorkeling in Jellyfish Lake
Below: Traditional war canoe
Following pages: World War II tank on Peleliu; Ngardmau Falls, Palau

Where to Eat

Inexpensive

Abai Coffee House Just like your hometown coffee shop, Abai Coffee House offers a variety of hot and cold coffee drinks, teas, and smoothies, as well as artisan sandwiches, salads, and muffins. Stop in to Abai Coffee Shop for your morning fix of caffeine or for a cold drink in the afternoon. Daily, weekly, and monthly internet passes are available. *Downtown Koror across from the Palasia Hotel. Hours: Mon-Sat 7 AM-5 PM, Sun 7 AM-2 PM; Cost: drink $2-5*

Rock Island Café Known to the local ex-pat community as the "poor man's Denny's," Rock Island Café, located in downtown Koror across from the Palau High School gymnasium, serves local and international food, including foods from home like meatloaf and beef brisket. The restaurant serves breakfast, lunch, and dinner, but it is closed Friday nights and during the day on Saturday. Credit cards are accepted. *Downtown Koror. Hours: Sun-Thurs 6:30 AM-9 PM, Fri 6:30 AM-6 PM, Sat 6-10 PM; Cost: meal $4-8; 488-1010*

Emaimelei Restaurant A local favorite, Emaimelei serves local and Asian dishes, as well as delicious pizza. Located behind the WCTC building in downtown Koror, this restaurant offers big portions for small prices. The restaurant serves breakfast, lunch, and dinner. Credit cards are accepted. *Downtown Koror; Hours: 7 AM-9 PM; Cost: meal $4-8; 488-5905 or 488-5576*

Suriyothai Restaurant Located in downtown Koror across from Asahi Ball Field, Suriyothai Restaurant serves yummy Thai food at great prices. If you like spicy food, try the Pad Kra Pao. The restaurant serves lunch and dinner and only accepts cash. *Downtown Koror; Hours: 11 AM-2 PM, 4-8 PM; Cost: meal $4-8; 488-8160*

 Fresh Noodle The building located beside Koror Elementary School in downtown Koror does not look like much from the outside, but inside you will enjoy dinner and a show as you watch the cook make the noodles right in front of you. Fresh Noodle serves big portions at good prices at lunch and dinner, but only cash is accepted. *Downtown Koror; Hours: Mon-Sat 11 AM-2PM, 5-9 PM; Cost: meal $4-8*

Bem Ermii Burgers & Fries This burger cart in downtown Koror in the Ministry of Education parking lot is great for a quick meal or a late night snack. Open until 4 AM on weekends, you will find this place teeming with locals when the bars close. Bem Ermii serves the best milkshakes in Palau! The venue accepts cash only. *Downtown Koror; Hours: Sun-Thurs 10:30 AM-2 AM, Fri-Sat 10:30 AM-4 AM; Cost: burger $4-8; 488-4354*

Keam Restaurant Keam Restaurant features a small menu with plenty to brag about! Try the fish burrito and the fried ice cream. The restaurant serves lunch and is closed on Sundays. Only cash is accepted. *At Belau National Museum; Hours: Mon-Fri 11 AM-4 PM; Cost: meal $4-8; 488-2265*

Sarah's Yum Yum An eclectic array of offerings makes Sarah's Yum Yum a great place to visit. From tacos to udong noodles, Sarah's is sure to please those eating on a budget. Sarah's is located on Ngerkebesang Island, just past the Belau National Hospital. *Ngerkebesang Island; Hours: 11 AM-8 PM; Cost: meal $4-8; 488-5590*

Moderate

 Kramer's Bar and Restaurant This local haunt found near the Palau Royal Resort on Malakal Island is a favorite of the ex-pat crowd, which convenes nightly to enjoy great food, cold drinks, and lively conversation. The staff is friendly, the fish is always fresh, and the food is delicious. Try the Black Bean Tostada Salad or the Fisherman's Spear! Kramer's is open for lunch and dinner and is closed on Sundays. Credit cards are accepted. *Malakal Island; Hours: Mon-Sat 11 AM-2 PM, 6 PM-midnight; Cost: meal $9-15; 488-8448*

Penthouse Café The menu at Penthouse features local and international dishes, and be sure to try the dessert; Penthouse has some of the best cakes and pies on the island. The restaurant is open for breakfast, lunch, and dinner and accepts credit cards. *At the Penthouse Hotel in downtown Koror; Hours: 6:30 AM-10:30 PM; Cost: meal $9-15; 488-1941*

Bar-Ra-Cu-Da Bar and Restaurant Where the Mediterranean meets the Pacific, Bar-Ra-Cu-Da Bar at Fish n' Fins Dive Shop offers some of the best hummus and falafel on island. Unfortunately, due to the restaurant's proximity to the local trash repository, flies can be bothersome at this outdoor restaurant. If the wind is not in your favor, order takeout, and enjoy your Mediterranean platter indoors. The bar and restaurant is open for breakfast and lunch and accepts credit cards. *At Fish n' Fins Dive Shop in downtown Koror; Hours: 6 AM-6 PM; Cost: meal $9-15; 488-2637*

Jive Café and Restaurant Perfect for a light meal or tapas style dining, this Japanese restaurant also provides a nice atmosphere for a few drinks with friends. The restaurant is open for dinner and accepts credit cards. Jive Café is located just before bridge to Malakal Island. *Downtown Koror; Hours: 7-10:30 AM, 4:30-11 PM; Cost: meal $9-15; 488-5483*

Drop Off Bar and Grill at Neco Marine The home of Survivor Palau, Drop Off is a great place to enjoy a tasty bite on the water. Grab a beer and a burger and swap dive stories with other patrons. Do not forget to try the Poke Sashimi! Located behind Neco Marine and Dolphins Pacific in Malakal, the restaurant is open for lunch and dinner. Credit cards are accepted. *Malakal Island; Hours: 11 AM-2 PM, 4:30-10 PM; Cost: meal $9-15; 488-1755*

Bottom Time Bar and Grill The Bottom Time Bar, located at Sam's Tours in Malakal, is a great place to eat before or after a water adventure. Serving bar fare and fresh fish every day, Bottom Time is open for breakfast, lunch, and dinner. Credit cards are accepted. *Malakal Island; Hours: 7:30 AM-8 PM daily; Cost: meal $9-15; 488-4382*

Carp Restaurant A local favorite, this hard-to-find restaurant offers large servings of local and Asian-inspired dishes at great prices. Try the sautéed kangkum, a leafy green similar to spinach. Carp Restaurant is open for lunch and dinner. Credit cards are accepted. *Malakal Island; Hours: 11 AM-2 PM, 4:30-8 PM; Cost: meal $9-15; 488-3314*

Red Rooster Café Though a little off the beaten path, the Red Rooster Café has a large menu full of delicious dishes. Try the restaurant's locally brewed namesake beer, Red Rooster! The restaurant accepts credit cards. *On T-Dock in Koror; Hours: 4-10 PM; Cost: $9-15; 488-5291*

Rip Tide Bar and Grill Rip Tide has atmosphere to spare with its private beach and views of the Rock Islands, but the menu selections fall a little flat. The restaurant is open for lunch and dinner, but it is often rented out on the weekends by locals; if you are looking for a quiet meal, call ahead. Credit cards are accepted. *At the end of Malakal Island; Hours: 11 AM-2 PM, 5-9 PM; Cost: meal $9-15; 488-3486*

Sakura Restaurant Sakura hits a homerun by fusing Japanese flavor and locally grown vegetables. Try the Cold Soba Salad or the Cheesy Tofu! Sakura serves lunch and dinner and accepts credit cards. *Next to the Bank of Guam in downtown Koror; Hours: 11 AM-10 PM; Cost: meal $9-15; 488-8793*

Expensive

Palm Bay Bistro Perfect for a nice night out, Palm Bay Bistro aims to please with an array of dishes. Enjoy your meal by the water on the outdoor deck or relax in the air-conditioning in one of the big booths. Try the Char-grilled Herb Chicken or the Stuffed Pork Chops. Palm Bay Bistro, located near the West Plaza Malakal Hotel, is open for lunch and dinner. Credit cards are accepted. *Malakal Island; Hours: 4-9 PM; Cost: meal $15 and up; 488-3476*

The Taj The Taj brings a taste of India to Palau. Serving deliciously rich curries, tandoori grilled meats, and fresh nan, the Taj is not to be missed during your stay in Palau. Many vegetarian options are also available. For a great deal, visit the Taj on Friday for the all-you-can-eat lunch buffet. The Taj, located above the Bank of Guam in downtown Koror, is open for lunch and dinner and accepts credit cards. *Downtown Koror; Hours: 11 AM-2 PM, 4:30-10 PM; Cost: meal $15 and up; 488-2227*

Coconut Terrace Although the buffets are a budget buster, the food is delicious. Treat yourself to the Sunday brunch and you will not be disappointed. Enjoy local dancing on Saturday nights. The restaurant is open for breakfast, lunch, and dinner and serves dishes buffet or a la carte. Credit cards are accepted. *At the Palau Pacific Resort; Hours: 6 AM-9 PM; Cost: meal $15 and up; 488-2600*

Dragon Tei Dragon Tei offers an authentic Japanese experience with a menu to satisfy all. Portions are small and a bit pricy, but enjoyed tapas-style Dragon Tei will be a hit. Try the carpaccio! Dragon Tei is open nightly for dinner. Credit cards are accepted. *Topside, Koror; Hours: 5-11 PM; Cost: $15 and up; 488-2779*

Elilai One step into Elilai and you will feel like you have been transported to a chic restaurant in Los Angeles until you take in the spectacular views of downtown Koror and the Rock Islands from this hilltop retreat. The menu features many delicious options, but all elegance comes with a price. Try having lunch for a more budget-friendly option. Elilai serves lunch and dinner and accepts credit cards. *At the Belvedere Apartment complex on Ngerkebesang Island; Hours: 11 AM-2 PM, 5-11 PM; Cost: meal $15 and up; 488-8866*

What to Do

SIGHTS

Palau is a diverse country filled with wonder and adventure for those who are willing to seek it. In this section, we have arranged the sights by state. Although many sights of interest are in Koror and the Rock Islands, you will learn that every state has something worth seeing. The best way to travel around Babeldaob, where many states are located, is to rent a car (see pg 189 more information on car rentals). There are also many land and sea tours that you can book though various providers.

Koror and the Rock Islands

The **Belau National Museum** (Mon-Thurs 8 AM-4:30 PM, Sat 10 AM-4:30 PM; admission $5; 488-2265, www.belaunationalmuseum.org) is a great place to go to learn about the history, culture, and traditions of Palau. Exhibits include ancient Palauan pottery, information about the explorers and traders that came to Palau, Palau's relationship with ruling nations, crafts and traditional items from surrounding Pacific Islands, and much more. If you have to choose only one museum to visit, make it the Belau National Museum.

The **Etpison Museum** (Mon-Sat 9 AM-5 PM; 488-6730) is more a display of depictive art than a historical exhibit, but it is still worth a visit if you are stranded on land for a day.

Though there are many ways to see Palau's sea life up close, the **Palau International Coral Reef Center** (9 AM-5 PM; admission $5-7; 488-6950, www.picrc.org) is a good place to learn about the different ecosystems and creatures inhabiting Palau's waters. You can also learn about the ways Palau is trying to preserve their underwater world through reef and fish monitoring and coral and clam farming.

Dolphins Pacific (7:30 AM-4 PM; 488-4973, www.dolphinspacific.com) is a natural dolphin sanctuary located a five-minute boat ride from Koror in the Rock Islands. Visitors of all ages can go to Dolphin Bay to find a happy family of dolphins and trainers, learn about dolphin behavior, and even snorkel with the dolphins! The facility is also equipped to facilitate disabled patrons. Close encounters start at $30; see the website for more pricing details. Reservations must be made at least one day in advance.

A day in the **Rock Islands**, which are interspersed throughout the inhabited islands of Palau, is not to be missed on any trip to Palau. Just zipping though the emerald islands in a speed boat, with the wind in your hair and the sun on your face, is enough to make you think of heaven. You could also spend a day picnicking on one of the many beaches throughout the Rock Islands. Boat transportation can be arranged through one of the many tour providers. Ask your hotel to recommend a tour company, or contact one of the snorkel tour operators, kayak tour operators, or dive shops.

One of the most amazing things you will experience in Palau is **Jellyfish Lake**. This marine lake, located about 20 minutes by boat from Koror, is filled with thousands of stingless jellyfish and you are invited to

> Jellyfish Lake has been featured on the Survivor television series several times.

snorkel along with them. Most tour operators run daily or weekly trips to the lake.

Tucked in a Rock Island cove, the **Milky Way** is a fun place to stop on a snorkeling expedition or Rock Island tour. When you arrive, you will notice the water is not the clear turquoise you are used to but a milky shade of blue. The white mud that gives this place its name, has been referred to as "beauty mud." Go ahead and rub it on your skin; it is a lot less expensive than a day at the spa.

The **helicopter tour of Palau** (488-6669) offers tourists a heavenly view of the Rock Islands. This tour offers amazing photo opportunities and the very rare chance to spot the endangered dugong, an animal similar to a manatee. Low tide is the best time for the ride, as it exposes more of Palau's intricate reef formations.

Airai

The **Airai** *Bai* is the oldest *bai* in Palau. It is thought to be more than 200 years old. Traditionally, *bais* were used as meeting places for village chiefs. Today, *bais* are very sacred places; please, be respectful and expect to pay a small fee.

Aimeliik

One of only four standing *bais* in Palau, **Aimeliik** *Bai* was built by the people of Aimeliik.

Many years ago, Malsol, a great warrior, killed the son of a prominent woman. She convinced her chief to help her capture Malsol and bring him to their village where the women proceeded to stone him to death. Today, you can see the stones that make up his grave at **Malsol's Tomb**.

Ngchesar

The **Jungle River Cruise** (488-1188, www.palaujunglerivercruise.com) is a 40 minute boat ride down the Ngerdorch River offering guests the opportunity to see local plants, such as ancient ferns and cannonball trees, as well as birds and animals like Palau's saltwater crocodile. The Jungle River Cruise is an excellent opportunity for photography. Advance notice is required, and rides to and from your hotel can be arranged. Adult tickets run about $45 per person.

Ngatpang

After a ride down a bumpy road and a 20 minute hike on a slippery jungle trail you will encounter the beauty of the **Ngatpang Waterfall**. The falls are about 20 feet (6 meters) tall and stand among towering trees and rock outcrops. You can enjoy swimming and picnicking while surrounded by the sounds of nature.

Just off the Compact road, a pyramid-shaped **WWII monument** is dedicated to the souls of the American and Japanese soldiers and the people of Palau who were killed during WWII.

Melekeok

If you are headed north on the east side of the Compact road, take the second Melekeok exit to find the nation's capital. **Palau's capitol building** sits atop a hill with breathtaking panoramic views. No official tour of the capitol, which was completed in 2006, is offered, but if you ask nicely you will be allowed to roam the halls. Be sure to check out the impressive collection of local artwork adorning the walls.

After the capitol, continue down the road until it ends, and turn right. In front of the corner house is the **largest stone face in Palau**. A red hibiscus plant is seemingly growing out of its head. Continue south for just a few more moments to reach **Okemii Deli and Internet Café**, a delightful restaurant that is open Monday through Saturday for breakfast and lunch. Ironically, the venue is neither a deli nor an internet café, but it does serve up is reasonably priced meals.

Continue down Hibiscus Lane another mile or so until you reach **Bailechesau**, the Melekeok State office. Stop in and check with the state employees before hiking up to the *bai* that is directly behind the office. They sometimes charge tourists to see the *bai*, but the nominal fee you may have to pay will be worth it. This *bai*, constructed in 1992 by Melekeok residents, was built using the original techniques without the aid of nails or power tools. It is about 10 minutes uphill by foot on an ancient stone path through the jungle. Across the street is a **public beach** area, the only spot in Palau where you can surf from the shore.

When leaving Melekeok continue north on the Compact road. About a mile (one and a half kilometers) up the road on the left is **Ngardok Lake**, the largest natural body of freshwater in the entire region. If you come at dawn or dusk you may catch a glimpse of the lake's small population of crocodiles. The lake is free to see, but you will have to hike 20 minutes to reach it. A longer path can take you all the way around the lake. Please note, however, there is no swimming allowed in Ngardok Lake.

Ngaremlengui

Tucked up a red clay road, you will find two **Japanese cannons** and a **bunker** that were used to ward off U.S. ships during WWII. From the hilltop vantage point, you can enjoy a beautiful view of the Philippine Sea and the barrier reef.

Native Religion on Palau

Today, the most widely practiced version of ancient Palauan beliefs is a religion called Modekngei. Believed to be introduced by Christian missionaries in the early 1900s, Modekngei religion is a hybrid of ancient Palauan customs and Christianity. Followers of the religion believe in the Christian God and recognize Jesus Christ as their savior while simultaneously making appeasements to ancient Palauan goddesses. Only about 8% of Palauans practice Modekngei, most of whom reside in the same village, Ibobang. This small town of less than 100 in Ngatpang state is a community devoted to the practice of Modekngei.

Citizens of Ibobang attend daily church services. One of the many Modekngei customs requires members of the community to walk silently to church each morning. To speak, especially loudly, before a church service is considered disrespectful or even blasphemous. Women in Ibobang usually dress in Western apparel, but they are required to always wear a dress skirt when entering or passing the church building. As a result, it is not uncommon for a woman wearing pants to take a longer route to her destination to keep from crossing the church grounds without the proper attire.

One custom that most Palauans observe, regardless of religious affiliation, is the prohibition of any alcohol or tobacco within the city limits of Ibobang. According to ancient belief, violating this religious law will bring terrible rainstorms upon the village until the sin has been forgiven by the Modekngei goddess.

Another customary activity that takes place in Ibobang is the blessing of the roads. This particular custom coincides with the moon's cycle. A few days before each full moon, the community works together to clean the entire village. Lawns are cut, trash is cleaned, and houses are scrubbed. Then, the evening before the full moon dawns, everyone who lives in Ibobang waits inside their houses while a village elder walks up and down the streets chanting prayers and blessings over the village. According to Modekngei belief, this practice is necessary because it is believed that during a full moon the Modekngei goddess is better able to see the malpractices of her people.

To experience a piece of ancient Palauan history, visit **Imeong Traditional Village**. Here, you can walk along ancient stone roadways, view stone platforms, building sites, a stone bridge, burial locations, and cultural sites.

Ngardmau

Ngardmau Waterfall, Palau's largest waterfall, is well worth the hike one must take to get there. The trail leads down a steep set of steps, across a very muddy trail, past defunct Japanese mining tracks, and onto a crest where you can enjoy a view of the waterfall from the top. The journey then continues down another steep set of stairs to the river where you can swim in several cool pools. From there, you can continue to follow the river down to the falls or take a muddy trail into the jungle. The amount of water that rushes over the edge at the top of the 60-foot (18-meter) high, 60-foot (18-meter) wide waterfall is truly astounding.

Ngaraard

The **Stone Path** cuts clear across the state, from the Pacific Ocean to the Philippine Sea, and is the longest stone path in the country.

Ngarchelong

The origins of the ancient site of **Badrulauch** are unknown, but some say the stone monoliths were the foundation of a *bai* that the gods were building before they were tricked into stopping construction by an evil god. Today, you can see ancient stone faces, some weighing five tons (4,500 kilograms), arranged in rows.

Ngiwal

The **Sunken City of Ngibital** is a fascinating spot for divers or snorkelers. There is a legend about a breadfruit tree that when cut would spout fish. Greedy villagers chopped the tree down to get all the fish they could, and so much water poured from the tree that the whole village was flooded and engulfed by the ocean. If you scuba dive off the coast, you can still see the walking paths of this sunken city.

WATER AND OUTDOOR ACTIVITIES

Diving

Palau, listed as one of the Seven Underwater Wonders of the World by CEDAM International, is world renowned for its scuba diving. Home to over 1,300 species of fish and more than 700 species of coral, Palau's naturalist diving is unparalleled. Palau features crystal clear waters with average visibility ranging from 165 to 200 feet (50 to 60 meters). Schools of sharks, manta rays, sea turtles, and a spectrum of vividly colored reef fish can be seen on any dive. The currents of Palau allow divers to drift along the walls or above the labyrinths of stunning hard and soft coral or to hook into the reef and float like an underwater balloon as the wonders of underwater life float by. In addition to the world class naturalist diving, the waters of Palau also offer exclusive opportunities to explore World War II wrecks.

Many of the smaller shops offer divers the freedom to explore a bit more on their own and are popular option for very experienced divers seeking to save a bit of money. However, guests should keep in mind that many of the dive sites of Palau are drift dives and are considered advanced. It is recommended that less experienced divers dive with larger shops offering better guide per guest ratios.

See pg 37 for more information on diving safety.

Dive sites such as Blue Corner are justifiably world famous, but it is important not to overlook the less celebrated dive spots. Often, particularly during the peak season, sites such as Blue Corner and German Channel will be overburdened with divers. This not only adversely impacts the sea life but also creates a less special ambiance for divers. All of Palau's dive sites are mesmerizing, and divers may seek a more singular experience at a less illustrious site.

Yellow Wall/Peleliu Express is well-known for its ripping and unpredictable currents and offers the apex in drift diving. Yellow Wall is named for the yellow tube corals that cover the area, creating the appearance of a glowing yellow wall. The strong currents are known to attract large sea creatures such as sharks, rays, Napoleon wrasse, and barracuda. Schools of smaller fish are also common, and green and hawksbill turtles visit the site to snack on the yellow tube coral. Although a trip to the sites of Peleliu requires special arrangements, as they are outside the reef and further than other sites, they are a crucial stop for any dive trip to Palau.

Ulong Channel, near the popular Siaes Tunnel, is another of Palau's famous drift dives. The 1,600-foot (490-meter) channel offers amazing coral gardens, close encounters with marine life, and two shark feeding stations. Ulong Channel is one of the premier sites to experience large numbers of reef sharks.

Blue Hole begins with a euphoric drop down one of four vertical shafts leading into a large cavern. Divers watch a variety of fish swimming upside down and sideways through the coral-adorned tunnel. The walls of the cavern are great places to search for nudibranchs and encounter the electric disco clam. Reef and leopard sharks are often found napping on the cavern's sandy bottom. Divers should visit Blue Hole during an outgoing tide and ride the current out to Blue Corner after a visit to the cavern.

Blue Corner is the most popular dive site in Palau and has been rated the single best dive site in the world by a multitude of dive magazines. Blue Corner has received this reputation due to the greatest variety and largest numbers of fish found anywhere in the world. Sharks, sea turtles, wahoo, tuna, eagle rays, grouper, and barracuda are just some of the species of large fish which populate the Corner, showing off for some of the best underwater photo opportunities found in the world. Blue Corner features a reef wall running parallel to Ngermelis Island dropping from 30 feet (9 meters) to over 100 feet (30 meters) before making a sharp left turn. This dive generally entails a drift along the wall and exploration of the plateau above.

German Channel is the dive site in Palau for encountering the majestic manta ray. German Channel boasts a cleaning station where cleaner wrasse and butterfly fish service mantas and reef sharks in search of a good scrub. In the late afternoon, the mantas are known to barrel roll through the mouth of the channel, feasting on plankton and krill. German Channel is a mandatory stop for divers visiting during manta season, from November through February. Divers should note that when the mantas are not present, the channel is less than a spectacular dive. Mantas, however, are seen year round and the chance to witness these creatures should not be missed.

Sam's Tours Sam's Tours is the largest and most popular dive shop in Palau. Although Sam's can be a bit more expensive than its competitors, the shop provides high end equipment and quality boats and employs knowledgeable, professional guides who cater to the needs of divers at any experience level. Sam's boasts a maximum of six divers per guide, a good ratio for less experienced divers. Also, compared with any other shop in Palau, Sam's best caters to English-speaking divers as it is staffed by American and fluent local guides and is owned by an ex-pat. Trips to Jellyfish Lake are included with a dive. *488-7267, www.samstours.com*

Neco Marine Neco Marine advertises "luxury diving," and charges a higher price than its competitors. Neco employs international guides from Europe and Japan and caters to Japanese and Western guests. *Cost: two-tank dive $150; 488-1755, www.necomarine.com*

Fish n' Fins Fish n' Fins Dive Shop was established by Francis Toribiong, the local pioneer of scuba diving and the man responsible for the discovery of the majority of the dive sites in Palau. Fish n' Fins offers competitive prices and is centrally located in Koror. They employ guides from Japan, the Philippines, Israel, and Austria as well as local guides. *M-Dock, Koror; Cost: two-tank dive $130; 488-2637, www.fishnfins.com*

Blue Marlin Blue Marlin Dive Shop offers the wonders of Palauan diving at reasonable prices. Located at the Palau Royal Resort, Blue Marlin is a convenient option for guests staying at that resort. However, divers should keep in mind that Blue Marlin employs mostly Japanese guides and mostly caters to Japanese tourists. *At Palau Royal Resort; Cost: two-tank dive $110; 488-2214, www.meluis.com*

Daydream Daydream offers diving at reasonable rates, but they cater mostly to Japanese tourists. Less experienced divers may feel uncomfortable with the language barrier. *Beneath Kramer's Bar and Restaurant; Cost: two-tank dive $120; 488-3551, www.daydream.to/palau*

Maml Maml Dive Shop specializes in diving Peleliu sites. Maml also offers diving at the sites around Koror at competitive prices. Although most of the dive shops offer trips to Peleliu sites, Maml is a good option for divers looking to stay on the island of Peleliu for part of their trip and dive the amazing sites nearby. *In Koror and on Peleliu; Cost: two-tank dive $120; 488-8029, www.mamldivers.com*

Splash Located beside Palau Pacific Resort's beautiful beach, Splash Dive Shop offers inexpensive diving with friendly and enthusiastic guides. Splash is prepared to accommodate Japanese and Western tourists alike, as four of their six guides are locals fluent in English. Jackson, Angelo, and the rest of the staff at Splash love to dive and their enthusiasm shows. *At Palau Pacific Resort; Cost: two-tank dive $120; 488-2600, www.splash-palau.com*

Fishing

Fishing is one of the cornerstones of life on the islands of Palau, playing a great role in the country to this day. Tourists visiting Palau have the opportunity to share in a Palauan fishing experience in some of the most abundant waters in the world. From shore or chartered boat, tourists can experience a variety of sport fishing techniques including casting, trolling, bottom-fishing, fly fishing, bone fishing, and spear fishing, the local preference.

> Visitors fishing independently should always check with authorities prior to casting as many areas around Palau are protected.

Fly and light tackle fishing tours are available for anglers looking to reel in barracuda, tuna, tarpon, and trevally. Those looking for rougher seas and a bigger fight should charter a tournament rigged boat and take it out to the reef to troll for marlin, tuna, wahoo, sailfish, and billfish or cast for trevally, grouper, snapper, and barracuda.

All of the major dive shops offer guided fishing trips and equipment rental, and it is advisable that visitors select a bigger shop to charter a boat, as the boats and equipment are generally of higher quality. Sam's Tours, Neco Marine, and Fish n' Fins are particularly recommended. IMPAC Tours (pg 212) is also recommended.

Serious sport fisherman may choose to visit Palau during the Etpison Cup, Palau's largest annual fishing derby, which usually takes place around the end of May. Anglers interested in competing in the fishing derby should contact the Palau Sports Fishing Association (488-3993, ypyalap@hotmail.com) in advance as preregistration is required.

Hiking

Much of the allure of Palau is in the undeveloped, natural beauty found in the country. Many of the marvels must be earned by visitors through majestic hikes in the nation's jungles. The hiking in Palau offers each visitor an opportunity for their own unpredictable adventure. Refer to the Sights section on pg 204 for some possible hike locations.

Jet Ski

Tourists looking to explore the waters of Palau with a bit more speed and adrenaline may want to cruise around the Rock Islands on a Jet Ski. Jet Ski rentals are available through the Sea Passion Hotel (488-0066, www.palauseapassion.com) and Blue Marlin Dive Shop (pg 210).

Kayaking

Take a Rock Island kayak tour and paddle into the heart of the limestone Rock Islands which surround the city of Koror. On one of the guided tours offered, guests will paddle through the islands as knowledgeable local guides educate them as to the environmental and historical features of the area, showing everything from WWII relics to secluded caves and the beautiful birds of Palau. The tours will also provide the opportunity to snorkel and experience the majestic underwater world of Palau.

Single day tours, overnight trips, or expeditions up to ten days are available depending on the time and interests of the guests. The locations of kayak trips vary depending on tides and weather conditions.

Planet Blue Kayak Tours Planet Blue offers the most knowledgeable guides and the highest quality kayaks and paddles; however, guests will be paying a higher rate for the tour. History buffs and nature enthusiasts alike will be impressed by the information provided in addition to the beauty of the surroundings. Planet Blue best caters to the individual needs and requests of their guests, and it is the only tour company offering multiple day expeditions. Expeditions include boat support, camping site setup, food, and drinks. *At the Sam's Tours Dive Shop; 488-7267, www.samstours.com*

IMPAC ToursIMPAC Tours offers kayak tours through the same waters as the other companies at less expensive prices. IMPAC caters mostly to Asian tourists, and the kayaking equipment is of a lesser quality. However, it is a less expensive choice for tourists interested more in kayaking and snorkeling and less in taking a guided tour. IMPAC offers only day tours of the Rock Islands. *488-0666*

Fish n' Fins Fish n' Fins offers guided kayak tours to the same major locations as other companies with accompaniment by naturalist guides. Tours can be booked by contacting Fish n' Fins Dive Shop. Fish n' Fins offers both day and overnight tours as well as a full moon tour. *488-2637, www.fishnfins.com*

Snorkeling

For visitors not interested in the depths of scuba or for divers looking for extra sea adventure during their surface time, snorkeling is a great way to experience the underwater wonders of Palau. It is recommended that all visitors bring a mask and snorkel with them as opportunities for independent snorkeling are very common. Tourists have the option to snorkel from shore, from a kayak, or with a guided boat tour. Many of the waters right around Koror offer great snorkeling opportunities. The beach at the Palau Pacific Resort offers access to some of the best snorkeling in Palau with both mandarinfish and nudibranchs waiting to be found. For guided snorkeling tours, refer to the dive shops (see pg 210) or kayak tour operators (see pg 211).

> For travelers on a budget, IMPAC Tours offers great snorkeling tours at reasonable prices.

Stand up Paddle Boarding

The newest trend in aquatic travel through the Rock Islands is paddle boarding. Clear, flat waters make Palau the ideal location for this up-and-coming water sport. Paddling combines good exercise and customizable sightseeing for a truly unique Rock Island experience. Paddle boarding is not only lots of fun, but it is easy to learn, too. More daring paddlers can take their boards out to the reef and ride some waves. Tours are available through Pleasure Island Palau (palau@pleasureisland.me, www.pleasureislandpalau.com) or through Stand Up Paddle Palau (488-0760, www.standup-paddle-tours.com).

> Contact Fuanes Oiterong at Stand Up Paddle Palau for a bit of instruction and a highly recommended tour around the island with Fuanes and his dog.

Surfing

There are a few places to surf in Palau, but conditions can be very unpredictable. The best time of the year to surf in Palau is from December to February. The only place to surf from shore is off the pier in Melekeok. Surfers can also find nice waves by boating off the coast of Ngaremlengui. The island of Angaur is another popular surf site. For surfing tours, lessons, and board rentals, contact Pleasure Island Palau (palau@pleasureisland.me, www.pleasureislandpalau.com). For daily surf conditions, email surfpalau@gmail.com or become a fan of Surf Palau on Facebook.

Swimming

There are plenty of opportunities to swim in Palau. However, currents can be unpredictable, and although attacks are very rare, dangerous animals such as crocodiles do reside in the waters of Palau. Visitors should always swim responsibly and check with locals prior to taking a dip. The beach at the Palau Pacific Resort is a beautiful location for swimming.

SHOPPING

Souvenirs

The **Palau Shop** (10 AM-9 PM; 488-1816), located in downtown Koror across from the post office, offers island style decorations and jewelry, as well as beautiful sarongs, women's apparel, swim trunks, and iron transfer T-shirts. Sadly, most of what you will find was not made locally.

Rur (10 AM-9 PM; 488-8852), also located in downtown Koror across from the post office, is a funky little shop catering mostly to Asian tourists and has nice but pricey souvenirs, including locally made teas, soaps, and jewelry. They also have some really unique, though expensive, T-shirts with Palauan language slogans. If you have the time, it is worth stopping in for a look.

You will find some truly Palauan gifts in **Yolt Gift Shop** (open afternoons and early evenings; 488-3665) including everything from jewelry to tea and sea salt as well as some imported trinkets. The store is located in downtown Koror next to the post office.

> Yolt is also a good place to start if you are looking to rent a bicycle while in Palau, but call first to find out if the bike guys are actually there.

Basibik Arts & Crafts (10 AM-9 PM; 488-6444), located near the Palau Visitors Authority in downtown Koror, is filled with traditional woven goods and jewelry from Palau and the surrounding islands. This is a great place to find a unique basket or purse.

The **Etpison Gift Shop** (Mon-Sat 9 AM-5 PM; 488-6730) in the Etpison Museum in downtown Koror has many posters and postcards of original Palauan art and photography by Mandy Etpison. You will also find plush goods, jewelry, seashell gifts, and more. There is no entrance fee to go to the gift shop.

The **Belau National Museum Gift Shop** (Mon-Fri 7:30 AM-5 PM; 488-2265) is a must-stop for Palauan gifts. Here, you can find locally made gifts, like hand carved spear fishing guns, coconut bras, storyboards, coconut rope, and traditional canoe replicas as well as books about the language and history of Palau, postcards, and posters. There is no entrance fee to go to the gift shop.

You might feel a little strange walking into Palau's only prison, but the staff and inmates are surprisingly welcoming. Just ask the officer on duty to take you to the **Subilik Gift Shop** (10 AM-6 PM daily; 488-2654) where you will find some of the most beautiful hand carved storyboards on the island. The boards are made by the inmates and the funds go either to the prison, to cover expenses like food and utilities, or to the inmates' families. The prices marked are ridiculously high, so do not be afraid to try to negotiate a more reasonable price. Give yourself some time to look around; there are many different stories and styles available.

Featuring original art, prints, and jewelry by artist Michael Glinsky, the **Belau Art Gallery** (Mon-Sat 10 AM-10 PM, Sun 10 AM-7 PM; 488-2000 ext. 207) at the Palau Royal Resort is a great place to find a unique and beautiful souvenir that you can appreciate forever.

Islander Arts and Crafts (10 AM-9 PM; 488-6889), located in the "Mansion" building of downtown Koror, is filled with gifts like shell purses, wood carvings, jewelry, and locally made soaps. Although some of the stuff is made locally, most of what you will find comes from elsewhere. If you want a truly local gift, make sure to read the labels or ask an employee.

For gifts of more refined taste, the **Duty Free Shop** (10 AM-10 PM; 488-1898) is a good place to look. Items for sale include beautiful sarongs, silver jewelry, logoed shirts, purses, and knick knacks. Duty Free Shops are located at the Palau International Airport, Palau Pacific Resort, and Palasia Hotel.

Story Boards

Many years ago men would meet in houses called *bais*. These houses were decorated with intricately carved depictions of local legends. As time went on and *bais* stopped being used, locals tried to find a way to capture these legends in a more portable form; thus, the storyboard was born. Today you can take home a piece of Palauan history in the form of a Palauan storyboard, the most uniquely Palauan souvenir you will find. They are sold many places on the island, and most locals can tell you all about the legends depicted.

Groceries

If you pay attention you'll realize that the Surangel family has their hand in just about every type of business venture on the island. Check out **Surangels grocery store** (Sun-Thurs 8 AM-10 PM, Fri 8 AM-5 PM, Sat 5 PM-10 PM; 488-8768), located in downtown Koror across from WCTC, if you are missing some of the comforts from home. Venture upstairs for their surf and sport shop filled with the latest in teen fashion and fishing equipment. There is also a department store with office supplies and discount clothing.

Other

The **West Caroline Trading Company** or **WCTC** (8 AM-9 PM; 488-1484), located across from Surangels in downtown Koror, is Palau biggest "department store." Upstairs you will find U.S. name brand clothing, Palau T-shirts, sweatshirts, and swim trunks, island-style souvenirs, electronics, and much more.

Overdrive Dive Shop (10 AM-8 PM; 488-6691), located in downtown Koror across from Asahi baseball field and next to Suriyothai Restaurant, is a good place to stop for dive gear favored by the Japanese. They have a variety of Gull rubber fins, BCDs, masks of all different sizes and shapes, diving apparel, plush gifts, and toys.

Featuring dive and snorkel gear, logoed apparel, witty T-shirts, and sundries, **Sam's Tours Dive Shop** (7:30 AM- 6 PM; 488-1062) has everything you will need for a fun day out on the aquamarine waters of Palau. The shop is located on Malakal Island in Koror.

Neco Marine Dive Shop (7:30 AM- 6 PM; 488-2009), located on Malakal Island, is expensive, but it offers a wide selection of logoed apparel, dive gear, and accessories. When you stop in, be sure to say hello to their resident parrot.

At **Splash Dive Shop** (7:30 AM-6 PM; 488-1601) on Ngerkebesang Island, dive gear, sundries, logoed apparel, bathing suits, and gifts are available.

Nightlife

Riptide Bar and Grill Located at the very southern tip of Malakal Island in Koror, Riptide is a great place to mix with the locals while enjoying refreshing ocean breezes. During the day, you can take a dip or play some volleyball at the private beach. *Malakal Island; Hours: 11 AM-9 PM; Cost: drink $3-5; 488-3486*

Joe's If you visit this bar before 10 PM you might think it is pretty dead, but Joe's fills up late at night with locals looking for a few drinks and a good time. Joe's is located in downtown Koror on Lebuu Street. *Downtown Koror; Hours: 5 PM-2 AM; Cost: drink $3-5; 488-8000*

Port Area Disco Located on Malakal Island in Koror, Port Area Disco offers karaoke and dancing. If you are looking for a smoky little spot to belt out tunes in your most off key voice and then shake your booty, this is the place for you. *Malakal Island; Hours: 8 PM-2 AM; Cost: drink $3-6; 488-8596*

Kramer's Bar and Restaurant Kramer's, located near the Palau Royal Resort, will quickly become the bar where everyone knows your name. This haunt is a favorite of ex-pats, and German owner Rene is always happy to welcome a new face (sometimes with a kiss on the forehead). The bar features two dart boards and a foosball table. The music varies wildly, and late at night, you might even encounter an impromptu dance party. *Malakal Island; Hours: Mon-Sat 11 AM-2 PM, 5 PM to midnight; Cost: drink $4-8; 488-8448*

Jive Café Located in downtown Koror, just before the bridge to Malakal Island, Jive is a great place to grab a quick bite and a cold drink and watch the boats pull back into town in the evening from the large deck. *Downtown Koror; Hours: 7-10:30 AM, 4:30-11 PM; Cost: drink $4-8; 488-5483*

Drop Off Bar and Grill Located behind Neco Marine and Dolphin's Pacific on Malakal Island, Drop Off is a favorite of locals and visitors. Enjoy the fresh Poke sashimi and a cold Red Rooster beer while listening to classic tunes. *Malakal Island; Hours: 11 AM-2 PM, 4:30-10 PM; Cost: drink $4-8; 488-1755*

Bottom Time Bar Grab a burger and a beer while listening to the tales of ocean conquests told by members and visitors to the Belau Yacht Club. *At Sam's Tours on Malakal Island; Hours: 7:30 AM-8 PM; Cost: drink $4-8; 488-4382*

The Taj Located in downtown Koror, the Taj is a great place to sip a cocktail and chat up the regulars. You are even likely to run into a few big players in the local government. Try the hand-shaken espresso martini! *Downtown Koror; Hours: 11 AM-2 PM, 4:30-10 PM; Cost: drink $4-10; 488-2227*

Outer Islands

KAYANGEL

For a little rest and relaxation during your vacation, do not miss a trip to Kayangel, Palau's only true coral atoll. Located an hour's boat ride off the northern tip of Babeldaob, these islands do not have much to offer in the way of creature comforts or entertainment, but what Kayangel lacks in excitement, it makes up for in natural beauty, peace, and serenity. Spend an enchanting weekend among the banana trees, swimming off the sandy beaches or getting to know some of the friendly locals. Make sure to visit the **Nguerangel Conservation Area** for great snorkeling! The area is packed with sea turtles, sharks, and other marine creatures.

There are no guest houses on Kayangel, but visitors can arrange a homestay or spend the night outdoors at the *sita*, or summer house (similar to a covered deck). There is also the opportunity to spend a weekend on your own private island, equipped with a *sita*, outhouse, and rustic cooking area. The best way to coordinate a trip to Kayangel is to call the **state office** (488-2766) in Meyuns, Koror. The state government provides transportation to and from the island every other weekend in coordination with the government pay schedule. You can ride on the boat for a small fee or arrange private transportation if you wish to visit on an off week. Typically, the boat makes a run to Kayangel on Friday morning and returns on Sunday afternoon. The trip takes about two hours if you depart from Koror or one hour if you depart from Ollei dock in Ngarchelong.

For accommodations on outer islands, see pg 190.

PELELIU

Just an hour south of Koror by speed boat or two and a half hours by slow state boat rests the isle of Peleliu. Once a desolate war zone, nearly 70 years has allowed the island to heal and reclaim its natural splendor. Today, Peleliu is a dense jungle island, scattered with WWII tanks, bunkers, planes, and memorials that remind visitors and locals of what happened here long ago.

Visitors to Peleliu have a few options for touring the island. Tour companies, out of Koror and out of the Peleliu resorts, can arrange transportation to the island from Koror on a speed boat. Once there, visitors are taken in an air-conditioned bus or van around the island to various spots of interest. Guides are informative and can give your information on Peleliu's role in the War, the history of the island, and details about the surroundings.

A less expensive option is to take the state boat to the island with the locals. It takes a little longer, since the boat moves much more slowly, but it will give you a chance to relax and watch the Rock Islands go by. The boat runs several times per week; contact the **Peleliu state office** (488-1817) in Koror for details.

Once there, you can rent a bicycle from Dolphin Bay Resort for about $10 and ride your way around the mostly flat island. **Bloody Nose Ridge**, the highest point on the island, offers spectacular views of the rest of the island. To obtain this view, visitors must walk the paths between the ridges, which U.S. Marines struggled through during the Battle of Peleliu. Peleliu is filled with **World War II remnants** which you can explore either through a guided tour or on your own. Some of the major attractions include American tanks, Japanese cannons and tanks, and numerous monuments. The largest monument on Peleliu is the **Japanese Peace Memorial Shrine,** located at **Peleliu Peace Memorial Park**, on the southern tip of the island. In addition to the memorial, the park offers a chance to enjoy the natural beauty of the volcanic island. **The Peleliu World War II Memorial Museum** was built in a damaged Japanese warehouse. The museum houses many artifacts from the war, letters from the marines who survived, and

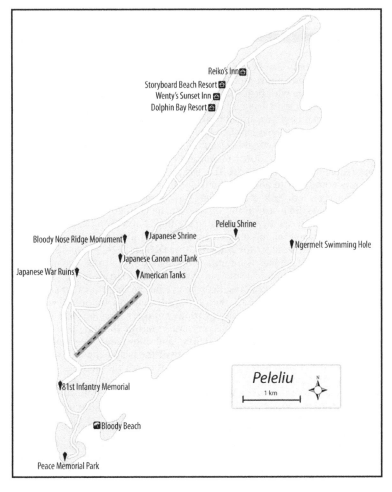

photographs of the destruction. The museum is very simple, but also very moving. To set up a time to visit the museum, contact the **state office** (345-2967). Guests should cool off from a day of visiting the monuments and remnants at **Ngermelt**, the saltwater swimming hole, which is frequented by locals and tourists alike.

Bloody Nose Ridge

Bloody Nose Ridge is the sight of one of the bloodiest World War II battles in the Pacific. Previously known as the Umurbrogol Mountain, Bloody Nose Ridge received its nickname from the soldiers of the U.S. 1st Marine Division, who engaged in a particularly bloody month-long battle to secure the mountain. During the first eight days of the attack, the marines suffered approximately 50% casualties. The marines, with the eventual aid of reinforcements, battled their way up the mountain through the Japanese troops, who were defending the mountain from caves and ridges running up the sides of the mountain.

ANGAUR

For an island only 3 miles (5 kilometers) long, Angaur combines enough tranquility and adventure to fill much more than a single weekend. Angaur welcomes visitors with beautiful jungles, pristine beaches, WWII remnants, challenging surf, and even a bit of relaxed nightlife.

Visitors can charter a speed boat to Angaur from Koror at any time. The cost of chartering a boat can be high, but doing so will give you flexibility in your schedule and will get you to the island quickly. There is also a local state boat that travels down to Angaur every other weekend; tickets are approximately $20 round-trip. The trip is between three and four hours one-way compared to about an hour on the speed boat. Also, the boat can get a bit crowded. Still, it is a great way to meet locals. Get to the state boat early to claim a seat in the shade near the railing for amazing views of the Rock Islands. See if you can catch a glimpse of a flying fish. To charter a boat contact one of the tour companies based in Koror. For information on the state boat, contact the **Angaur State Office** (277-2967 or 488-5282).

The island of Angaur is an untamed jungle waiting to be explored. The island is small enough to walk, but the wide trails cut through the jungle making for excellent bike rides. Keep an eye on the trees to catch a glimpse of the crab-eating macaques, the only wild monkeys found anywhere in Palau. It is also common for these curious monkeys to come right onto the path for a closer view of you. Be sure cruise out of the jungle to some of the beautiful beaches, inspiring cliffs, and blowholes overlooking the breaking waves of the ocean. The majority of the island can be explored in a day by bike. Bike rental can be arranged through the house or motel at which you are staying.

There are some amazing **World War II remains** left from the Battle of Angaur. Head to the end of the old runway on the north side of the island for an amazing view overlooking the ocean. Then, duck into the jungle to check out the **WWII Airplane Graveyard.**

Angaur also features sights preserved from Palau's colonial period. During colonization, Germany established phosphate mines on Angaur. Evidence of these mines, such as the **conveyer belt ruins,** remains throughout the island. Also, a visit to the **Abandoned Lighthouse** from this era, rewards visitors with an amazing view down the west coast of Angaur.

Guests may also enjoy a peaceful moment at one of the religious monuments on Angaur. The **Virgin Mary Statue** and **Buddhist Monument** are both located at the northwest corner of the island, near a series of breathtaking blowholes.

The **Banyan Tree Bar** offers guests the chance to hang out with the locals. This small, open-air bar features pool, karaoke, and a bit of dancing. The locals of Angaur are some of the friendliest people you will find in Palau.

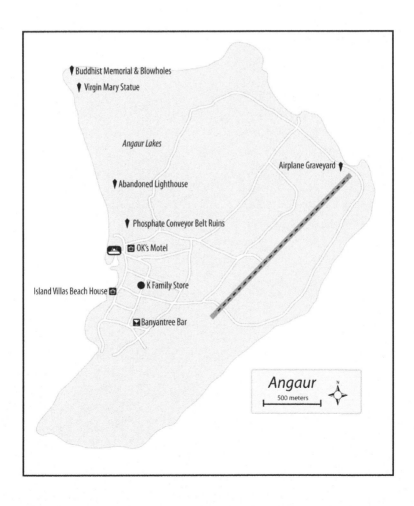

Further Reading

BOOKS

Some Things of Value: Micronesian Customs and Beliefs by **Gene Ashby**
This is a good introduction to some Micronesian cultural practices.

Island of Angels by **Elden Buck** Written by a member of the United Church of Christ clergy who lived in Micronesia for over two decades, this is an excellent history of Kosrae.

Micronesian Legends by **Bo Flood, Beret E. Strong, and William Flood**
This great compendium of stories and legends from throughout Micronesia can be hard to find, but it is well worth the search.

Legends of Micronesia: Book One by **Eve Grey** A fantastic collection of traditional stories from Micronesia.

Upon a Stone Altar: A History of the Island of Pohnpei to 1890 by **David Hanlon** Authored by a former Peace Corps volunteer who spent many years living in Micronesia, *Upon a Stone Altar* is the best history of Pohnpei available.

Atlas of Micronesia by **Bruce G. Karolle** You may not want to read this reference from cover to cover, but if you are looking for a basic introduction to the geography of the region, it is difficult to beat Karolle's *Atlas*.

His Majesty O'Keefe by **Lawrence Klingman and Gerald Green** Written in 1950, this narrative about O'Keefe and his life was later adapted for the screen.

The Edge of Paradise: America in Micronesia by **P. F. Kluge** This engaging read is a collection of stories from various islands in Micronesia that provide insight into U.S. presence in the region of Micronesia. The book offers not only information on the recent history of these islands but also recounts the author's personal experiences.

Diving the Pacific: Volume 1: Micronesia and the Western Pacific Islands **by David Leonard** Of the several books on diving in Micronesia, this is the most useful and up-to-date. Leonard's maps and descriptions of dive sites are particularly helpful.

Micronesian Reef Fishes **by Robert F. Myers** This impressive work catalogues all the species of fish found in the reefs of Micronesia with descriptions, illustrations, and color photographs. Divers interested in fish should check out this book.

The Island of the Colorblind **by Oliver Sacks** Written by the famous neurologist, this fascinating book recounts the author's two trips to Micronesia. The title refers to Pingelap, an island with a high rate of a rare form of colorblindness, but the book also describes Sacks's voyages to Pohnpei, Majuro in the Marshall Islands, Guam, and Rota in the Northern Marianas.

WEBSITES

micsem.org This is the website of the Micronesian Seminar, a Jesuit-run research institution. The site is a vast mine of academic information about Micronesia, including its history and current events.

www.pacificworlds.com An educational site about selected places in Pacific. The site includes a wealth of information about Airai in Palau and Ulithi in Yap.

www.visit-fsm.org The FSM Visitor Board's website includes information on all the states of the FSM.

www.visit-palau.com The Palau Visitors Authority's website provides information for planning a visit to Palau.

yapstategov.org Yap state's official information outlet is a great source for day-to-day information about the state.

Language Reference

Micronesia is an amateur language-learner's nightmare. Every main island and many outer islands have distinct languages, many of which are quite challenging for native English speakers. Because of this, some visitors can be tempted to speak only English, which is spoken on all the islands. By learning just a few phrases, however, visitors can earn the respect of locals and experience the rich linguistic heritage of Micronesia and Palau.

Pronunciation

Phonetic pronunciations are given in square brackets after each phrase. Stress goes on the syllable in all capital letters. Vowel sounds are indicated as follows:

Symbol	Pronounced like underlined vowel sound
\a\	apple
\ā\	ape
\ä\	father
\au\	out
\e\	men
\ē\	bean
\i\	kit
\ī\	kite
\o\	hot
\ō\	cone
\u\	full
\ü\	too

English	Kosraean
Hello	None; use "Good morning," "Good afternoon," etc. as appropriate
Goodbye	Kuht fah osun [kud fä ō-SÜN]

Please	Nuhnahk muhnas [NU-näk mu-näs]
Thank you	Kulo [KÜ-lō]
You're welcome	Kulo pac [KÜ-lō pak]; ke kulang [kā kü-LANG]
How are you?	Kom fuhkah? [kōm fü-KA]
I'm fine	Nga wona [ngä WŌ-ne]
Good morning	Tu wo [DÜ wō]
Good mid-day	Len wo [LĀN wō]
Good evening	Eke wo [e-KĀ wō]
Good night	Fong wo [FUNG wō]

English	**Pohnpeian**
Hello	Kaselehlie maing (to one person) [kä-sä-LĀ-lē-ye mīng]; Kaselehlie maing ko (to a group) [kä-sä-LĀ-lē-ye mīng kō]
Goodbye	Same as "hello"
Please	Menlau [men-LAU]
Thank you	Kalahngan [ke-LÄNG-än]
You're welcome	None
How are you?	Ia iromw? [yä ē-RŌM]
I'm fine	I kehlail [ē KĀ-līl]
Good morning	Menseng mwahu [men-seng MWA-ü]
Good mid-day	Souwas mwahu [sō-wäs MWA-ü]
Good evening	Soutik mwahu [sō-chik MWA-ü]
Good night	Pwohng mwahu [pwäng MWA-ü]

English	Chuukese
Hello	Ran annim [rän ä-NĒM]
Goodbye	Kene nom [ke-nā NŌM]
Please	La mochen tungurok [lä mō-chen TÜN-ge-rōk]
Thank you	Kinissou [kē-ne-SŌ]
You're welcome	Kote puan afani [KŌ-tā pon ä-fä-NĒ]
How are you?	Ifa osum? [ē-fä ō-SÜM]
I'm fine	Pechekul [pe-che-KÜL]
Good morning	Neesor annim [ne-sōr ä-NĒM]
Good afternoon	Nanowas Annim
Good evening	Nenkunuion Annim [ne-KÜN-ē-on ä-NĒM]
Good night	Neepwong annim [ne-pong ä-NĒM]

English	Yapese
Hello	Mogethin [MŌ-ge-thin]
Goodbye	Kefel [ke-FEL]
Please	Wenig ngom [we-NĒG ngōm]
Thank you	Kammagar [KÄ-me-gär]
You're welcome	Dariy [DÄ-rē]
How are you?	Ke uw rogom boch? [ke ü RŌ-gōm bōch]
I'm fine	Maenigiil [mī-ne-GĒL]
Good morning	Maenigil e kakadbul [mī-ne-GĒL e kä-KÄD-bul]
Good mid-day	None

Good evening	Maenigil e balayal [mī-ne-GĔL e bä-LĪ-yal]
Good night	None

English	Palauan
Hello	Alii [ä-LĔ]
Goodbye	Mechikung (to one person) [me-Ĕ-kün]; Ak morolung (to a group) [äk-mō-rō-lün]
Please	Adang [A-dang]
Thank you	Kmal mesulang [kmäl MES-ü-lang]
You're welcome	Ng diak [eng DĪ-ak]
How are you?	Ke ua ngerang? [ke wä nge-RANG]
I'm fine	Ak messisich [äk MES-ā-sē]
Good morning	Ungil tutau [üng-ĔL tü-TÄ]
Good mid-day	Ungil suelb [üng-ĔL sü-ELB]
Good evening	Ungil kebesengei [üng-ĔL ke-be-seng-Ä]
Good night	Ma tutau [mä rü-TÄ]

During your trip, you may find that things have changed since this guide was written. Establishments go out of business, phone numbers change, and even cultural practices evolve. We would love to hear your feedback so that we can make the next edition of this book better.

To provide feedback on this guide, please contact Other Places Publishing (info@otherplacespublishing.com, www.otherplacespublishing.com).

OTHER PLACES PUBLISHING
www.otherplacespublishing.com